LIFE AS A BILINGUAL

About half the world's population knows and uses two or more languages in everyday life, and an increasing number of parents are raising their children bilingual. This makes a resource on what it means to become and be bilingual all the more necessary. This book brings together a selection of posts from the author's highly successful *Psychology Today* blog, grouped by topic into fifteen chapters. The topics covered include, among others, what it means to be bilingual, the extent of bilingualism, how someone becomes bilingual, how bilingualism is fostered in the family, the bilingual mind and brain, and bilingualism across the life span. It also includes the author's lively interviews with other experts, delving into their research and their own experience as bilinguals. Written in a highly engaging, readable style, this book is suitable for anyone who wants to better understand those who live with two or more languages.

A bilingual himself, François Grosjean is a world-renowned expert on the topic. He started his academic career at the University of Paris 8 and then taught and completed research in psycholinguistics at Northeastern University in Boston. In 1987, he was appointed professor at Neuchâtel University, Switzerland, where he founded the Language and Speech Processing Laboratory.

LIFE AS A BILINGUAL

Knowing and Using Two or More Languages

François Grosjean

University of Neuchâtel

with contributions from Aneta Pavlenko

CAMBRIDGE
UNIVERSITY PRESS

CAMBRIDGE
UNIVERSITY PRESS

University Printing House, Cambridge CB2 8BS, United Kingdom

One Liberty Plaza, 20th Floor, New York, NY 10006, USA

477 Williamstown Road, Port Melbourne, VIC 3207, Australia

314–321, 3rd Floor, Plot 3, Splendor Forum, Jasola District Centre,
New Delhi – 110025, India

79 Anson Road, #06–04/06, Singapore 079906

Cambridge University Press is part of the University of Cambridge.

It furthers the University's mission by disseminating knowledge in the pursuit of
education, learning, and research at the highest international levels of excellence.

www.cambridge.org
Information on this title: www.cambridge.org/9781108838641
DOI: 10.1017/9781108975490

First published 2021

Printed in the United Kingdom by TJ Books Limited, Padstow Cornwall

A catalogue record for this publication is available from the British Library.

Library of Congress Cataloging-in-Publication Data
Names: Grosjean, François, author. | Pavlenko, Aneta, 1963– contributor.
Title: Life as a bilingual : knowing and using two or more languages / François
Grosjean ; with contributions from Aneta Pavlenko.
Description: Cambridge ; New York, NY : Cambridge University Press, 2021. | Includes
bibliographical references and index.
Identifiers: LCCN 2020046978 (print) | LCCN 2020046979 (ebook) | ISBN
9781108838641 (hardback) | ISBN 9781108972116 (paperback) | ISBN
9781108975490 (ebook)
Subjects: LCSH: Bilingualism.
Classification: LCC P115 .G758 2021 (print) | LCC P115 (ebook) | DDC 306.44/6–dc23
LC record available at https://lccn.loc.gov/2020046978
LC ebook record available at https://lccn.loc.gov/2020046979

ISBN 978-1-108-83864-1 Hardback
ISBN 978-1-108-97211-6 Paperback

To Ismaël and Mia, my bilingual grandchildren,
and their generation of young bilinguals

Contents

CONTENTS

Figures

Introduction

In early June 2010, Carlin Flora, a Senior Editor for the New York based, *Psychology Today*, wrote to me to ask me if she could interview me after having read my new book, *Bilingual: Life and Reality*. We emailed back and forth concerning the matter and then, a few days later, she asked me, "I wonder if you'd like your own blog on bilingualism? . . . The website gets two million visitors per month."

I was totally taken aback as I had been, up to then, a rather traditional academic who mainly wrote scholarly papers, chapters, and books. Blog posts seemed a bit short at first – some 800 to 1,000 words per post as compared to tens of pages for papers – and maybe a bit too personal – I am more used to using the passive voice than the active voice. But then I looked around and saw, among others, David Crystal's blog on English linguistics. Here was a well-known academic, author, and lecturer, who had been blogging for several years and doing so most successfully.

So, after a few weeks, I accepted for a number of reasons. First, I have always wanted to put to rest the many myths that surround bilingualism, as well as tell the general public about findings in my research field. Since about half of the world is bilingual, that is, uses two or more languages or dialects in everyday life, and studies on bilinguals have been far less numerous than those on monolinguals, I feel that we researchers have the added duty of communicating our results on bilinguals to all those who might be interested in them.

Not all research has a direct impact on everyday life, and one must accept that. But some findings can play a role in our lives as bilinguals or in the lives of bilingual children, whilst others can change our attitudes toward bilingualism. It is therefore important we inform the general public.

Another reason is that there is the need to reassure bilinguals about their own bilingualism and to give those involved with children – parents and other caretakers, educators, speech/language pathologists, and so on – some basic knowledge about growing up with two or more languages. Hopefully, a blog can help them understand why and how bilingual children behave the way they do, such as develop a dominant language, show a person–language bond, refuse to speak a particular language at some point, mix their languages in certain situations, and so on.

I also wanted to constitute a small online resource on the bilingual person, adult and child, that people can come back to at any time. And finally, there was a more personal reason. Since I was no longer teaching and I missed it, I thought it would be enjoyable to write introductory posts about various aspects of bilingualism for a general audience.

Ten years later, at the time of writing, my blog with the same title as this book, "Life as a bilingual," has been visited by more than 2.2 million readers, much to my amazement. There are some 150 posts, comprising short texts and interviews, that can be consulted by anyone throughout the world[1].

In 2014, my colleague, Aneta Pavlenko, kindly joined me and for the following five years, we took turns writing posts for the blog. She authored wonderful texts in her areas of specialty and greatly diversified our offerings. She left the blog in 2019 but her posts are still there, and she has very kindly agreed to have some appear in this book.

But why now a book with a selection of posts? Blogs have many advantages but also some inconveniences: They can be removed by the owner of the platform at any time; the posts are organized from latest to earliest, which makes selecting a topic and finding follow-up posts very difficult; and categories of posts are not easily identifiable. In addition, an electronic medium often lacks some of the advantages of books such as ease of manipulation, durability, and transportability. When I approached Cambridge University Press with a proposal to publish a selection of my

---

[1] The blog can be found here: www.psychologytoday.com/intl/blog/life-bilingual. For an index by content, see here: www.francoisgrosjean.ch/blog_en.html

posts, they showed very real interest – confirmed by five outside reviewers they consulted – and for this I am grateful.

The 121 posts written between 2010 and 2020 in this book, including twenty-three interviews, are organized by topic, in fifteen different chapters. The first four set the stage: describing bilinguals, the extent of bilingualism, using two or more languages, and bilingualism across the life span. These are followed by chapters on becoming bilingual, bilingualism in the family, bilingualism in children with additional needs, and second language learning. Next comes a chapter on biculturalism and personality. It is followed by a special chapter, "When the heart speaks," with posts that concern emotions in bilinguals and how they express and process them in their languages.

The next three chapters concern language processing in bilinguals, the bilingual mind including the lively debate on whether bilinguals are advantaged cognitively, and the bilingual brain, its study, and what happens when it is impaired. This is followed by a chapter on special bilinguals such as translators, interpreters, teachers, and bilingual writers who have both a regular and a unique relationship with their languages. In the last chapter, much shorter than the others, I reminisce on a few events that I lived through during my career studying bilingualism and bilinguals.

To help readers choose the texts they wish to peruse, each chapter starts with an introduction that presents the posts that it contains. Then, each post is preceded by a short abstract. Finally, there is a fair amount of cross referencing within posts to other posts and other chapters.

Since the emphasis in this book is on the bilingual person, adult or child, other topics that relate to the sociology, anthropology, and politics of bilingualism, such as language minorities, language and power, language ideologies, language planning, language and nation building, are not covered[2].

---

[2] Cambridge University Press offers numerous handbooks that deal with these topics. Among these we find *The Cambridge Handbook of Bilingualism* (edited by Annick De Houwer and Lourdes Ortega), *The Cambridge Handbook of Sociolinguistics* (edited by Rajend Mesthrie), and *The Cambridge Handbook of Linguistic Anthropology* (edited by Nick J. Enfield, Paul Kockelman, and Jack Sidnell).

This book would not have been possible without the help of a number of people. Carlin Flora who encouraged me to start a blog, and the subsequent *Psychology Today* editors who continued to assist me; Aneta Pavlenko who was such a fine co-blogger for five years; the many colleagues who accepted to be interviewed on topics they are experts in; my wife, Lysiane, who read the posts before they were published and helped me choose the accompanying photographs; and all those who encouraged me all these years if only by putting the links of the posts up on social media.

I also wish to thank those at Cambridge University Press who believed in this book from the outset: Helen Barton, the Language and Linguistics Commissioning Editor who has seen this book through the stages of evaluation, preparation, and production; Isabel Collins, her editorial assistant; Joshua Penney, the Content Manager; Jayavel Radhakrishnan, the Project Manager; and Padmapriya Ranganathan, the Copy Editor.

This book is dedicated to my two grandchildren, Ismaël and Mia, both bilingual, and to all those other children of their generation who also live with two or more languages.

1

Describing Bilinguals

INTRODUCTION

The posts here will help set the stage for many of those that follow in later chapters. In Post 1.1, it is shown how language proficiency has ceded its place to language use when defining bilingualism. Bilinguals are now seen as those who use two or more languages (or dialects) in everyday life.

A monolingual (or fractional) view of bilingualism is presented at the start of Post 1.2. According to this view, the bilingual is, or should be, two monolinguals in one person. A more recent view is then discussed – the holistic view of bilingualism – that I proposed some time ago. It states that bilinguals have a unique and specific linguistic configuration. The coexistence and constant interaction of the two or more languages in bilinguals have produced a different but complete language system.

In Post 1.3, a grid is presented that allows one to visualize a person's bi- or multilingualism. It takes into account language proficiency and language use in each language known. An example is discussed, and an empty grid is proposed for the reader to use.

In Post 1.4, bilinguals tell us about their own bilingualism – the many advantages they see and the few inconveniences they report on.

Posts 1.5 and 1.6 deal with important linguistic aspects of bilingualism. In the first, the Complementarity Principle is explained, which is the fact that bilinguals usually acquire and use their languages for different purposes, in different domains of life, with different people. It accounts for interesting bilingual phenomena, one of them being language dominance, which is dealt with in a separate post (Post 1.6).

The last three posts deal with having an accent in one or more languages. In Post 1.7, the myth that real bilinguals have no accent in their different languages is discussed. In Post 1.8, the factors that explain why some retain an accent whereas others do not are examined. Maturational reasons are important but so are the type and amount of input from the language in question. Finally, in Post 1.9, a report is given on a study that looked at the impact that accented speech has on our understanding of what is being said. Contrary to what one might think, even if some speak with a foreign accent, there is a good chance that they will be understood.

1.1 WHO IS BILINGUAL?

Bilinguals are those who use two or more languages (or dialects) in their everyday lives. But this definition is fairly recent.

> "No, I'm not bilingual; I'm not fluent in all my languages."
>
> "I don't consider myself bilingual since I don't know how to write my other language."
>
> "I didn't grow up with two languages, so I'm not bilingual."
>
> "I have an accent in Spanish so I can't be considered bilingual."

I have heard such remarks repeatedly and I have always been dismayed that so many bilinguals depreciate their language skills.

The main reason is that the criterion of how proficient bilinguals are in their languages has long been dominant in how we characterize them. Even some linguists have put it forward as the defining characteristic. Hence, the American linguist, Leonard Bloomfield, stated that bilingualism is the native-like control of two languages.

The "real" bilingual has long been seen as the one who is equally, and fully, fluent in two languages. He or she is the "ideal," the "true," the "balanced," and the "perfect" bilingual. All the others – in fact, the vast majority of bilinguals – are "not really" bilingual or are "special types" of bilinguals.

This view of a bilingual person as two monolinguals in one has been assumed and amplified by many bilinguals themselves who criticize their own language competence, or strive to reach monolingual norms, or even hide their knowledge of their weaker language(s).

If one were to count as bilingual only those people who pass as complete monolinguals in each of their languages – they are a rarity – one would be left with no label for the vast majority of people who use two or more languages regularly but who do not have native-like proficiency in each. The reason they don't is quite simply that bilinguals do not need to be equally competent in all of their languages. Where, for what, and with whom they use their languages are crucial aspects in understanding how much each language will be developed.

One of the fathers of bilingualism research, Uriel Weinreich, a linguist in the second part of the twentieth century, recognized this and proposed, along with Canadian linguist William Mackey, a more realistic definition of bilingualism – the alternate use of two or more languages. My own definition is very similar: Bilinguals are those who use two or more languages (or dialects) in their everyday lives.

This other way of looking at bilinguals allows one to include people ranging from the professional interpreter who is fluent in two languages all the way to the established immigrant who speaks the host country's language but who may not be able to read or write it. In between we find the bilingual child who interacts with her parents in one language and with her friends in another; the scientist who reads and writes articles in a second language (but who rarely speaks it); the member of a linguistic minority who uses the minority language at home only and the majority language in all other domains of life; the deaf person who uses sign language with her friends but uses the written form of the spoken language with a hearing person; and so on. Despite the great diversity that exists between these people, they all lead their lives with more than one language.

The more recent and more realistic view of bilingualism has allowed many people who live with two or more languages to accept who they are – bilingual, quite simply.

Reference

Grosjean, F. (2010). *Bilingual: Life and Reality.* Cambridge, MA: Harvard University Press.

1.2 A HOLISTIC VIEW OF BILINGUALISM[1]

Two views of bilinguals are compared, a monolingual (or fractional) view whereby bilinguals are considered as two monolinguals in one person, and

---

[1] The post's original title was "What Do Bilinguals and Hurdlers Have in Common?"

a holistic view which states that bilinguals have a unique and specific linguistic configuration.

The monolingual (or fractional) view of bilingualism, which we mentioned briefly in Post 1.1, has been prevalent – and still is among some people – when we talk about those who use two or more languages (or dialects) in their everyday lives.

According to a strong version of this view, the bilingual has (or should have) two separate and isolable language competencies. These competencies are (or should be) similar to those of the two corresponding monolinguals, therefore, the bilingual is (or should be) two monolinguals in one person.

This monolingual view of bilingualism has had a number of consequences. One of them is that bilinguals have been described and evaluated in terms of the proficiency and balance they have in their two languages. Another is that language skills in bilinguals have almost always been appraised in terms of monolingual norms. The evaluation tools used with bilinguals are often quite simply those employed with the monolinguals of the two corresponding language groups. These assessments rarely take into account the bilinguals' differential needs for their two or more languages or the different social functions of these languages, that is, what a language is used for, with whom, and where (see Post 1.5).

Even experimental work has sometimes led to a straightforward comparison of monolinguals and bilinguals. Some researchers talk of "a bilingual disadvantage," others more recently of "a bilingual advantage" when the results obtained by bilinguals are unlike those of monolinguals. Why not simply talk of "a bilingual difference"? This clearly shows that for some the monolingual is the norm.

One other consequence that has always saddened me is the fact that bilinguals themselves often find fault with their own language competence: "Yes, I use English every day at work, but I speak it so badly that I'm not really bilingual," or "I mix my languages all the time, so I'm not a real bilingual," or even "I have an accent in one of my languages so I'm not bilingual" (see Post 1.7). Other bilinguals strive their hardest to reach monolingual norms, and still others hide their knowledge of their "weaker" language(s).

Over the years, I have defended the bilingual or holistic view of bilingualism which proposes that the bilingual is an integrated whole that cannot easily be decomposed into separate parts. Bilinguals are *not* the sum of two, or more, complete or incomplete monolinguals; rather, they have a unique and specific linguistic configuration. The coexistence and constant interaction of the two or more languages in bilinguals have produced a different but complete language system.

The analogy I use comes from the domain of track and field. Hurdlers blend two types of competencies, that of high jumping and that of sprinting, into an integrated whole. When compared individually with sprinters or high jumpers, hurdlers meet neither level of competence, and yet when taken as a whole, hurdlers are athletes in their own right. No expert in track and field would ever compare hurdlers to sprinters or high jumpers, even though the former blend certain characteristics of the latter two.

In many ways, bilinguals are like hurdlers: unique and specific communicators. Apart from a few exceptions (e.g. translators and interpreters; see Posts 14.2 and 14.3), bilinguals use their two (or more) languages, separately or together, in different areas of life and with different people. Because the needs and uses of the two languages are usually quite different, bilinguals are rarely equally or completely fluent in their two or more languages. Levels of proficiency in a language will depend on the need for that language and will be domain specific.

This holistic view of bilinguals has been emphasized by other colleagues such as Newcastle University Professor Vivian Cook who studies the multicompetence of second-language learners and bilinguals, as well as by researcher Madalena Cruz-Ferreira who has examined, among other things, multilingual norms in the evaluation of bilingual children and adults.

Many others defend this view in their thinking and in their research – a real plus for all of us who are bilingual!

Reference

Grosjean, F. (2010). The bilingual as a competent but specific speaker-hearer. In M. Cruz-Ferreira, ed., *Multilingual Norms*. Frankfurt am Main, Germany: Peter Lang, pp. 19–31. This chapter originally appeared as an article in the Journal of Multilingual and Multicultural Development in 1985.

1.3 VISUALIZING ONE'S LANGUAGES

The defining factor of bilingualism has shifted over time from language proficiency to language use. And yet both factors are important when portraying the languages of a bilingual or a multilingual. A new grid takes into account each factor and is easily filled in.

When describing bilinguals – and not just defining them – it is important to take into account both language use and the level of proficiency that bilinguals have in their different languages. I set about finding a way of doing so visually and the outcome is in the form of a grid that is presented in Figure 1.1.

Language use is presented along the vertical axis (from Never used at the bottom all the way to Daily use at the top) and language proficiency is on the horizontal axis (from Low proficiency on the left to High proficiency on the right). These labels can be replaced with numerical values if necessary. Based on the two factors – measured objectively or based on self-reports – a bilingual's two or more languages can be placed in the appropriate cells of the grid.

To illustrate how the grid functions, I have inserted the three languages of a given bilingual, Lucia: English (E), Spanish (S), and French (F). Her most fluent and most used language is English (E), and it can be found at the top right corner of the grid. She is also fluent in Spanish (S) but slightly less so, and hence it is slightly to the left of E. In addition, she does not use it as much as English and so it is slightly lower than E.

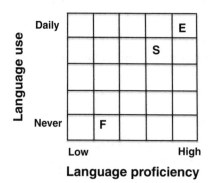

Figure 1.1 A bilingual described in terms of language use and language proficiency

As for French (F), a language Lucia learned in school, her proficiency is between low and medium, and she never uses it. Hence its position is in the bottom left part of the grid. This is not uncommon in bilinguals who, in addition to the languages they use on a regular basis, know one or two other languages to a much lesser degree and use them quite rarely.

Examining a grid such as this one is instructive. Thus, in our example, Lucia is clearly bilingual (she uses English and Spanish on a regular basis), and she also knows one other language, French. Had her French been situated at the top of the grid, and toward the middle- or the right-hand side, she could have been considered to be trilingual. When I filled in my own grid with four languages, it came out clearly that I am bilingual in English and French and that I also know two other languages, but to a much lesser extent, and that I rarely use them.

Any bilingual can fill in his/her own grid. An empty grid is presented in Figure 1.2 and can be copied and saved for personal use. Once filled in, it can be compared to the grid of other bilinguals or multilinguals.

Separate grids can be used for each of the bilingual's four language skills (speaking, listening, writing, and reading) since it is often the case that amount of use and degree of proficiency can be quite different in these skills in the different languages. Thus, some bilinguals may have very good oral comprehension of a language but may not speak it very well; others may know how to read and write one of their languages but not the other(s); and so on.

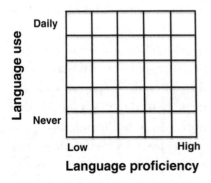

Figure 1.2 Empty grid to be filled in by the reader

To represent a bilingual's language history, one will need several grids, with one grid for each important linguistic period in the person's life. That way, major linguistic milestones will appear, such as the age of onset of each of the bilingual's languages, changes of language dominance, moments when the bilingual stopped using a language, and so on. An example of a person's language history is given in Post 4.1.

Of course, there are many other factors that are important when describing bilinguals, most notably how languages are distributed across different domains of life (see Post 1.5), the bilinguals' movement along the monolingual–bilingual language mode continuum (see Post 3.1), as well as whether they are also bicultural (see Post 9.1). But this visualization of language proficiency and language use is a first step in portraying a bilingual's linguistic configuration.

Reference

Grosjean, F. (2010). Describing bilinguals. Chapter 2 of *Bilingual: Life and Reality*. Cambridge, MA: Harvard University Press.

1.4 WHAT IS IT LIKE TO BE BILINGUAL?

We all have an opinion about what it means to be bilingual even if we are not bilingual ourselves. Here we let bilinguals tell us about the many advantages – and a few of the inconveniences – of being bilingual.

Practically everyone has an opinion about the advantages and inconveniences of being bilingual – educators, psychologists, linguists, sociologists – even if they are not bilingual themselves. With the aid of two short surveys and many personal testimonies, I propose we let bilinguals tell us what it is like to be bilingual.

The dominant picture that emerges is that bilinguals are quite positive about their bilingualism. A first advantage they put forward concerns the ability they have to communicate with different people, of different cultures, in different regions or countries. Linked to this is the fact that being bilingual allows you to read more (if you are literate in several languages naturally) and to sometimes express yourself with greater clarity and with a more diverse vocabulary (when all languages are taken into consideration, of course).

A second advantage put forward by bilinguals is the fact that knowing several languages seems to help you learn other languages. Not only might the new language be linked to one that you already know, hence facilitating its learning, but the more the mind learns about the workings of different aspects of language, the more it can help with a new language. A Marathi/Hindi/English trilingual verbalized this by stating that being bi- or multilingual helps understanding how a language has a different logic.

Bilinguals also stress the fact that bilingualism fosters open-mindedness, offers different perspectives on life, and reduces cultural ignorance. As a sign language/oral language bilingual wrote to me, "Bilingualism gives you a double perspective on the world."

Bilinguals are also very practical when they state that bilingualism gives you more job opportunities and greater social mobility. Other advantages they put forward are that bilingualism allows you to help others, create a bond with other bilinguals (even if they do not share all your languages), and understand what others do not.

The two surveys also inquired about the inconveniences of being bilingual. Surprisingly, a third of the respondents stated that there weren't any. Of the disadvantages that were listed, one was the fact that not knowing a language well makes communication – spoken or written – tiring and error prone. In fact, some bilinguals sometimes feel that they do not know either of their languages well (for the beginning of an explanation, see Post 1.5). There are also those who regret having an accent in one of their languages.

A few bilinguals state that when speaking monolingually, they struggle to keep out code-switches and borrowings (see Post 3.4). Interferences can also appear (see Post 3.7), which increase in number when bilinguals get tired, angry, or nervous. Having to use the "wrong language," that is, the language not usually used in a particular situation, can also be difficult and frustrating (see Post 3.2).

Bilinguals note the inconvenience of being asked to translate and interpret from time to time. They may not be able to refuse, so they struggle through and find it quite stressful. One particularly vivid testimony is given by Paul Preston who interviewed English/American Sign Language hearing bilinguals. This particular person had to interpret at her father's funeral because there was no one else who could do it: "I just kept sobbing and signing, all mixed up, all at the same time."

A final inconvenience that is mentioned is linked to biculturalism and reflects the fact that some bicultural bilinguals are still in the process of adjusting to their cultures and working out how they wish to identify themselves (see Post 9.2).

Despite these disadvantages, it clearly emerges from the surveys that bilinguals are very positive about their knowledge and use of two or more languages. Had they been asked, they would probably have made their own this trilingual's testimony:

I have achieved greater stature in my work environment; I have developed my lingual capacities; I have become more open-minded toward minorities and more aware of their linguistic problems; I have enjoyed various forms of literature and felt a certain amount of pride in being able to read in three different languages ... Life never becomes boring, because there is more than just one language available.

References

Grosjean, F. (2010). Attitudes and feelings about bilingualism. Chapter 9 of *Bilingual: Life and Reality*. Cambridge, MA: Harvard University Press.
Preston, P. (1995). *Mother Father Deaf*. Cambridge, MA: Harvard University Press.

1.5 WHAT A BILINGUAL'S LANGUAGES ARE USED FOR

Bilinguals usually acquire and use their languages for different purposes, in different domains of life, with different people.

"Antoine, how do you say 'download a file' in French?"
"Hem, I'm not quite sure."
"But I thought you were bilingual?"

How many bilinguals have found themselves in Antoine's situation, trying to translate a term or expression into another language, or attempting to describe something, or simply talking about a topic normally covered by their other language?

When I returned to Europe after twelve years in the United States and offered to teach an introductory course in statistics at my university,

I suddenly found myself in trouble. I simply didn't know how to say simple things – albeit for someone who knows some statistics – such as "scattergram" or "hypothesis test" in French.

Antoine's predicament and my own can be explained quite simply: Bilinguals usually acquire and use their languages for different purposes, in different domains of life, with different people. Different aspects of life often require different languages. I have called this the "Complementarity Principle."

If we were to take a bilingual's domains of language use, such as immediate family, distant relatives, work, sports, religion, school, shopping, friends, going out, hobbies, and so on, and if we were to attach languages to these domains, we would see that some domains are covered by one language, some others by another language, and some by several languages. Rarely do bilinguals have all domains covered by all their languages.

Figure 1.3 helps us visualize this. Each quadrilateral represents a domain of life such as work/studies, home, family, shopping, leisure, administrative matters, holidays, clothes, sports, transportation, health, politics, and so on. The person who is depicted here, a trilingual in languages a, b, and c, uses language a (La) in seven domains of life, Lb in three domains, both La and Lb in five domains, and all three

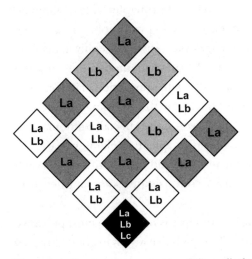

Figure 1.3 The domains covered by a bilingual's three languages

languages (La, Lb, and Lc) in just one domain. Some domains, therefore, are specific to one language (ten in all), and others are shared by two or three languages (six in all). Any bilingual can be characterized in this way and will have a pattern that is specific to him or her.

I have met many bilinguals who have shared the experience of suddenly having to use a language that they don't normally use in a particular domain. It is often a frustrating experience. Bilinguals tend to hesitate and fumble in that language. They are often tempted to draw from their other language(s), a strategy that works when they are speaking with other bilinguals. When this is not possible, they may still borrow words but they then have to explain them. They may also quite simply shorten the conversation.

The Complementarity Principle accounts for many interesting bilingual phenomena. The first is language proficiency. If a language is spoken in a reduced number of domains and with a limited number of people, then it will not be developed as much as a language used in more domains and with more people. This is true of certain language skills such as reading and writing as well as stylistic levels.

Well-learned behaviors are special cases of the principle – counting, doing arithmetic, praying, and so on – since one language usually has exclusive control of that behavior. How often have I had to think hard about my phone number in the "wrong" language!

Translation is another skill affected by the principle. Unless bilinguals have domains covered by two languages (as do professional translators), or have acquired their other languages via translation equivalents (I'm thinking here of traditional language learning methods), they may not have the resources to produce an adequate translation. Hence, even though bilinguals can usually translate simple things from one language to another, they often have difficulties with more specialized domains.

Children are also influenced by the principle. It explains, in part, why a language is more developed than another, and why children may switch over to the other language during a conversation, sometimes even in front of monolinguals.

Basically, the Complementarity Principle is one of the most pervasive aspects of individual bilingualism. Bilinguals live with it in good harmony until, on occasion, it interferes with their everyday language use.

Reference

Grosjean, F. (2016). The Complementarity Principle and its impact on processing, acquisition, and dominance. In C. Silva-Corvalán and J. Treffers-Daller, eds., *Language Dominance in Bilinguals: Issues of Measurement and Operationalization*. Cambridge: Cambridge University Press, pp. 66–84.

1.6 WHAT DOES IT MEAN TO BE DOMINANT IN A LANGUAGE?

An interesting concept in the study of bilingualism is language dominance. What does it mean? And does it depend, in part, on what a bilingual's languages are used for?

In the preceding post (1.5), I explained by means of the Complementarity Principle how different aspects of life often require different languages. The Principle plays a large role in various aspects of bilingualism, one of them being language dominance. Professor Li Wei of University College, London, defines the dominant bilingual as someone with greater proficiency in one of his or her languages and who uses it significantly more than the other language(s). In addition to language proficiency and language use, other factors are sometimes mentioned by researchers when accounting for dominance such as when the language was acquired, the bilingual's ability to read and write that language, the speed and efficiency with which it is processed, and so on.

Researchers have long tried to measure dominance. Outside judges can evaluate the bilinguals' languages such as their pronunciation and the extent of their vocabulary, or the bilinguals can be given various tests such as naming pictures, recognizing words, carrying out a command, or translating sentences from one language to the other. From the various measures obtained, specialists give the participants a dominance rating: the person is dominant in language A, or dominant in language B, or balanced in both languages (if such a person exists).

However, these various approaches have been criticized for reducing the complexity of the bilingual's language knowledge and behavior to a number of simple tasks often given in just one language. In addition, the cut-off point in the results of a particular task that is used to separate dominant from balanced bilinguals is arbitrary. It is also the case that many people use more than two languages in their everyday life which complexifies things even more.

Bilinguals can also be given language background questionnaires to fill in with questions that pertain to when and how the languages were learned, when the respondents started feeling comfortable speaking each language, how and when the languages are used, how proficient the bilinguals feel in each of their languages, and so on. A dominance index is then calculated based on the answers given.

All these measures, both objective and subjective, may produce a global measure of dominance and may confirm, for example, that bilinguals are globally dominant in one of their languages, but they do not take into account that some domains of life are specific to a language. In the figure in Post 1.5, the bilingual depicted is globally dominant in La (thirteen domains counting shared domains), but there are three domains in which she uses Lb exclusively. With adequate assessment tools, it would probably be fairly easy to show that this bilingual is dominant in Lb in these domains. Thus, one can be globally dominant in a specific language but be dominant in the other language for particular domains of life.

Even though the Complementarity Principle puts the emphasis on language use, it has an indirect effect on proficiency, the other variable in Li Wei's description of dominance in the bilingual. If a language is spoken in a reduced number of domains and with a limited number of people, then it will not be developed as much as a language used in more domains and with more people. It is precisely because the need and use of the languages are usually quite different that bilinguals do not develop equal and total proficiency in all their languages.

This is also true for certain skills such as reading and writing. Many bilinguals do not need to read and write in some of their languages and hence have not developed these skills. Even if they do have reading and writing skills in their two or more languages, the levels of competence are probably different because the needs for these skills are not the same in each language.

Fortunately, researchers are starting to take the Complementarity Principle into account when describing language dominance. In 2016, Carmen Silva-Corvalán of the University of Southern California and

Jeanine Treffers-Daller of the University of Reading edited a book on the topic and they proposed a new definition which takes into account the Principle: "... we define dominant language, a relative notion, as that in which a bilingual has attained an overall higher level of proficiency at a given age, and/or the language which s/he uses more frequently, and across a wider range of domains."

The book contains nine chapters by other researchers in addition to the ones by the editors, and it raises many unresolved issues relating to language dominance in children and adults. It also offers different theoretical perspectives on the question and a number of approaches to get at dominance. It has quickly become *the* book to read on the topic!

References

Wei, L. (2007). Dimensions of bilingualism. In L. Wei, ed., *The Bilingualism Reader*. London and New York: Routledge, pp. 3–24.

Silva-Corvalán, C. and Treffers-Daller, J. (2016). *Language Dominance in Bilinguals: Issues of Measurement and Operationalization*. Cambridge: Cambridge University Press.

1.7 BILINGUALS AND ACCENTS

There is a longstanding myth that real bilinguals have no accent in their different languages. In fact, having an accent in one or more languages is the norm for bilinguals; not having one is the exception.

Do you recognize the distinguished looking gentleman in the photo? He was trilingual in Polish, French, and English; he wrote outstanding prose in his *third* language, English, and he is now recognized as one of English literature's great authors. His name is Joseph Conrad and, as it happens, he had a very strong Polish accent in English!

There is a longstanding myth that real bilinguals have no accent in their different languages. Joseph Conrad and many other bilinguals, in all domains of life, show how unfounded this myth is. Having a "foreign" accent in one or more languages is, in fact, the norm for bilinguals; not having one is the exception. There is no relationship between one's knowledge of a language and whether one has an accent in it.

Figure 1.4 Joseph Conrad in 1904 taken by George Charles Beresford

Researchers do not agree on an accent age limit – no accent if a language is acquired below it, the presence of an accent if it is acquired later. Some have proposed that a language can be "accent-less" (in the sense of not being influenced by another language, normally one's first language) if acquired before age six; others extend the window to age twelve. Personally, I have met bilinguals who acquired their second or third language even later who do not have an accent in it.

Usually a first language will influence a second language that is acquired later, but it is not uncommon that a second language may influence the first. This happens when the second language is used much more than the first, over an extended period of time. Bilinguals who start having an accent in their first language are usually very conscious of it and often comment on it; some even excuse themselves. But it is a normal linguistic phenomenon explained by the circum-stances of life.

As for the origin of accents in a third or a fourth language, one must examine the bilingual's language history. It really depends on when and where the person acquired the language and which other language was dominant at the time.

Some bilinguals even have an accent in all of their languages. This happens when they spent their early years moving between language communities. Once again, this is not an indication of how well they master their languages.

We are all conscious of our accents; some see disadvantages to them whereas others see advantages. Among the disadvantages, the one that is mentioned the most is that it makes you stand out from others when you want to blend in. If the society you live in is not positively inclined toward the group you belong to, an accent can have a negative effect on the way you are perceived and treated.

Another disadvantage is that an accent may signal that the speaker has not tried hard enough to learn the language when, in fact, it is due to neuromuscular factors that are difficult to control. Finally, although having an accent does not normally impede communication, when it is very strong, it may do so, even though the person may be fluent in the language being spoken (see Post 1.9).

But there are also many advantages to having an accent. Some accents are seen positively by people or groups (e.g. a French accent in Germany, a British accent in France, etc.). I have also known of cases in which an accent was a major factor in a person's falling in love with someone, although not the only factor, one hopes.

An accent also clearly marks you as a member of your group if you do not want to be seen as a member of the other group. Linked to this is that an accent can be self-protective. It prevents members of the group you are interacting with from expecting you to know their language perfectly as well as all their cultural and social rules.

In sum, having an accent when you know and use two or more languages is a fact of life; it is something you get used to, as do the others you interact with.

Reference

Grosjean, F. (2010). Having an accent in a language. Chapter 7 of *Bilingual: Life and Reality*. Cambridge, MA: Harvard University Press.

1.8 RETAINING AN ACCENT

Many different factors explain why some people retain an accent in a second language whereas others do not. The pioneering work of Professor James Flege over the years has helped us understand this intriguing phenomenon.

Some time ago, a friend wrote to me to ask why it is some people retain an accent and some do not. She was quite aware of the maturational aspect that underlies the phenomenon (accents are maintained beyond a certain age in adolescence) but she rightly pointed out that some people who acquire a language before age ten, for example, have an accent whereas others who acquire it later do not. Why is that?

I relayed her question to my colleague, Professor Emeritus James Flege of the University of Alabama, who is the world's expert on the question. He very kindly directed me to a few of his papers and sent me a keynote lecture he had given at an international conference in 2012.

James Flege mentions a number of factors that explain the presence of a foreign accent. Among them we find the maturational factor (see Post 1.7) as well as interference from the other language(s). In a 1995 paper with his colleagues Murray Munro and Ian MacKay, he divided the latter into two sub-factors: "habit formation" (first language sounds are substituted for second language sounds) and "incorrect perception" (language learners fail to perceive accurately the phonetic details of a second language). Other factors James Flege mentions are motivation to produce the exact sounds required (it can decrease, for example, if articulatory errors do not impede communication), individual differences (they include language history, language habits, as well as sometimes not wanting to sound like a native speaker), and finally, the phonetic input bilinguals have received (for example, hearing others speak the second language with or without a foreign accent).

In their 1995 study, James Flege and his colleagues examined the English pronunciation of 240 adult native Italian speakers of English who had begun learning English when they emigrated to Canada between the ages of two and twenty-three years. When recorded, they had been there for an average of thirty-two years and reported speaking English more than Italian. The authors found that the age of learning English exerted a systematic effect on the bilinguals' production of English. The earlier the age of arrival, the weaker the accent. This can be explained by the maturational factor but also by the amount of English heard and spoken since their arrival.

But clearly other factors were present too. For example, in a later study that used a subpart of this vast database, James Flege and other colleagues found that those who spoke Italian relatively often had significantly stronger foreign accents than those who seldom spoke Italian. It was as if the more frequent activation of their first language, Italian, had an impact on the pronunciation of their second language.

In his 2012 keynote lecture, James Flege came to the conclusion that the second language input heard by bilinguals over the years will eventually be shown to be more important than other determinants that account for the pronunciation level reached in that language. The evidence he brought was based in part on an unpublished study Ian MacKay and he conducted a bit more than ten years after their 1995 study. They wished to see if their already very experienced users of English were capable of improving their pronunciation of that language. To do this, they rerecorded 160 of the original 240 Italian immigrants with identical procedures and equipment.

A first analysis of the results obtained seemed to show that there was no change in the speakers' pronunciation of English; the correlation they found between the results of the earlier and the later study was an amazing 0.97. Could this be a sign that the pronunciation of their participants was "fossilized"? In fact, a closer analysis of the results showed that the pronunciation of a bit more than a third of the participants had become slightly worse over the ten-year period whereas the pronunciation of some 14 percent had improved slightly.

To try to understand this, the researchers defined three groups: a group that used less English (as compared to 1992), a group that used English more, and a group where there was no change. For each group, they examined the pronunciation of a number of consonants (these are clear indicators of the presence of an accent or not) and they found that the group which had used more English in the interval showed the most improvement in pronunciation. The group that had not changed in their use of English showed some improvement, but less, and the group that had used less English remained at the same pronunciation level.

James Flege believed that the group that used English more probably came into contact with a greater number of English monolinguals with whom they had to speak English. Hence they heard more accentless English which in turn had an impact on the pronunciation of their English sounds. This reinforced his hunch that input (both type and amount) is an important factor in second language pronunciation. As he so nicely put it, "You are what you eat . . .. phonetically."

References

Flege, J. E. (2012). The role of input in second language (L2) speech learning. Keynote address, VIth International Conference on Native and Non-native Accents of English Łódź, Poland, December 6–8.

Flege, J. E., Munro, M. J., and MacKay, I. R. A. (1995). Effects of age of second-language learning on the production of English consonants. *Speech Communication*, 16, 1–26.

1.9 UNDERSTANDING SOMEONE WITH A FOREIGN ACCENT

We sometimes interact with a person who has a strong foreign accent. What impact does it have on our understanding of what is being said?

How foreign accents are perceived, that is, the impression they make on us, and how well accented speech is understood, are topics that have led to some very interesting studies. Here is just one example. Two Canadian researchers, Murray Munro at Simon Fraser University and Tracey M. Derwing at the University of Alberta, asked native speakers of English to listen to English recordings made by native speakers of Mandarin who had learned English after puberty. They were proficient in English but their pronunciation ranged from moderately to heavily accented.

The English native speakers were asked to do three tasks. In one of them, they had to give an accentedness rating, that is, to rate the degree of foreign accent in each recording sample they were given. They used a 9-point scale, where 1 corresponded to no foreign accent and 9 to a very strong foreign accent. The final distribution of these ratings was basically flat, with almost as many samples falling in the 1–3, 4–6, and 7–9 accentedness groups. Thus, there were as many samples considered to have been spoken with no foreign accent, as there were with a moderate accent, and with a very strong accent.

Would this distribution be reflected in how well the samples were understood? Would a sample judged to be heavily accented be badly understood? And likewise, would a sample judged to have been spoken with no foreign accent be easily understood? The participants were given two tasks to get at this. In the first, a judgment task, they had to assign a comprehensibility rating to each sample, where 1 corresponded to extremely easy to understand, and 9 to impossible to understand.

To the authors' surprise, the comprehensibility distribution was quite different from the one obtained for accentedness: 22 percent of the samples here were given a rating of 1 (extremely easy to understand) – only about 4 percent had received a 1 in the accentedness ratings – and a full 64 percent of the samples fell in the 1–3 comprehensibility categories. Basically, many of the samples were perceived to be comprehensible even though they had been judged to be accented. Thus, even if someone is speaking with a foreign accent, there is a fair chance that they will be understood.

The real test though is to move away from perceived comprehensibility to actual comprehension. To do this, the participants were given an intelligibility task. They were asked to transcribe exactly what they had heard. The transcriptions were then given an intelligibility score on the basis of the number of words that exactly matched what had been said. The results were quite amazing. Close to two-thirds of the samples received a score in the 91–100 percent intelligibility range. Basically, the presence of a foreign accent did not impact intelligibility to a large extent.

Thus, listening to someone with an accent does not normally affect the comprehension and hence impede communication. Of course, from time to time this can happen, and we all have a few examples in mind when we found communication difficult. The accent was so strong that it almost seemed as if the person was speaking their other language. However, if we interact with someone periodically, we often adapt to the specificities of their accented speech marked by vowel and consonant changes, word stress misplacement, inappropriate pause placement, different pitch contours, and so on.

We also adopt various perception and communication strategies. Here is one described by an English–Spanish bilingual listening to her mother, originally from Guatemala, when she was speaking English to her: "She ... struggled with differentiating 'b' and 'v.' In Spanish they sound alike, unlike English. So whenever she was writing, and she asked me for the spelling of an unfamiliar English word that began with one of those letters, I would say, 'It starts with V, like vaca or B, like bebé?'"

Of course, at times, we may have to shorten the interaction we are having with a person with heavily accented speech, but such instances are relatively rare. In sum, as I wrote in Post 1.7, having an accent when you know and use two or more languages is a fact of life; it is something you get used to, as do the others you interact with.

References

Munro, M. J. and Derwing, T. M. (2019). Phonetics and second language teaching research. In W. F. Katz and P. F. Assmann, eds., *The Routledge Handbook of Phonetics*. Abingdon: Routledge, pp. 473–495.

Munro, M. J. and Derwing, T. M. (1999). Foreign accent, comprehensibility, and intelligibility in the speech of second language learners. In J. Leather, ed., *Phonological Issues in Language Learning*. Oxford: Blackwell, pp. 285–310.

2

The Extent of Bilingualism

INTRODUCTION

People are often surprised that those who use two or more languages (or dialects) in their everyday lives make up more than half of the world's population. In Post 2.1, a few examples of the extent of bilingualism are given and it is explained why the phenomenon is so widespread.

In Post 2.2, the difficulty in obtaining clear data on the number of bilinguals in different countries is discussed. Two examples are given. In the first, the United States, which does not address bilingualism as such in its census or annual surveys, asks three language questions that allow one to obtain a fairly good estimation of the number of bilinguals. In the second, it is shown how Switzerland has a more restrictive view of bilingualism. This impacts the number of bilinguals the census reports on.

Post 2.3 hunts down the claim that 65 percent of the world's population is bilingual, a far larger percentage than what is normally accepted. It makes for an interesting story and illustrates perfectly the difficulties of getting a good numerical grasp of the extent of bilingualism.

The last two posts concern bilingualism in the United States. In Post 2.4, its extent is explained, and those who are bilingual – who they are, where they live, and which languages are involved, in addition to English – are described. And in Post 2.5, I go back all the way to 1980, when I first started being interested in bilingualism in the United States, and I then move forward. I show by means of statistics how the situation has evolved quite amazingly since then without endangering in any way the prominence of English as the country's main language.

2.1 BILINGUALISM'S BEST KEPT SECRET

It is estimated that those who use two or more languages (or dialects) in their everyday lives make up more than half of the world's population.

Whenever I give a talk on bilingualism, I surprise my audience with the following estimate: more than half of the world's population uses two or more languages (or dialects) in everyday life. Bilingualism is present on all continents, in all classes of society, in all age groups.

We know, for example, that in Asia and Africa, many people are bi- or multilingual although precise figures are often lacking. In Europe, a bit more than half of the population is at least bilingual. Smaller countries such as Luxembourg, Switzerland, and the Netherlands are home to many bilinguals, whereas larger countries such as Great Britain and France have fewer of them.

In North America, some 35 percent of the population in Canada is bilingual and although the percentage is smaller in the United States – close to 23 percent[1] – this still corresponds to an estimated seventy million inhabitants. Bilingualism in the United States is very diverse, pairing English with Native American languages, older colonial languages, recent immigration languages, and so on.

How can one explain such large numbers of bilinguals? One reason is simply that many countries house numerous languages: 722 in Indonesia, 445 in India, 207 in Australia, and so on. Contact between communities means learning other languages or, at the very least, acquiring a common language of communication and hence being bilingual.

In addition, some countries have a language policy that recognizes and fosters several languages – at the very least their official or national languages. Children learn these languages (or some of them) and many may well be educated in a language that is not their native language.

Trade and business are a major cause of language contact, and hence bilingualism. For example, Greek was the language of buyers and sellers in the Mediterranean during the third, fourth, and fifth centuries BCE and, of course, English has become a major language of trade and business today. I have known business people in Sweden, Switzerland,

---

[1] Based on 2018 data from the American Community Survey; see Posts 2.4 and 2.5.

and Singapore who speak English all day at work and return home to speak their native language.

An important cause of bilingualism is the movement of peoples. The reasons are many – political, religious, social, economic – and go back to the beginning of time. For instance, people have always moved to other regions or countries in search of work and better living conditions, and this has led to substantial bilingualism. It is with this in mind that American linguist Einar Haugen, a pioneer of bilingualism studies, stated that the United States has probably been the home of more bilingual speakers than any other country in the world.

That said, bilingualism will never be very extensive at any one time in the United States because it is usually short-lived and transitional. For generations and generations of Americans, bilingualism has covered a brief period, spanning one or two generations, between monolingualism in a minority language and monolingualism in English. Things are changing though (see Post 2.5). More and more families are keeping their linguistic and cultural heritage alive in addition to making sure their children know the majority language. And more and more professions need people who speak two or more languages. In addition, bilingualism allows you to communicate with different people and hence to discover different cultures, thereby giving you a different perspective on the world.

Reference

Grosjean, F. (2010). *Bilingual: Life and Reality.* Cambridge, MA: Harvard University Press.

2.2 ON THE DIFFICULTY OF COUNTING PEOPLE WHO ARE BILINGUAL[2]

We don't know for sure how many people in the world are bilingual. Official data, when they exist, can produce quite surprising results.

It has been estimated that probably more than half of the world's population is bilingual, that is, uses two or more languages (or dialects)

---

[2] The original post was entitled "How Many Are We?"

in everyday life (see Post 2.1). But this is just an estimation, and, unfortunately, we are still a long way away from knowing exactly how many
people are indeed bilingual. Why is that?

It is rare that a national census or survey has a question pertaining to
bilingualism itself. Usually, there are questions on the languages known
by the inhabitants of the country and the results obtained are then used
by researchers to work out the number of bilinguals. This can be rendered difficult when the questions asked are not quite appropriate or
when they reflect a certain partiality concerning what it means to know
a language or to be bilingual.

I will take two examples of national censuses – the one in the United
States and the one in Switzerland – and show how quite official data can
sometimes produce very surprising results. In this instance, it would
appear that there are proportionally more bilinguals in the United
States than in Switzerland even though the latter country is known the
world over for the bi- or multilingualism of its inhabitants.

In the United States, language questions have been asked on and off
in the censuses or in surveys conducted by the US Census Bureau for
more than a hundred years. These questions have been quite straightforward, and estimating the number of bilinguals from the data has not
been too difficult, although the results are invariably tentative. In 1940,
for example, the question was addressed with, "Language spoken in
home in earliest childhood," and in 1960, for a person born outside the
United States, the question was, "What language was spoken in his home
before he came to the United States?". Since 1980, three questions have
been asked: "Does this person speak a language other than English at
home? What is this language? How well does this person speak English
(very well, well, not well, not at all)?"

The 2018 American Community Survey (ACS), using these questions,
found that a bit more than sixty-seven million inhabitants spoke
a language other than English at home. Among those people, some sixty-
three million also knew and used English and hence were bilingual. This
represents 20.55 percent of the population. A rough estimate of the final
proportion of bilinguals in the United States, taking into account those
not counted by the survey, is probably around 23 percent of the
population.

Let's now turn to Switzerland and the language questions asked in its 2010 national census. I will concentrate on the first one as it is so very different from the questions that have been asked in the United States. In addition, it is the data obtained with this question that have been used by Swiss Statistics to estimate the number of bi- or multilinguals in the country. Here is a translation of the question: "What is your main language, i.e. the language in which you think and that you know the best? If you think in several languages and know them very well, then name these languages." This was followed by a number of language categories that often grouped together a national language and a dialect such as "German or Swiss German."

Clearly, the people who thought of the question had a very restrictive view of bilingualism given that the most used definition of bilingualism today is simply that it is the regular use of two or more languages or dialects in everyday life. In the census question, it was assumed that people have one main language and that if they have others, then they must know them very well. In addition, it was stipulated that one must think in each of one's languages to be able to list them. The fact that thinking can take place independently of language and can be visual-spatial or involve nonlinguistic concepts was not taken into account (see Post 12.1).

Finally, speakers of Swiss German and German, among others, were given just one category to check and hence could not list their two languages. And yet, the majority of the Swiss German population (close to two-thirds of Swiss people) use both Swiss German and German in their everyday lives.

The outcome was that Swiss Statistics stated that a mere 15.8 percent of the Swiss population is bi- or multilingual (less than the 23 percent found for the United States therefore) when, in fact, most Swiss people know several languages, which they use frequently. The estimated percentage of bi- or multilinguals, based on the other language questions, was later figured out to be 42 percent.

Faced with such issues as what a language is as opposed to a dialect, what knowing a language means, how to define bilingualism, and so on, it is not surprising that the results of language surveys do not give us a ready answer as to who is monolingual, bilingual, or multilingual. Where does that leave researchers in the field? They have no choice but to continue stating that probably more than half of the world's population uses two or more languages (or dialects) in everyday life – some even go up to 65 percent (see Post 2.3) – in the hope that they can have a definite number one day!

References

Grosjean, F. (2010). The extent of bilingualism. *Bilingual: Life and Reality*. Cambridge, MA: Harvard University Press.

Zeigler, K. and Camarota, S. A. (2019). 67.3 Million in the United States Spoke a Foreign Language at Home in 2018. Center for Immigration Studies, Washington, DC. https://cis.org/Report/673-Million-United-States-Spoke-Foreign-Language-Home–2018

2.3 CHASING DOWN THOSE 65 PERCENT

Humans love numbers and bilinguals are no exception. For a long time, most researchers said that half, or a bit more than half, of the world's population is bilingual but then 65 percent was proposed. Where does this percentage come from and is it possible?

When asked how many bilinguals there are in the world, I usually state that there are no precise figures but that probably half or slightly more than half of the world's population is bilingual, that is uses two or more languages (or dialects) in everyday life. When asked to be more precise, I usually stay around the 50 percent mark.

I immediately add that we are still a long way away from knowing exactly how many people are bilingual. Rare are the national censuses that have a question pertaining to bi- or multilingualism, and when they do, the meaning they give to this notion can be very restrictive (see Post 2.2). In addition, those countries that only ask about languages, not bilingualism, can reflect a certain partiality concerning what it means to know a language, and then there are those countries that do not even ask language questions in their censuses such as France and Belgium.

One day, a few years ago, as I was watching Dr. Kim Potowski, professor of Hispanic linguistics at the University of Illinois at Chicago, give her very stimulating TEDx talk, "No child left monolingual," I heard her say, "Now the fact is that 65% of the world today is bilingual or multilingual. . . ."

I was intrigued by this sudden jump in numbers and so I wrote to Kim Potowski to ask her what the source was for her figure. She kindly replied that she had found it in a book published in 2002 which I immediately consulted, but I had no success finding the figure. I left it at that although her number seemed really high to me.

More than a year later, it was a pleasant surprise to hear from Kim Potowski again who told me that she had finally found the source. The figure had been given by Professor Colin Baker and his colleague Dr. Sylvia Prys Jones, both of Bangor University in Wales, in the Preface to their monumental *The Encyclopedia of Bilingualism and Bilingual Education* published in 1998. They state, "... around two-thirds of the world's population are bilingual."

So the next stage in my quest was to write to Colin Baker to ask him where they had obtained that figure, or how they had worked it out. Over several exchanges of emails, he explained to me how they had guesstimated the figure. They put together a rough spreadsheet with estimates of each country's bilingual population. They used Ethnologue, *the* source about languages in the world today, to which they added several other sources. At the time, the language sources were incomplete (e.g. on the bilingual language minorities in China and in other large countries) or quite simply, the data were inaccurate.

Colin Baker continued,

> My memory is that we estimated that the "true" value was probably between 50% and 70% if we were rather generous in our definition of a "bilingual". Under 50% seemed too small and above 70% rather unlikely. While 60% would have been a midpoint, it would have been spurious and dishonest to suggest we could be that accurate. Hence "two thirds" became a less spurious way of giving our generous guess.

I asked Colin Baker if they had taken the mean of percentages worked out for each country, in essence giving each country the same weight even if the populations are of different sizes, or if they had taken the total estimated number of bilinguals, across all countries, divided by the world's population at the time. He replied that they had used the latter approach but that they had to exclude some countries from the total for sheer lack of data.

Colin Baker added an important remark to this. They had included those learning a second language, particularly English, which adds literally millions of people to the numerator. Based on this, and on the fact that at the time the numerical bilingual data were so poor, he now thinks that it would have been wiser to give upper and lower boundaries for the guesstimate, that is between 50 percent and 70 percent, ". . . as this would have better expressed what is not definable, measurable or likely to be agreed upon."

So where do we stand on this question today? Colin Baker summarized his answers to my emails with, "I suppose the real answer is: we do not know." In addition, his figure includes language learners, which may be problematic as many of them, unless they are new immigrants, are not active bilinguals but only bilingual potentially (recall the definition I use: bilinguals are those who *use* two or more languages, or dialects, in everyday life). Given all of this, I think that I will continue to state that probably more than half of the world's population is bilingual, and hope that one day we will be able to have a more precise figure.

But will that hope ever materialize? Let's give Colin Baker the last word and imagine a British gleam in his eyes as he says it: "And to add to the fun – perhaps the question about the percentage of the world's population who are more than bilingual (multilingual) could be posed. I'd not even offer a guess on that one!"

References

Baker, C. and Prys Jones, S. (1998). *Encyclopedia of Bilingualism and Bilingual Education*. Clevedon: Multilingual Matters.
Ethnologue: Languages of the World (2020): www.ethnologue.com/

2.4 BILINGUALS IN THE UNITED STATES

Bilinguals represent about 23 percent of the population in the United States. Who are they? Where do they live? What languages do they speak in addition to English?

Ever since I worked on my first book on bilingualism back in the early 1980s, I have been fascinated by the state of bilingualism in the United States. And over the years, I have followed its evolution.

As we saw in Post 2.2, the 2018 American Community Survey found that a bit more than sixty-seven million inhabitants spoke a language other than English at home. Among those people, some sixty-three million also knew and used English and hence were bilingual. This represents 20.55 percent of the population. If we add to this number bilingual children under five (not covered by the survey) as well as people who use a second or third language in their everyday lives but only English at home, then probably close to 23 percent of the population can be considered bilingual.

Bilingualism in the United States is on the rise (see Post 2.5) and it is also very diverse, pairing English with Native American languages, older colonial languages, recent immigration languages, American Sign Language, and so on. English–Spanish bilinguals represent 61 percent of all bilinguals and hence Spanish is definitely America's second language. Other important languages, but to a far lesser extent, are Chinese, Tagalog, Vietnamese, Arabic, French, and Korean.

Over the past forty years, many "traditional" immigrant languages have declined in number. Among these we find Italian, Yiddish, Polish, and Greek. This is largely due to aging populations and dwindling migrant flows from the countries where those languages are used.

Bilinguals are not equally distributed across the nation. Some states contain proportionally very few (e.g. West Virginia, Mississippi, Montana, and Kentucky) whereas others have a far greater proportion (e.g. California, Texas, New Mexico, New Jersey, and New York). As for cities, the ones with the most bilinguals are Los Angeles, Houston, New York, Phoenix, and Chicago.

If one considers the geographical distribution of language pairs (English and a minority language), then English–Spanish bilinguals are mostly found in the Southwest and Florida, English–Chinese bilinguals in California and New York, bilinguals with English and a Slavic language in Illinois, New York and New Jersey, and English–German bilinguals in the Dakotas and Pennsylvania.

Bilingualism in the United States has traditionally been transitional – a passage, over one or two generations, from monolingualism in a minority language to monolingualism in English.

However, there is an increasing awareness that the country's knowledge of the languages of the world is a natural resource that should not be wasted. Hence a growing number of families are fostering bilingualism, either by making sure the home's minority language and culture are kept alive, in addition to using English outside the home, or by encouraging their English-speaking children to acquire and use a second language.

With the rising number of bilinguals in the United States over the years (see Post 2.5), we can dream that President Obama's suggestion in 2008 during a rally may just be the beginning of a new trend: "You should be thinking about ... how can your child become bilingual. We should have every child speaking more than one language."

References

Shin, H. B. and Kominski, R. A. (2010). Language Use in the United States: 2007. American Community Survey Reports, ACS-12. U.S. Census Bureau, Washington, DC. www.census.gov/library/publications/2010/acs/acs-12.html
Ryan, C. (2013). Language Use in the United States: 2011. American Community Survey Reports, ACS-22. U.S. Census Bureau, Washington, DC. www.census.gov/library/publications/2013/acs/acs-22.html
Zeigler, K. and Camarota, S. A. (2019). 67.3 Million in the United States Spoke a Foreign Language at Home in 2018. Center for Immigration Studies, Washington, DC. https://cis.org/Report/673-Million-United-States-Spoke-Foreign-Language-Home–2018

2.5 THE AMAZING RISE OF BILINGUALISM IN THE UNITED STATES

The United States has long been seen as a mostly monolingual country. Things have changed rapidly in forty years, however, and now well over a fifth of the population is bilingual.

In Post 2.4, I described the state of bilingualism in the United States. The US Census Bureau does not keep track of those who use two or more languages in their everyday lives, but since 1980 it does ask three language questions: (1) Does this person speak a language other than English at home? (2) What is this language? (3) How well does this person speak English (very well, well, not well, not at all)? These questions were first asked in the census, every ten years, but are now part of the annual American Community Survey (ACS).

The data that we now have cover 1980, 1990, and every year since 2000 until 2018. Even though children under five were left out, as we saw in Post 2.4, as were people who use a second or third language in their everyday lives but only English at home, they give us an idea of the number of bilinguals in the United States and how the numbers have evolved since 1980.

Researcher Jeffrey Bloem at the University of Minnesota helped me extract the appropriate numbers from the IPUMS database which contains the census and ACS data. For each year, we tabulated those who spoke a language other than English, as well as English to varying degrees (we removed those who did not know English at all as they were not bilingual), and we worked out a percentage based on the total population. I then plotted the results obtained.

As can be seen in Figure 2.1 (top function), there is a steady increase in the percentage of bilinguals between 1980 and 2018. Back in 1980, the percentage of bilinguals was 10.68 percent whereas in 2018, the last ACS survey for which we have data, it was 20.55 percent, that is, sixty-three million inhabitants. The percentage has practically doubled in thirty-eight years. If we add a few percentage points to take into account

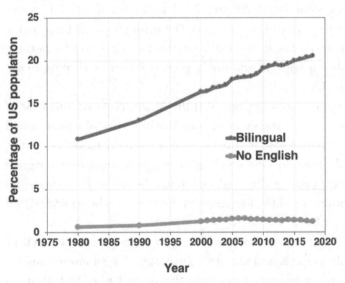

Figure 2.1 Percentage of US population that is bilingual (top function) and that knows no English (bottom function)

those not included in the survey, the proportion of bilinguals today is probably close to 23 percent of the total population.

Of course, this percentage is still low compared to traditionally multi-lingual countries (e.g. in Switzerland some 42 percent of the population use two or more languages in everyday life) but it is similar to that of other countries with a world language as a national language (e.g. France with its 20 percent).

One will want to study the reasons for this constant rise since 1980. There is, of course, the arrival of new immigrants who learn English and hence become bilingual. Some maintain their languages from gener-ation to generation and hence bilingualism continues. Other reasons may be the (re)learning of some older immigration languages, as well as of Native American languages, and of American Sign Language. To these should be added the effort that is being made to allow children and adolescents to acquire and use a second language in the home, as well as more natural language learning opportunities in some schools with immersion and dual language programs.

Some might say that the increasing number of bilinguals goes hand in hand with an increase of inhabitants who know no English. I have plotted the results of those who report that they do not know any English in the same graph (Figure 2.1: bottom function) and, as can be seen, the percentages remain very low throughout all these years. English is so important in the United States that close to 98.7 percent of the population know it, and use it in everyday life, according to the 2018 ACS results.

Back in 1986, I wrote an op-ed in the Miami News on the state of languages other than English in the United States. I had observed, as had others, the extremely fast shift between two monolingualisms – that of newly arrived immigrants in a non-English language, and that of the great majority of the population in English. I stated, "A national resource – the country's knowledge of the languages of the world – is being wasted and is not being replaced."

I am now happy to observe, more than thirty years later, that an effort is being made to speak and use other languages in addition to English. The position of prominence that English has in the United States is in no danger, but some room is now being made for other languages. This can only lead to a person's personal enrichment, increased ties between generations and cultures, and more diversity in job opportunities.

References

Grosjean, F. (1982). Bilingualism in the United States. Chapter 2 of *Life with Two Languages: An Introduction to Bilingualism*. Cambridge, MA: Harvard University Press.

Zeigler, K. and Camarota, S. A. (2019). 67.3 Million in the United States Spoke a Foreign Language at Home in 2018. Center for Immigration Studies, Washington, DC. https://cis.org/Report/673-Million-United-States-Spoke-Foreign-Language-Home–2018

3

Using Two or More Languages

INTRODUCTION

When communicating with others, bilinguals have to decide which language to use – this is called language choice – and they also have to decide whether they can bring in their other language(s) in the form of code-switches and borrowings.

Post 3.1 concentrates on language choice, a fascinating but also complex phenomenon that is governed by numerous factors. Post 3.2, on the same topic, examines non accommodation, that is, those instances when bilinguals use different languages with one another when normally they would have agreed on speaking the same language. And Post 3.3 looks at cases where bilinguals simply refuse to speak one of their languages on a more permanent basis. Various reasons – political, social, linguistic, communicative – explain this behavior.

Three posts follow which examine how bilinguals can bring in their other language(s) when talking to bilinguals, that is, when they are in a bilingual language mode. Post 3.4 examines code-switching, the complete shift to the other language for a word, a phrase, or a sentence. Reasons for code-switching are given and its use in literature is evoked.

Posts 3.5 and 3.6 cover borrowing whereby bilinguals take a word or expression from the other language and adapt it into the base language. First, the intricacies of borrowing are examined, and then Dr. Shana Poplack, who has studied borrowing extensively, is interviewed on her book dedicated to the topic.

The last four posts discuss what happens when bilinguals are in a monolingual language mode, that is, they are interacting with monolinguals and have to keep to just one language. Bilinguals are usually incredibly adept at this but they may nevertheless produce interferences from time to time, that is deviations from the language being spoken (or written) due to the influence of the other, deactivated, language(s). Posts 3.7 and 3.8 introduce the notion of interference, and give explanations and examples. Post 3.9 examines how with time a bilingual's first language may be restructured under the constant pressure of the second language. And Post 3.10 looks at how a manual language, American Sign Language, influences the use of gestures in a spoken language, English.

3.1 QUESTIONS BILINGUALS ASK THEMSELVES WHEN COMMUNICATING WITH OTHERS

When talking to others, bilinguals are always faced with two questions, but they are rarely aware of them.

The first question bilinguals ask themselves when communicating with others relates to language choice: Which base language should be used? The second question concerns whether another language can be brought in, or not, into the base language. Bilinguals stick to one language in many situations (they are said to be in a monolingual mode) and they intermingle their languages when talking to other bilinguals they feel comfortable with (they are then in a bilingual mode).

Here is an example of the latter situation. A French family in the United States is watching some ice fishermen in the dead of the winter and their son, Marc, is right in the middle of the action. The mother is getting very cold and says to her husband: "Va chercher Marc *and bribe him* avec un chocolat chaud *with cream on top*." (The French parts mean "go fetch Marc" and "with a hot chocolate," respectively.) In this case, the base language is French and the other language, English, is brought in for short segments (see Post 3.4).

We will concentrate on language choice here. The "which language to use" question is an intriguing bilingual phenomenon even though, at first, it may appear to be pretty straightforward. This is so when only one language is possible but it is far more complex, and quite subtle, when several languages can be chosen. Four groups of factors explain language choice: participants, situation, content of discourse, and function of the interaction.

As concerns participants, one important factor is the language proficiency of the interlocutors. Bilinguals usually use the language that will be the most successful for communication. How often have I seen a group of bilingual speakers change over to another less known language when someone arrives, and change right back to their language of communication when the latter has a side conversation or steps away for a few minutes!

There is also the language one customarily uses with a person. When this "agreed upon" language fails to be used in a particular exchange, for example, on the phone, the interlocutor may be surprised and may ask why at some later time (see Post 3.2). Other factors include attitude toward a language, age, degree of intimacy, and so on.

Concerning the situation, the location of the exchange will be a major factor. In some countries, members of a language minority may decide to speak the majority language in public even though, in private, they use their other language.

The content of discourse concerns the fact that some domains and topics are better dealt with in a particular language (see Post 1.5). As for the function of the interaction, we all communicate to achieve something and not just to pass information along to someone else. Bilinguals can choose one language over another to create a social distance, raise their status, request something, give a command, and so on.

They can also exclude someone by changing language but this sometimes backfires, as in the following example. A Russian–English student once told me that she and a friend were seated in a park when a round little man sat down on the bench opposite them. Switching over to Russian, one said to the other, "He's like a balloon, he's going to blow up!" They then continued their conversation in English but were startled when, sometime later, the man walked past them and said, in Russian, "You see, I didn't blow up!" All bilinguals reading about this little "incident" will probably have one or two examples of their own.

Usually several factors taken together explain a bilingual's language choice, and some factors have more weight than others. However complex though, language choice is a well-learned behavior that takes place smoothly and rapidly. Bilinguals are usually quite unaware of the many factors behind their choice; it is just part of being bilingual.

References

Grosjean, F. (2010). Language mode and language choice. Chapter 4 of *Bilingual: Life and Reality*. Cambridge, MA: Harvard University Press.

Grosjean, F. (1982). Language choice. Chapter 3 of *Life with Two Languages: An Introduction to Bilingualism*. Cambridge, MA: Harvard University Press.

3.2 WHY AREN'T YOU SPEAKING THE RIGHT LANGUAGE?

Monolinguals rarely have to worry that their interlocutor is not speaking the right language when it is the main means of communication. But this can happen to bilinguals who share the same languages but who find themselves in a situation where a non optimal language is being used by one of them. This non accommodation may cause puzzlement and even distress.

We saw above (Post 3.1) that deciding which language to speak with another bilingual is a rather subtle and complex behavior that nevertheless takes place smoothly and rapidly. Bilinguals often have a habitual language of interaction with people they interact with regularly (e.g. family members, colleagues, friends, etc.). When they are with others, then other factors intervene, as we noted.

When bilingual speakers use *different* languages with one another in the same interaction (A is using language X and B language Y), and this is not an accepted means of communication, then one talks of non accommodation. If this is at the start of an exchange, a rapid adjustment usually follows, with one of the two languages usually prevailing. And yet, sometimes non accommodation may persist. It may even occur as the conversation is taking place. This is noticed invariably by at least one of the bilinguals, triggering questions such as, "Shouldn't we speak X?" or reflections later on of the type, "What happened just there?".

Non accommodation might even make one of the interlocutors upset, as Susan Gal, professor at the University of Chicago, reports in her study of language choice between Hungarian and German bilinguals in Oberwart, Austria. She relates that an elderly man told his friends during a game of cards how insolent a young bilingual salesman at the grocery store had been to him. "The little creep answered me in German" he stated, when he should have replied in Hungarian, the language he had been addressed in.

Several reasons may explain non accommodation. A rather trivial one is when a bilingual wants to stop someone overhearing what is being said. This is typical during a phone conversation when suddenly one of the two speakers starts using another language because someone has walked into the room or into hearing distance. The person on the other end may not know this and may therefore be surprised by the change of language. She may inquire what the reason is without being guaranteed that an answer will be forthcoming if the person is still there.

Status-raising is another reason for a change of language. Professor Carol Myers Scotton of Michigan State University, and her colleague, William Ury, reported on some fascinating cases in the Luhya region of Kenya. In one of them, a passenger on a bus in Nairobi and a conductor (fare collector) were conversing in Swahili. The passenger said that he wanted to go to the post office, and the conductor replied that it would cost him fifty cents. The passenger gave him a shilling and the conductor told him to wait for his change. As the bus neared the post office, the passenger became worried and asked for his change again. The conductor simply replied that he would receive it. No longer convinced, the passenger changed over to English and said, "I am nearing my destination." and the conductor replied in English, "Do you think I could run away with your change?".

According to the authors, the passenger's change over to English was a bid for authority, changing his role from one of equal status with the conductor to a higher status (English is the language of the educated elite in Kenya). This was a way of making sure that he would obtain his change before he got off. But the conductor countered the shift in status by replying in English, thereby reestablishing equality.

A further reason for non-accommodation is simply to show off one's knowledge of a language or to get practice using one's weaker language. The latter may occur when one interlocutor is not very fluent in language X and instead of speaking language Y with the other interlocutor, their optimal language of communication, he or she insists that it be language X. This happened to me just recently. A student came into my office and asked me in hesitant French, and a strong American accent, if she could speak to me. Mindful of the importance of establishing clear communication between us, I suggested we speak English. She continued in

French and I reiterated my offer in English. She then told me that she had come over to learn French and wanted to speak it.

In such situations, friends can discuss why one of them refused to speak language X, but when the two are mere acquaintances, there may be no explanation offered, and once the – usually shortened – interaction is over, one of them will probably walk away wondering why the other did not reply in the appropriate language.

References

Grosjean, F. (1982). Language choice. Chapter 3 of *Life with Two Languages: An Introduction to Bilingualism*. Cambridge, MA: Harvard University Press.
Gal, S. (1979). *Language Shift: Social Determinants of Linguistic Change in Bilingual Austria*. New York: Academic Press.
Myers Scotton, C. and Ury, W. (1977). Bilingual strategies: The social functions of code-switching. *Linguistics*, 193, 5–20.

3.3 REFUSING TO SPEAK A LANGUAGE

For many monolinguals, being bilingual and hence being able to know and use two or more languages in everyday life is seen as a real advantage. And yet some bilinguals, be they adults or children, refuse to speak one of their languages. Why is that?

Major life changes such as immigration, the loss of a close family member, a separation, a change of jobs, or simply growing up and leaving one's community may lead some bilinguals to no longer use a language. Since it is no longer needed, it is put aside. This is a normal consequence of the wax and wane of languages in bilinguals.

But there are also instances where a decision is made *not* to use a language any longer. The reasons vary and cover both adults and children. For example, members of stigmatized minorities may opt to no longer use the language of the majority when they are able to do so. Thus, many German Jews during World War II refused to continue using German after emigrating to a new country. This was also true of some members of the resistance movement. For example, Austrian-born historian and author, Gerda Lerner, joined the resistance in her home country. When she arrived in the United States in 1939, she rejected

German even though it was her first language. It was only many years later that she reconciled herself with her native language.

Strong negative attitudes toward a minority language will also lead speakers of that language to refuse to speak it in public. This was the case for many speakers of regional languages in nation-states in Europe in the nineteenth and twentieth centuries. And it is true of certain recent immigrant languages among second and third generations today.

To these political and social reasons should be added individual linguistic reasons. Some bilinguals, for example, fear that a particular language will taint their other language too strongly and so they decide to no longer use it, or to use it on very rare occasions. A well-known example is the surrealist writer and poet, André Breton, who spent some time in the United States during World War II. He is said to have refused to speak and write English because he didn't want his native language to be affected by it!

And, of course, there are those – I am one of them – who know a third or fourth language so badly that they simply decide to no longer speak it. Of course, they still understand it to some extent but if they start using it, their interlocutor might think they know it better than they do, and miscommunication will take place. It is simply easier, and safer, to close it down, often with regret though.

Children are also well known for their decision at times not to use a language. Many very young bilingual children have an agreed upon language they use with the adults they know well (see Post 6.9). If someone uses the wrong language with them, they may become quite upset in addition to simply refusing to answer back in that language.

Older bilingual children and adolescents who become conscious of which language their peers speak may well reject a language, usually the home language, so as not to be different from them. An Arabic–English bilingual once wrote to me that as an adolescent he pretended he did not know Arabic. He continued, "I did this because I wanted very badly not to be different from the rest of my friends."

Researchers Stephen Caldas and Suzanne Caron-Caldas tracked language use in their English–French bilingual children over a six-year period in Louisiana, and in Quebec in the summer. The perception of peer pressure outside the home was such that the children were basically English monolinguals in Louisiana, and French monolinguals in

Quebec. In a revealing anecdote included in the study, the father, who spoke French to his children in Louisiana, was with his twelve-year-old daughter, Stéphanie, at a football game. He was getting ready to say hi to one of her friends when Stéphanie hissed to him, "Don't speak French to her." The authors tell us that the father did so anyway!

Parents often have to find creative ways of encouraging the use of the rejected language in order to ensure the development of active bilingualism in their children. It is no mean feat as their testimonies show!

References

Caldas, S. and Caron-Caldas, S. (2002). A sociolinguistic analysis of the language preferences of adolescent bilinguals: Shifting allegiances and developing identities. *Applied Linguistics*, 23, 490–514.

Grosjean, F. (2010). Family Strategies and Support. Chapter 17 of *Bilingual: Life and Reality*. Cambridge, MA: Harvard University Press.

3.4 INTERMINGLING LANGUAGES

When interacting among themselves, bilinguals may well intermingle their languages. What may seem to be haphazard behavior is governed in reality by linguistic and social constraints, and is even used to literary ends by some bilingual authors.

When bilinguals are communicating with other bilinguals who share their languages, and with whom they feel comfortable, they may well intermingle their languages. They choose a base language and then bring in the other language when the need arises (see Post 3.1).

One common way of doing so is to code-switch, that is, to shift completely to the other language for a word, a phrase, or a sentence, and then revert back to the base language. (Another way is to borrow a term from the other language; see Post 3.5.) The following code-switch was reported by Aurelio M. Espinosa: "Vamos a ir al *football game* y después al baile a tener *the time of our lives.*" (The Spanish parts mean "let's go to the" and "and then to the dance to have"). Any bilingual reading this post can add one of two preferred examples from their own bilingual speech or that of others.

Even though it is widespread, code-switching has been criticized by some who feel that it is done out of pure laziness and that it is a grammarless mixture of two languages. Many pejorative names have been used to characterize this bilingual form of communication such as Tex-Mex and Franglais. Even the word "mixing" has now taken on negative overtones. One consequence of this is that some bilinguals never code-switch and may look down upon others who do, while others restrict it to a situation in which they will not be stigmatized for doing so.

Linguists have spent many years studying the intermingling of languages and one clear outcome has been that code-switching has been found to follow very strict linguistic constraints requiring good competence in more than one language. In addition, the cognitive mechanisms that lead to spontaneous code-switching are both complex and exceptionally fine-tuned.

Why do bilinguals code-switch? One reason is that some concepts are simply better expressed in the other language. Using a word or expression from that language allows you to be more precise than trying to find an equivalent in the base language. I compare this search for *le mot juste* to having cream with coffee instead of just having it black; it adds a little something to your drink, at least for those who don't drink their coffee black!

Since a bilingual's domains of life are rarely covered by just one language (see Post 1.5), one will also code-switch to fill a linguistic need. You prepare a word or phrase in the other language and since your interlocutor knows that language, you insert it into your conversation. Another reason is to report what someone has said in that other language. It would be unnatural to translate it for someone who understands the language perfectly.

There are also interesting communicative and social reasons for code-switching such as personalizing a message, emphasizing a point, changing one's role (e.g. from friend to employer), including or excluding someone, emphasizing group identity, and so on. An example of the latter was related by linguist Robert J. DiPietro who noticed that Italian immigrants would tell a joke in English and give the punch line in Italian. Not only was it better said in that language but it stressed the fact that they all belonged to the same community, with shared values and experiences.

In recent years, some Hispanic American contemporary authors have used the full richness of their two languages by resorting to code-switching in their prose. For example, Susana Chávez-Silverman, a professor at Pomona College in California, expresses her bilingual creativity by making extensive use of code-switches in a manner that is rarely found in the written mode.

Here is a short extract taken from her book, *Killer Crónicas: Bilingual Memories:* "Como northern Califas girl, of course, habiá visto mucho nature espectacular; the Pacific Ocean como yarda de enfrente, for starters, y los sequoia giant redwoods. Yes, especially los redwoods."

Listening to Susana Chávez-Silverman reading extracts from her book[1] is an even more fascinating experience and shows how enthralling code-switching can really be.

References

Chávez-Silverman, S. (2004). *Killer Crónicas: Bilingual Memories.* Madison, WI: University of Wisconsin Press.

Grosjean, F. (2010). Code-Switching and Borrowing. Chapter 5 of *Bilingual: Life and Reality.* Cambridge, MA: Harvard University Press.

3.5 HOW BILINGUALS BORROW WORDS FROM THEIR OTHER LANGUAGE(S)[2]

Borrowing is a fascinating process, not only because it occurs widely, but also because it can have an interesting impact on language understanding.

- "Did you see Helen yesterday?"
- "Oh, do you mean *Hélène*" (pronounced in French)?
- "Um ... yes ..."

In addition to code-switching, bilinguals can also borrow, that is, bring in a word or short expression from the other language and adapt it morphologically, and often phonologically, into the base language. For example, a French–English bilingual in the United States might say to

---

[1] https://uwpress.wisc.edu/books/2616-audio.html
[2] The original title of this post was "Helen or Hélène."

another bilingual, "Tu viens *bruncher* avec nous?" (Are you coming to brunch with us?). Here the word "brunch" has been borrowed from English and integrated into the French sentence.

Another form of borrowing is to take a word in the language being spoken and to add a meaning to it based on a word in the other (guest) language. Thus, the French word "réaliser" is now often used not only with the meaning of "to do or carry out something" but also with the meaning of "to begin to understand something," borrowed from English. This particular loanshift, as it is called, first started with bilinguals and it is now quite common among French speakers who know no English whatsoever.

Bilinguals borrow for many of the same reasons they code-switch: they want to use the right word; the word they need belongs to a domain they normally talk about in the other language (see Post 1.5); the language they are speaking does not have a word for what they want to say, and so on.

Those who have migrated to a different country have often found themselves faced with having to speak about new realities and new distinctions in their native language. The latter simply does not have the vocabulary needed and hence borrowing ready-made words is more economical than describing things afresh. As bilingual researcher, Uriel Weinreich, once wrote, few language users are poets!

Spoken borrowings are usually recognized quite easily – if the listeners are bilingual, of course – but sometimes processing issues do occur. For example, if there is a word that is quite similar in the base language, then an ambiguity may arise. Thus, one day, I heard a French–English bilingual child, Olivier, ask his mother, "Maman tu peux me *tier* mes chaussures." I understood, "Mummy, can you sharpen my shoes?" (the borrowing "tier" was pronounced like the French word "tailler" (to sharpen)), and it took me some time to realize that Olivier was in fact asking his mother to "tie" his shoes! A cognitive conflict had occurred in my mind between the English borrowing and the existing French word.

Another moment of difficulty may come when, by adapting the guest language word into the base language, the speaker changes its configuration considerably. Thus, cognitive scientist Ping Li of the Hong Kong Polytechnic University has shown that English words such as "flight" borrowed into Chinese can be difficult to perceive by Chinese–English bilinguals. This is because when they are adapted into Chinese, consonants are softened or even dropped. Thus "flight" sounds something like "fie" and takes more time to identify.

Finally, let us return to our opening example concerning Helen or Hélène. It concerns what to do with proper names that belong to the other language – first names, family names, names of cities or of landmarks, and so on. Do you bring them into the language you are speaking without adapting them (you code-switch) or do you adapt them into the base language (you borrow)? We have probably all been made aware of the problem in the different renditions we have heard of Cairo's Tahrir Square in the media, from the totally English pronunciation of "Tahrir" (borrowing) to the totally Arabic pronunciation (code-switch).

There are no clear rules here. Bilinguals don't want to sound too sophisticated by using the "real" pronunciation, especially if there are monolinguals among those listening, but at the same time they want to respect the phonetics of the word and make sure their listeners understand who or what they are talking about. The problem is all the more complex if the two pronunciations (in the base language or in the guest language) refer to different places or people, as in the case of Helen and Hélène (hence the hesitation in the dialogue above). The ultimate strategy becomes: do everything you can to make sure your interlocutor understands you!

References

Grosjean, F. (2010). Code-switching and borrowing. Chapter 5 of *Bilingual: Life and Reality*. Cambridge, MA: Harvard University Press.

Ping, L. (1996). Spoken word recognition of code-switched words by Chinese-English bilinguals. *Journal of Memory and Language*, 35, 757–774.

3.6 BORROWING WORDS[3]

(Interview with Shana Poplack)

Many bilinguals borrow words from one language to another. Dr. Shana Poplack, an expert on this phenomenon and author of the book, Borrowing, tells us how this takes place.

---

[3] The original title of this post was, "When bilinguals borrow from one language to another."

Code-switching – the shift from one language to another for a word, phrase, or sentence – has been the object of much research but this has not been the case for borrowing. Professor Shana Poplack of the University of Ottawa published a much-awaited book entitled, *Borrowing: Loanwords in the Speech Community and in the Grammar*. She has kindly accepted to answer a few of our questions and we thank her wholeheartedly.

You are known the world over for your pioneering work on code-switching. And now you have published this impressive book on borrowing. Can you tell us the reasons behind it?
I came to borrowing as a result of many years of studying code-switching. The latter involves juxtaposing sequences of one language with sequences of another, as in this sentence, "Quand il marchait là, il marchait *over dead bodies*," spontaneously produced by one of the participants in our studies. Code-switching is conspicuous, salient and endlessly fascinating. Yet, despite intense scholarly scrutiny, it remains controversial. Analysis of bilingual behavior on the ground suggests that this is a consequence of failing to recognize borrowing in all its manifestations. Speakers, on the other hand, make a fundamental distinction between borrowing of all types and code-switching (CS) (as your own early experimental work suggested).

In contrast to CS, borrowing, as in "Je *groovais* comme si j'étais à un *show* de *rap*" ("I was grooving like I was at a rap concert"), has been treated as a poor relation. By virtue of its major property, integration, it often passes unnoticed. This is a shame, because systematic analysis of borrowing in the thirteen language pairs my team and I studied showed that the linguistic and social processes involved are at least as complex and startling as those underlying CS. So I had to write a book about them!

How frequent is borrowing in bilingual discourse as opposed to code-switching?
Ironically enough, given the neglect it has suffered, borrowing turns out to be the major manifestation of language mixing by far. In the French-English materials we studied it outweighs CS by a factor of 20. In many bilingual data sets, that's all there is. I regularly send my graduate students out to collect samples of CS from communities they describe as rife with mixing, and nine times out of ten they return with nothing but examples of lexical borrowing.

Are some bilinguals code-switchers and others borrowers? If so, what accounts for being one or the other?
Definitely, and for good reason. The ability to access a sequence like "*over dead bodies*" necessarily requires knowledge of English. The ability to juxtapose it with a French sequence so as to result in a sentence that is well-formed in both languages simultaneously requires (even greater) knowledge of both languages. And indeed, our research has shown, not surprisingly, that CS is the province of the most proficient bilinguals.

A borrower, on the other hand, doesn't need to know the other, donor, language at all. English speakers, for example, utter words borrowed from Italian, Spanish, French and Japanese every time they say "*espresso*," "*arroyo*," "*diamond*" or "*tsunami*" respectively, whether they know it or not. We studied bilinguals who engage in these strategies, as well as spontaneous ("nonce") borrowing of novel words, and found no correlation. Copious code-switchers are not necessarily copious borrowers. Rather these strategies, and the speakers who favor them, are independent.

When a bilingual borrows a new word from the other (donor) language, it is termed a nonce borrowing. Can you tell us about the linguistic operations that take place when she produces such a word in the other (recipient) language?
When English speakers use old established loanwords like "*terrace*", "*boil*" or "*court*", they are often unaware that they were originally French. This is because these words have been refashioned according to English grammar, taking English plural markers ("*terraces*"), English verb endings ("*boiling*"), and entering into English word orders ("<u>criminal</u> <u>court</u>"). Such integration of donor-language material to the morphology, syntax and optionally, the sound system of the recipient language, is the major mechanism underlying borrowing.

The actual linguistic operations involved are those of the recipient, and can therefore vary wildly from one language to the next, depending on the specific grammatical properties of each. These may include assigning a gender if the recipient language features that category ("<u>la</u> *drop*") or applying complex vowel harmony rules ("*nà-a-hallucinate*"). These characteristics are amply evident in the loanword stock of all languages.

Our studies of nonce borrowing on the ground show that speakers also appeal to them when incorporating other-language words spontaneously: they treat novel borrowings exactly like their established loanwords (by imbuing them with the grammar of the recipient language), and distinguish both from their CS, which retain the grammar of the donor language.

When nonce borrowings do become established loans (which you term loanwords), what linguistic transformations, if any, have they gone through to get to that end point?
Thank you for asking that question! I'm actually in a position to answer it, based on analysis of bilingual speech data spanning an unprecedented century and a half. One of our most startling discoveries is that nonce borrowings are not transformed into loanwords gradually, as scholars have long believed. Instead, bilinguals decide whether to borrow (as opposed to CS) right off the bat. If they opt for the former (which by the way, they almost always do), they imbue the word with the full complement of recipient-language grammar. Remarkably, they engage in these complex operations at their very first mention of the other-language word!

It's the *social* integration of borrowed items that is gradual. As the word diffuses across the community, it stands a greater chance of becoming a bona fide, or established, loanword. Still, in the grand scheme of things, this almost never happens – another surprising finding of our research.

As bilinguals, we produce many nonce borrowings but they are ephemeral and very few make it into the language as established loans. Why do some obtain this distinction?
That's the $64,000 question! We discovered that the overwhelming majority of borrowed words disappears after the first mention. We don't know which will persist or why. All we can say is that the received wisdom – that words designating cultural items like "*hamburger*" or "*yoga*" get borrowed, while core words like "*mom*" do not – definitely doesn't hold. Of course, all languages feature plenty of such words ("*pizza*," "*jihad*," "*origami*," etc.). But their numbers pale in comparison to the body of loanwords that don't designate such things.

The words that persist over time and go on to achieve the status of established loanwords often turn out to be the least expected. Why do we need to borrow words like "*friend*," "*weird*," or "*game*," as the Quebec francophones we have studied have done, when there are perfectly good French words for them? We don't! Need is not *the* motivating factor in borrowing. Rather, words are borrowed through implicit community compacts, and become part of the community *norms*.

These norms may differ from one community to the next, *even when the same languages are involved*. This is why you hear *"parking," "shopping,"* and *"weekend"* in France, while in Canada, *"stationnement," "magasinage,"* and *"fin de semaine"* are de rigueur (a French loanword in English). Canadians prefer *"chum"* to *"ami"* and *"cute"* to *"mignon"*. When it comes to language mixing strategies, the community rules.

Reference

Poplack, S. (2017). *Borrowing: Loanwords in the Speech Community and in the Grammar*. New York: Oxford University Press.

3.7 INTERACTING IN JUST ONE LANGUAGE AND KEEPING OUT THE OTHER(S)[4]

Researchers have long been interested in the way bilinguals manage to control the language they are speaking and keep out their other language(s). But how "language tight" is the process?

As we saw in Post 3.1, when bilinguals are in the presence of monolinguals, or of bilinguals with whom they only share one language, or with whom they do not feel they can intermingle their languages, they have to use only one language and not let their other language(s) intervene.

It never fails to impress me how well bilinguals can keep to just one language. If, in addition, they speak the language fluently and have no accent in it, then they may "pass" as monolinguals. How many of us have not been taken aback to hear a monolingual, so we thought, suddenly start speaking another language we knew nothing about. The surprise is probably as great as if we had heard Natalie Wood suddenly switch into fluent Russian during the movie West Side Story. Although artistically impossible, it was linguistically feasible as she had been raised in a Russian-speaking family and was bilingual in Russian and English.

Researchers have long been interested in the way bilinguals manage to control the language they are speaking monolingually and keep out their other language(s). Cognitive scientists such as Ellen Bialystok at York University examine the executive control needed for such an operation

---

[4] The original title of the post was, "Interacting in just one language."

and neuroscientists study the neural structures that supervise the selection of the appropriate language.

How "language tight" is the process? Despite the fact that bilinguals are adept at keeping out their other language(s) when they are speaking or writing monolingually (as I'm doing right now, keeping out my French), the other language(s) may sometimes seep through, most of the time in the form of interferences, that is deviations from the language being spoken (or written) stemming from the influence of the other, deactivated, language(s).

Interferences, also called transfers or cross-language influences, follow bilinguals throughout their lives, however hard they try to filter them out. They are, in a sense, their uninvited hidden companions! Static interferences reflect permanent traces of one language on the other such as a permanent accent (see Post 1.7), specific syntactic structures taken from the other language (see Post 3.9), and so on.

Dynamic interferences, on the other hand, are the episodic deviations from the language being used. Examples are the accidental pronunciation of a sequence based on the rules of the other language, or the momentary use of a word or grammatical structure from the wrong language (see Post 3.8 for examples). Bilinguals are not usually aware of these latter types of interferences. It is only when their interlocutor asks what they meant by word X, or corrects their syntax, or looks at them in a strange way that they realize, after the fact, that the other language has slipped in.

Bilinguals are often left with the feeling that they were sure that they had used the appropriate word or structure in the language they were speaking when in fact that was not the case. Things get even more difficult when they are dealing with homographs or homophones. Einar Haugen, a pioneering researcher in bilingualism, gives the following example. When a young bilingual Norwegian–American was asked by a stranger in English where his father was, he replied quite spontaneously, "Oh, he's in the *stove*," This was due to the fact that "stova" means a living room in Norwegian.

This said, monolinguals who live or work with bilinguals grow accustomed to language that can be influenced by the other tongue. They get used to hearing an accent, a strange sentence structure, or a word that is not quite appropriate, and this often makes communication easier.

The positive side of interferences is that they often render what is said more original and less stereotypical. Thus, the prose of bilingual writers such as Joseph Conrad and Samuel Beckett, among others, is greatly enriched by the influence of their other language(s).

Eva Hoffman, the contemporary author of *Lost in Translation*, and herself bilingual in Polish and English (see Post 14.10), states this fittingly when she writes: "Each language modifies the other, crossbreeds with it, fertilizes it. Each language makes the other relative. Like everybody, I am the sum of my languages." (p. 273).

References

Hoffman, E. (1989). *Lost in Translation*. New York: Penguin.
Grosjean, F. (2010). Speaking and writing monolingually. Chapter 6 of *Bilingual: Life and Reality*. Cambridge, MA: Harvard University Press.

3.8 FALSE FRIENDS AND OTHER UNWANTED COMPANIONS

Living with two languages is full of mysteries. One of them is how a language that has been deactivated when we speak or write monolingually nevertheless sometimes comes through in the form of interferences.

It is worth spending a bit more time on dynamic interferences, introduced in Post 3.7, as they are a bilingual's unwanted companions throughout life. They are the episodic deviations from the language used due to the influence of the other, deactivated, language(s) and they can occur at all levels of language. For example, at the level of pronunciation, interferences may come through if the person is tired or under stress. They materialize when you mispronounce certain sounds (e.g. the English "th" sound, the French "ou" sound), when you put equal stress on all syllables of a word which only requires one stressed syllable, or when you use an intonation pattern based on your other language.

At the level of words, there are the infamous false friends (the constant fear of translators and interpreters, among others) which correspond to near homophones or near homographs in two languages, but with different meanings. How many times have I not said, "librairie" in

French (it means "bookstore"), basing myself on English "library," when I should have said "bibliothèque." (The same false friend exists between Spanish and English – a "librería" is not a library but a bookstore.)

There are also those words that are unreliable friends such as Spanish "historia" which does mean "history" but which also means a story or a tale. Nancy Huston, the Canadian and French bilingual writer, reports that she ends up avoiding the use of false friends such as French "éventuellement" ("possibly" in English) and "eventually" to make sure that she doesn't mix them up.

Syntactic interferences happen, for example, when bilingual speakers use the word-order pattern of one language in the other, insert determiners where they are not needed, put the wrong gender marking on an article, or use prepositions inappropriately.

Idiomatic expressions are well-known traps when they are translated word-for-word since all the words uttered are perfectly fine but the overall meaning is not. For example, "I'm telling myself stories" uttered by a French–English bilingual should be replaced with, "I'm kidding myself" (the person based herself on French, "Je me raconte des histoires").

It is at times like this, when the person being spoken to asks what is being said or reacts in some way, or even offers a correction, that bilinguals are taken aback. They suddenly realize that all was not totally clear when they were certain they had spoken correctly.

Those bilinguals who write in both their languages have to be particularly careful with the spelling of near homographs. French–English bilinguals have to stop to think how many d's there are in "address" (only one in French), how many h's in "rhythm" (again only one in French), and so on. The best present bilinguals received with the advent of word processors were spell checkers!

If bilinguals are clearly dominant in their first language, then it is usually this stronger language that influences their second or weaker language. However, when bilinguals are fluent in both languages, interferences are often two-way, with each language being able to influence the other from time to time. This leads some bilinguals to think that maybe they don't speak either language well when, in fact, these are very small bumps on what is usually a smooth road.

We should keep in mind that once a bilingual has attained a stable level of proficiency, interferences rarely compromise communication. As I wrote in Post 3.7, they even render what is said more original, less stereotypical, and stylistically more interesting, as can be seen in the prose of many bilingual writers. As bilinguals, we should maybe heed Barbara Kingsolver's words of wisdom when we think of interferences: "The friend who holds your hand and says the wrong thing is made of dearer stuff than the one who stays away."

References

Grosjean, F. (2012). An attempt to isolate, and then differentiate, transfer and interference. *International Journal of Bilingualism*, 16(1), 11–21.
Grosjean, F. (2010). Speaking and writing monolingually. Chapter 6 of *Bilingual: Life and Reality*. Cambridge, MA: Harvard University Press.

3.9 HOW A BILINGUAL'S FIRST LANGUAGE CAN BE RESTRUCTURED OVER TIME[5]

It has long been held that a first language influences a second language, and not the other way round. However, there is now increasing evidence that a bilingual's competence in a first language can be modified durably by a second language, even when the latter is acquired in adulthood.

The influence of a first language on a second language in the form of interferences is well accepted and well documented. Yet some people find themselves using their second language more than their first language, in many more domains of life (see Post 1.5), and over a very long period of time. This has an impact on the competence of their first language as is seen by both dynamic and static interferences (see Post 3.7). A colleague of mine, Bernard Py, and I studied how this could lead to the restructuring of a first language.

We asked first-generation Spanish immigrants, who had spent some twenty years in French-speaking Switzerland, and who had known no French before the age of twenty, to tell us if they accepted a number of

---

[5] The original title of this post was, "Changing a first language permanently." It was dedicated to Bernard Py.

Spanish grammatical variants influenced by French. For example, did they accept, *"El león quería morder el hombre"* (The lion wanted to bite the man) when Spanish monolinguals would say, *"El león quería morder al hombre."* Did they accept, *"Decidió de llamar al médico"* (He decided to call the doctor) when Spanish monolinguals would say, *"Decidió llamar al médico."*

When we compared their results to those of monolingual Spanish speakers, we found that a fair number of these new Spanish variants were accepted by the first-generation immigrants. Of course, they still accepted the standard Spanish variants but they had made room in their Spanish language competence for some of these new variants.

When the study was over, I went to see Noam Chomsky (see Post 15.1) and asked him what he thought of our results. His position was that the native language competence of the immigrants had not in fact been changed. Rather, it was their cognitive style that was now different. He suggested that when you move into a foreign language environment, your standards on grammatical acceptability are lowered because you are confronted with many ways of saying things, in the one or the other language, or in both. This change in cognitive style may thus explain the way you react to your native language, but it should not influence your knowledge of your native language.

In an attempt to get to the bottom of this, some ten years later, one of our graduate students, Eliane Girard, moved away from acceptability judgments. She asked second-generation Spanish–French bilinguals who had produced similar acceptability results to those of the first-generation participants, to interpret sentences into Spanish.

Thus, for example, she got them to hear sentences such as, "Cet été nous allons en vacances en Espagne" (This summer we are going on vacation to Spain) and recorded their interpretations. When she analyzed the results, she checked to see if they responded with, *"Este verano vamos de vacaciones a España"* (Standard Spanish variant) or *"Este verano vamos de vacaciones en España"* (Swiss–French Spanish variant).

What she found was that the rank ordering of the grammatical features was the same as that found in the acceptability studies. Since interpreting is very different from making acceptability judgments, these new results would seem to speak against a simple change in cognitive style as suggested by Chomsky.

The conclusion we came to at the end of these studies that spanned some fifteen years or so is that the impact of a dominant language over a lengthy period of time can be quite profound even on the first language competence of adult native speakers. We had found that the Spanish of native speakers who did not know any French before the age of twenty had been modified due to the long-term impact of French. And this change had also been found in the grammatical competence of the next generation several years later.

References

Grosjean, F. (2008). The Complementarity Principle and language restructuring. Chapter 3 of *Studying Bilinguals*. Oxford/New York: Oxford University Press.
Grosjean, F. and Py, B. (1991). La restructuration d'une première langue: l'intégration de variantes de contact dans la compétence de migrants bilingues. *La Linguistique*, 27, 35–60.

3.10 THE CASE OF A MANUAL LANGUAGE INFLUENCING A SPOKEN LANGUAGE[6]

The languages of a bilingual influence one another, either momentarily or in a more permanent way. This is also true when one language is a sign language and the other is a spoken language.

Have you ever spoken with people who know sign language, such as American Sign Language (ASL), or who are learning it (see Post 7.3)? Have you noticed how their hands move much more than they would normally? It happened to me a lot when I was learning to sign and then conducting research on the language.

San Diego State University researchers Shannon Casey, Karen Emmorey, and Heather Larrabee set about studying the influence of ASL as a second language on the gestures (also called co-speech gestures) that are used when English is being spoken.

---

[6] This post was originally entitled, "When a sign language imposes itself on speech."

They asked English speakers, acquiring ASL, to re-tell in English two scenes of a *Tweety and Sylvester* cartoon. The students did this twice, in the same experimental conditions, once when they started their ASL acquisition and then again one year later, after six hours of instruction per week covering three ten-week quarters.

What they found is that the ASL learners, when speaking English, had increased their rate of gestures significantly after one year of language instruction, in particular iconic gestures, that is, gestures that represent the attributes, actions, or relationships of objects or characters, according to University of Chicago Professor David McNeill. An example would be making a downward movement with the hands to represent a bowling ball being thrown down a pipe (as in the *Tweety and Sylvester* cartoon). The authors also observed a significant increase of marked ASL handshapes (such as the L handshape) after one year of ASL.

Interestingly, students were aware of these changes in their gesturing. In another study done by the same authors, 75 percent of the students at the end of two semesters of ASL instruction felt that their co-speech gestures had indeed increased since they had started learning ASL. Practically the same percentage (76 percent) felt that their gestures had changed in some way during that time. According to them, they were bigger and used more space, as is the case when using sign language. They also felt that they used more gestures to express emotion or to explain what they were saying.

The authors propose several reasons for this change in number and type of gestures. Since signing involves manual articulators, the students may have become accustomed to moving their hands when communicating, and this carries over into monolingual speech environments.

Another reason they put forward is that learners of ASL become accustomed to signing and speaking at the same time when using sign language, that is, they produce a sign and whisper its English translation equivalent. This behavior, which is true of many hearing people who sign, not just learners, simply carries over into speech. Finally, a third possibility could be that the students' repertoire of conventional gestures (akin to crossing your fingers for "good luck") may simply have been increased by bringing in new gestures. The problem, of course, is that these new gestures are not meaningful to people who do not know sign language.

Whatever the reason, signing definitely influences gesturing in speech. Two questions come to mind though: Would a difference have been found in number and type of gestures if the students had retold the cartoons to English monolinguals, on the one hand, and to English–ASL bilinguals, on the other? We would expect this to be the case (see Post 3.1). And how long does this influence last when a person stops signing for good, as in my case regretfully?

Reference

Casey, S., Emmorey, K., and Larrabee, H. (2012). The effects of learning American Sign Language on co-speech gesture. *Bilingualism: Language and Cognition*, 15(4), 677–686.

4

Across the Life Span

INTRODUCTION

A person's bilingualism evolves over time as does the relative importance of the languages involved. In Post 4.1, I use my own language history to show how new situations, new interlocutors, and new language functions change a bilingual's language configuration over time.

In Post 4.2, dormant bilinguals are examined, that is, those who have moved from being active, regular bilinguals to single-language users. They are represented here by former President Obama who practically stopped using his Indonesian when he moved to Hawaii in his youth. By studying a speech he gave in Indonesia in 2016, we see that he can still say many things in that language.

In Post 4.3, heritage language speakers are described. They share many of the characteristics of other bilinguals but the way these characteristics are intertwined make them a distinctive type of bilinguals.

Post 4.4 looks at how we can keep a language alive despite not using it that much. Various possibilities exist for adults, but in the case of children, parents have to be creative so as to trigger a real communicative need and hence keep all their languages alive.

The two posts that follow, 4.5 and 4.6, examine language forgetting. In the first one, the process is examined in adults and then in children. In the second, Dr. Monika Schmid, a foremost researcher in the field, is interviewed on language attrition in bilingual adults.

The last three posts ask a fascinating question: Can a first language be totally forgotten when it stops being used in early childhood? In Post 4.7, experimental data are examined and the answer obtained is that some remnant of the first language remains. This is confirmed in Post 4.8 where we report on a functional magnetic resonance imaging (fMRI) study conducted on French–Chinese bilinguals in Quebec.

The final post describes a rather old, but quite amazing, study that used hypnosis. It showed that a forgotten childhood language can indeed reappear using age regression. Another study – only three are readily available to this day – confirms this pioneering research.

4.1 HOW A BILINGUAL'S LANGUAGES EVOLVE OVER TIME[1]

Significant life events can change the relative importance of a bilingual's languages over time and can explain why new languages are acquired and older ones are used less or even forgotten.

A bilingual's languages can wax and wane over time. Significant life events such as starting school, getting a job, moving to another region or country, settling down with a partner/spouse, losing a close family member with whom a language was used exclusively, and so on, may change the relative importance of a bilingual's languages as well as explain the acquisition of new languages and the forgetting of older ones.

To illustrate this, allow me to quickly skim through my own language history. I started as a monolingual in French and it is only at age eight that I acquired English by being put in an English-speaking boarding school. After a year or two, English became my dominant language and remained that way for some ten years. During that time, I also acquired Italian and became quite fluent in it.

At age eighteen, I went to college in France and little by little French won back its "most important language" status. Italian started declining as I no longer used it very much. After ten years in France, my family and I moved to the United States where we lived for twelve years. English became once again my dominant language and French dropped a bit in fluency and use. It was at that time that I learned American Sign Language (ASL) but I was never very fluent in it, much to my regret.

Finally, when I was forty, we moved to the French-speaking part of Switzerland and, once again, my languages reorganized themselves. Currently I use French daily as I do English (especially in its written modality), whereas ASL and Italian are slowly being forgotten.

---

[1] The original title of this post was, "The wax and wane of languages."

Stepping back from this quick overview of my own language history (other bilinguals have their own fascinating histories, sometimes far more complex than mine!), a few points come to mind. First, it counters a myth that real bilinguals acquire their two or more languages in their very early childhood (see Post 5.1). In fact, one can become bilingual at any time during one's lifetime. Even adults can become just as bilingual as those who acquired their languages in their early years, even though they may retain an accent in their new language(s).

A second point is that new situations, new interlocutors, and new language functions will create new linguistic needs, and these will change a bilingual's language configuration. There will be periods of stability and periods of linguistic restructuring. During the latter, a language may be strengthened, another may lose its importance and even start to be forgotten, yet another may be acquired, and so on.

A final point is that global dominance in a language can change over time. In my case, it changed four times due to my moving back and forth between countries. In addition, there were two periods of some ten years each where my first language was not my dominant language. Admittedly, it is not rare to find bilinguals who go from being dominant in their first language to being dominant in their second language, after a period of transition, of course. It is a bit rarer, though, to revert back to being dominant in your first language and then, some years later, to change once again, as in my case.

When speaking of language dominance, one should be careful to differentiate between overall dominance and dominance by domains of language use. Overall dominance may change, as shown above, but some domains of use (e.g. speaking to immediate or distant family members, using language for well-learned behaviors or for religious activities, etc.) may remain tied to one, and only one, language (see Post 1.6).

So next time someone asks you what your dominant language is, and how it has evolved over time, ask back, "Do you mean overall dominance or by domain of use?" If their eyes glaze over at that point, switch subjects or invite them to read my blog!

Reference

Grosjean, F. (2010). Languages across the lifespan. Chapter 8 of *Bilingual: Life and Reality*. Cambridge, MA: Harvard University Press.

4.2 DORMANT BILINGUALS[2]

Dormant bilinguals revert to using only one of their languages, and after a period of time, they may start forgetting their other language(s). President Obama is a prime example.

I have often been asked the following question: If bilinguals are those who use two or more languages (or dialects) in their everyday lives, what do you call people who now live their lives with just one language, even though they know several other languages and used them before? My reply is that they are dormant bilinguals.

It is not rare for bilinguals to go from being active, regular bilinguals, interacting with the world around them using their different languages, to being single language users. This can happen at any time and is usually due to a major life change such as immigration, the loss of a close family member, a separation, a change of jobs, or simply growing up and leaving one's language community. If this situation extends over time, then the language no longer being used on a regular basis will start to be forgotten.

President Barack Obama is a fine example of a dormant bilingual. He spent four years in Indonesia between the ages of six and ten. He attended local schools and spoke Indonesian (Bahasa Indonesia) quite fluently. He stopped using it with others though when he moved to Hawaii with the exception of his half sister and when on trips back to Indonesia.

This said, he can still hold a general conversation in Indonesian and it was interesting to hear him say a few words in his other language when he addressed students at the University of Indonesia in 2016[3].

Each time he switched over to Indonesian – "Selamat pagi" (Good morning), "Pulang kampung nih" (Back to/in my hometown) and so on – his audience applauded loudly. He also made them laugh

---

[2] The original title was, "Dormant bilinguals and President Obama."
[3] www.americanrhetoric.com/speeches/barackobama/barackobamaindonesiauniversity .htm

mimicking the calls of street vendors. He finished with a much longer sentence in Indonesian, clearly showing that he retained a lot of the language.

Even though one may feel shy speaking a language one no longer uses (this is my case when I say a few words in Italian), it can be a real pleasure to realize that people understand you nevertheless. Clearly President Obama was relishing such moments when he switched over to Indonesian. And when he stated, "Indonesia bagian dari didi saya" (Indonesia is part of me), he was clearly touched as was his audience.

By living those four years in a country, "made up of thousands of islands, and hundreds of languages, and people from scores of regions and ethnic groups," as he states in his speech, President Obama experienced bi- and multilingualism firsthand. This was reinforced later by his years in Hawaii with its two state languages (English and Hawaiian) and its many other languages.

It is no surprise therefore that President Obama defends bilingualism. When he was a candidate, in the summer of 2008, he stated at a rally, "You should be thinking about . . .. how can your child become bilingual. We should have every child speaking more than one language."

When uttering those words, he may have been thinking of himself when he was a bilingual child in Indonesia. He shared some of those happy memories with his audience during his 2016 speech, "I learned to love Indonesia while flying kites and running along the paddy fields and catching dragonflies. . . . I remember the people, the old men and women who welcomed us with smiles; the children who made a foreign child feel like a neighbor and a friend; and the teachers who helped me learn about this country."

4.3 HERITAGE LANGUAGE SPEAKERS

Heritage language speakers are a distinctive type of bilinguals. They are invaluable ambassadors between two or more linguistic and cultural groups, within a nation and across nations.

One day, I received an email from California-based Susanna Zaraysky, a polyglot, world traveler, language ambassador, and teacher. She told me of her recent trip to Kyrgyzstan and her experience as a Russian heritage speaker in a country where Russian is an official language along with Kyrgyz. It reminded me of my own experience as a returnee to France at age eighteen after spending ten years in English-speaking schools.

Heritage language speakers share many of the characteristics discussed in posts in this book, but the way these characteristics are intertwined make them a distinctive type of bilinguals.

They have usually been exposed to their heritage language (e.g. Spanish in the United States) at home and hence, for many, it is their first language. They acquired the majority language (e.g. English) either as very young children through contact with people outside the home or when they started going to school. In his book, *Hunger of Memory*, writer Richard Rodriguez relates how he started school in Sacramento knowing just fifty words of English.

Because the heritage language is usually their first language, these bilinguals often have little or no accent in that language. The advantages are many but there are also some disadvantages such as that people expect you to know the language fluently as well as the culture that goes with it. In her own blog[4], Susanna Zaraysky writes that the internet café clerk in Kyrgyzstan was rude to her because she was not familiar with the local computer practices. Had she spoken Russian with a strong accent, she writes, he would have been more understanding.

Heritage language speakers usually change their language dominance when they start going to school, and with time they may well use their home language less and less to the point of starting to forget it (see Post 4.5). Rodriguez evokes this vividly in his book when he writes, "As I grew fluent in English, I no longer could speak Spanish with confidence."

These speakers become literate in their school language but less often in their first language. And even if they do learn to read and write their heritage language such as when they take it as a subject in school, the level reached may not be the same as with their second, dominant, language. Personally, I recall having to struggle for a long time to bring my written French up to par when I came back to France at age eighteen,

---

[4] http://createyourworldbook.com/being-in-limbo-difficulties-of-a-russian-heritage-language-speaker-going-to-a-russian-speaking-country.htm

and even now I bless the developers of good French grammar and spell checkers which I sometimes call upon when I write French!

The domains of use of the heritage language may often be limited (e.g. home, family, and some friends), and very often these bilinguals may not know the vocabulary of more specialized domains. Susanna Zarayksy mentions a phone call she had with her landlord in Ukraine when the electricity broke down in her apartment. She didn't know the translation equivalent of words such as "circuit breaker" and "electric outlet" in Russian and consequently had problems understanding what he was telling her.

Having fewer domains of life covered by a heritage language makes translation into it more difficult. As we saw in an earlier post (see Post 1.5), unless bilinguals have domains covered by both languages, or have acquired their other languages via translation equivalents, they may not have the resources to produce an adequate translation.

Finally, heritage language speakers may not be fully bicultural. Of course, they know a lot more about their heritage culture than, say, someone who is learning the language and culture for the first time in school. As Susanna Zarayksy writes about meals in Kyrgyzstan: "Cottage cheese filled blini and dill laced salads at breakfast were like being at my mom's house." This said, there will be times when they may be surprised by certain behaviors and attitudes in their first culture.

Even though language heritage speakers are a special class of bilinguals, they have a real head start in their first language and culture which can blossom to more complete competence in the right environment. In addition, they are invaluable ambassadors between the two or more linguistic and cultural groups they belong to, within a nation and across nations. It is something they should be proud of!

References

Rodriguez, R. (1983). *Hunger of Memory: The Education of Richard Rodriguez.* New York: Bantam Books.

Bigelow, M. and Collins, P. (2019). Bilingualism from Childhood through Adolescence. In Annick De Houwer and Lourdes Ortega, eds., *The Cambridge Handbook of Bilingualism.* Cambridge: Cambridge University Press, pp. 36–58.

4.4 KEEPING A LANGUAGE ALIVE

One of the languages we know may start waning for different reasons. But there are ways of keeping it alive, both in adults and in children.

Some of us feel that we are no longer making progress in a language that we have learned. Others of us who have known and used a language for years may realize that we are no longer using it very much, or at all. We no longer need it to interact with others, nor do we need it in our studies or at work, or in our social activities. Whatever the reason, we may have become dormant bilinguals (see Post 4.2) and we may even feel that we are starting to forget the language. Although many of us allow our languages to follow their course, we are not always aware that there are ways of keeping a language alive – both in adults and in children – although special measures may be needed in the latter case.

If adult language users are not, or are no longer, in contact with a community or a group that speaks the language (e.g. they have moved to another region or country), then various strategies are open to them to maintain the language. In addition to regular trips to the region or country, they can find friends with whom to practice their language. A more formal way, especially for foreign language learners, is to join a language group or club (e.g. a French club) which meets regularly and where its members speak together in that language. This can be combined with various activities such as seeing a movie, hosting a guest speaker, having a meal together, and so on.

There are also so-called language exchange (or Tandem) programs where two speakers of different languages meet and agree to speak each language half the time. For instance, someone who wants to practice her Spanish can meet a Spanish speaker who wants to practice her English. They take it in turn to use the other's language and hence get practice that way. Such exchanges can also take place on the internet, via Skype, for instance.

In a more passive way, but still at the level of the spoken language, one can watch TV programs or DVDs in the language concerned, go on the internet and follow various news or entertainment programs, or put on some songs and sing along with them (this is great for pronunciation and rhythm).

At the level of reading and writing, all kinds of approaches are possible, such as keeping a diary in the language concerned, having a pen pal or friend, reading books and articles in the language, taking notes, and so on.

Things are not quite as easy with children as one must create a real communicative need to keep a language alive. In Post 5.10, I relate how two American kids, Cyril and Pierre, came to live for a year in a small Swiss village and acquired French during their stay. The family returned to the United States at the end of the year and very soon English took over again and became dominant even though the family remained bilingual in English and French.

Since there was no nearby language community on hand that spoke French, and no bilingual program in the local school, the parents decided to enforce a home language convention where only French would be spoken at home (both parents had originally come from France). However, like any parent in a bilingual family knows, this was easier said than done as the majority language – English – entered the home in multiple ways (peers and friends, homework, TV, DVDs, and so on).

So the parents, while doing their best to enforce the home language convention, devised other strategies. For example, they sought out newly arrived French-speaking families who had children the same age as their boys, and they organized get-togethers with them to see if they got along. It worked with one or two children and thus, for several months, while the latter were learning English, both Cyril and Pierre had monolingual French-speaking friends to talk to and play with.

The parents also invited some of the friends the two boys had made in Switzerland to come and visit. Since they were monolingual in French, Cyril and Pierre didn't have any choice but to speak French with them. In addition, the parents had French-speaking friends and relatives come and stay; this bolstered the presence of the home language in a natural way.

The parents had learned quite rapidly that forcing children to keep to just one language when they themselves, the parents, are bilingual can lead to frustration on both sides, especially if it is the weaker language that has to be spoken. Invariably, the children revert back to their stronger language. Thus Cyril and Pierre's parents always looked for situations where there was a real need for the weaker language; it worked well and both boys retained their French. In later years, they went on to acquire several other languages.

Reference

Grosjean, F. (2010). Family strategies and support. Chapter 17 of *Bilingual: Life and Reality*. Cambridge, MA: Harvard University Press.

4.5 LANGUAGE FORGETTING

Language forgetting is the flip side of language acquisition and it is just as interesting linguistically. Both adults and children forget languages but the latter do so much more rapidly.

- "I really should have kept up my Spanish";
- "I wish I could speak Chinese the way I used to as a child";
- "My German is going to pot."

We have all heard statements such as these from people of all ages, be they active or dormant bilinguals. They are often said with regret and sometimes a hint of sadness or even guilt.

One should keep in mind, though, that language forgetting is simply the flip side of language acquisition and that it is just as interesting linguistically. But the attitudes toward it are very different. Whereas language acquisition is seen positively ("Isn't it wonderful that you're learning Russian!"), language forgetting is not talked about in such terms.

The process of language forgetting begins when the domains of use of a language (see Post 1.5) are considerably reduced, if not simply absent. It extends over many years in adults and is marked by hesitant language production as the speaker searches for appropriate words or expressions. There is also the frequent intermingling of languages as he or she calls on the dominant language for help; pronunciation is marked increasingly by the other language or languages; "odd" syntactic structures or expressions are borrowed from the stronger language, and so on.

Language comprehension is less affected, although the person may not know new words and new colloquialisms in the language that is being forgotten. People who are in an extended process of forgetting a language avoid using it because they no longer feel sure about it and they do not want to make too many mistakes. If they do have to use it, they may cut short a conversation so as not to have to show openly how far the attrition has progressed.

There is increasing work being done on language forgetting in adults (see the next post) but there is less work on how bilingual children lose a language. Case studies have existed for a long time, however, and one that is well known was reported by anthropologist Robbins Burling. His family had moved to the Garo Hills district of Assam in India when their son, Stephen, was sixteen months old. There, Stephen quickly acquired Garo since he spent a lot of his time with a local nurse.

When the family left the Garo region a year and a half later, Stephen, was bilingual in Garo and English, maybe with a slight dominance in Garo. He translated and switched from one language to the other as bilingual children do.

The family then traveled across India and Stephen tried to speak Garo with people he met, but he soon realized that they did not speak it. The last time he tried to use the language was in the plane going back to the United States. He thought that the Malayan boy sitting next to him was a Garo and, as Robbins Burling writes, "A torrent of Garo tumbled forth as if all the pent-up speech of those weeks had been suddenly let loose." Within six months of their departure from the Garo Hills, Stephen was having problems with the simplest of Garo words.

At the end of his article, Robbins Burling raises an issue that is starting to be resolved by research (see Posts 4.7–4.9): "I hope that someday it will be possible to take him back to the Garo Hills and to discover whether hidden deep in his unconscious he may not still retain a remnant of his former fluency in Garo that might be reawakened if he again came in contact with the language."

I contacted Robbins Burling a few years ago and asked him if Stephen had indeed gone back to the Garo Hills. He replied that he hadn't but that he had acquired Burmese at age six in Burma. He spoke it fluently for a while but then forgot it. Robbins Burling finished his message by stating that in his early childhood Stephen had learned three languages and had forgotten two!

Stephen, now an adult, would probably agree with the following: All those who have a childhood language deep inside their minds have a hidden wish that one day they will be able to reactivate it and use it in their everyday life.

References

Burling, R. (1978). Language development of a Garo and English speaking child. In E. Hatch, ed., *Second Language Acquisition*. Rowley, MA: Newbury House, pp. 55–75.

Grosjean, F. (2010). Languages across the Lifespan. Chapter 8 of *Bilingual: Life and Reality*. Cambridge, MA: Harvard University Press.

4.6 UNDERSTANDING LANGUAGE LOSS

(Interview with Monika S. Schmid)

Languages can be acquired but they can also be lost. In this post, an expert on the topic of language attrition in bilinguals tells us about it.

The field that examines language forgetting is called language attrition and the bilinguals undergoing such changes, language attriters. One of the foremost researchers in the field is Monika S. Schmid, Professor of Linguistics at the University of Essex in England. In order to help us better understand her field and its recent findings, she has very kindly accepted to answer our questions. We thank her wholeheartedly.

Does language attrition concern language knowledge or language use or both?
If you define "knowledge" to be the deeply rooted fundamental structure of the language which allows you to produce and understand it in the first place, and "use" as any concrete instance of it, such as an individual utterance, language attrition tends to affect mainly "use."

People can develop a foreign accent in their native language, they make occasional grammatical mistakes, they become less fluent and use a less diverse vocabulary, but generally speaking they are still able to speak and understand the language, albeit with more effort or difficulty.

In your writings, you state that in adult bilinguals, as opposed to bilingual children, the atrophy of language knowledge of the first language is

minimal. Is there an age after which a language will no longer suffer as much?
The situation I describe above only pertains to those speakers who have lived in an environment where their first language (L1) is spoken as one of the majority languages until around age twelve, and then there is a change in their language situation. There are many indications that this age is a turning point.

Before then, language knowledge is extremely vulnerable, even if a child appears to be using a language in the same way as other native children of around the same age. Children can and do lose such languages almost entirely if they stop using them[5].

What are the linguistic manifestations of attrition?
One of the first things that most people experience is a lack of fluency. Attriters like myself tend to fumble for words an awful lot of the time, in particular when one of their languages has a word that could credibly belong to the other language. This is very similar to what people who learn a second language experience.

For example, just recently, I was warned that if I want to introduce myself in my very basic Spanish, I need to take care to use the verb *presentar*, as *introducer* in Spanish means "insert." Similarly embarrassing mistakes often creep into the native language, particularly when it is very similar to the language of the environment.

Apart from lack of fluency and getting words mixed up, attriters can also struggle with some of the more complex grammatical phenomena – the way in which a subordinate clause has to be structured, for example, or which grammatical case to use with a particular verb.

It is also often difficult to maintain the knowledge on how to speak "appropriately," for example in languages like French, which use different pronouns (*tu* and *vous*) depending on the relationship between the speakers. I often find myself confused as to how to address a particular person in my native German which also has the distinction.

For a long while, researchers thought that frequency of use of a language was a main factor in language attrition. You have shown that it really depends on the language mode the bilinguals are in. Can you explain?

[5] See the next three posts.

Over the years, research into attrition tended to assume that it is a form of "forgetting" the language, that the knowledge stored in the brain simply "evaporates" after some time – the "use it or lose it" assumption. However, we have found that even speakers who have not used their first language for decades can be all but perfect in it.

What seems to be more problematic is if you frequently speak the language with other bilinguals, and then mix and drop in words from your second language whenever you cannot think of them in your first language. This means that you may not use the "muscles" you need to push the second language out of the way in order to speak the native one. Of course, people can also pick up mixed speech from each other, and begin to think that these are the correct words to use, as you yourself showed in a study you did with Bernard Py in 1991 (see Post 3.9).

Some bilinguals lose their language(s) over the years more readily than others. What are the factors that explain this?
I think that this is one of the areas about which we still know the least. There are some people who are simply more talented at learning a second language, but we don't know whether it is the same people who will also experience more (or less) attrition. Other so-called "individual differences" might play a role, such as working memory capacity, or level of education. So far the experimental findings on these matters are slim.

In your first book based on your thesis, you showed that emotional factors can greatly influence attrition. Can you tell us about it?
What this study showed is that if you no longer want to be a native speaker of a particular language, that is a goal you can achieve. In that study, I looked at German Jews who fled from the Holocaust, and I showed that the degree to which their German had deteriorated was linked to how much persecution and trauma they had experienced. They had very good reasons for no longer wanting to be German, and this affected their language.

You wrote back in 2002 that the overwhelming majority of language attrition studies have concentrated on "what is lost" to the exclusion of "what is retained." Please explain.
I think you yourself were one of the first researchers to make the argument that people who use more than one language should not be seen as

deficient, as falling short of the "norm" of the monolingual native speaker (see Post 1.2). Instead, we should think of them as individuals who are capable of doing a wide range of things in several languages – the linguist Vivian Cook coined the term "multicompetent" for this.

In a similar vein, my assumption was that the way in which a monolingual speaker, and an attriter of the same language, use that language will probably overlap to a huge degree, and that it would be interesting to explore this, instead of staring at the relatively few mistakes they make.

Finally, language attrition is a very sensitive issue for those losing a language. Many feel ashamed, others refuse to speak the language they are losing, others still are in denial. What do you say to these people as a linguist?

Let me address them directly: Firstly, you should always keep in mind that anyone who mocks or denigrates you for such things probably knows fewer languages than you do. Secondly, you are not alone – pretty much anyone who has lived abroad for any length of time, or even uses a foreign language a lot while remaining in the same country, will have experienced the same thing.

Thirdly, why should we have such unrealistic and high expectations? As I said above, I'm now trying to learn Spanish. It is still extremely basic and I cannot say a single sentence without at least five mistakes, but I can't wait to go on holiday and try it out – that's the way a language develops.

After all, what is so terrible about making mistakes? And if anyone still remarks on any of your own mistakes, send them to my website[6].

References

Yilmaz, G. and Schmid, M. S. (2018). First language attrition and bilingualism: Adult speakers. In D. Miller, F. Bayram, J. Rothman, and L. Serratrice, eds., *Bilingual Cognition and Language: The State of the Science Across its Subfields.* Amsterdam: John Benjamins, pp. 225–249.

Schmid, M. S. and Köpke, B. (2017). The relevance of first language attrition to theories of bilingual development. *Linguistic Approaches to Bilingualism,* 7(6), 637–667.

---

[6] https://languageattrition.org

4.7 CAN A FIRST LANGUAGE BE TOTALLY FORGOTTEN? I

An intriguing question that has been asked over the years is whether a first language can be totally forgotten when it stops being used in early childhood. Recent research on adults who were adopted as very young children and who suddenly changed their home language is starting to give us an answer.

At the turn of this century, researchers started studying whether there are remnants of a first language that are left after it has been replaced at a very early age by a second language. In a study that is often cited, a group of Paris-based researchers, headed by Christophe Pallier, tested adults (mean age of 26.8) who had been born in Korea and who had been adopted by French families in their early childhood. All claimed that they had completely forgotten their native language, Korean, and all spoke French fluently with no perceptible foreign accent.

They were asked to do three tasks: a language identification task (they had to recognize Korean sentences amid other sentences spoken in five different languages), a word recognition task (here they decided which of two Korean words was the correct translation of the French word displayed on a screen), and a fragment detection task (they had to ascertain whether a short speech fragment came from a sentence which could be in one of four languages, one of them being Korean). During the latter task, brain imaging (fMRI) was performed.

The results obtained were clear. The adults who had been adopted as very young children could not distinguish sentences in Korean amid sentences from other languages. Nor could they choose the correct Korean word in the recognition task. And similarly, they could not detect fragments from Korean sentences any better than native French controls. The cortical regions that showed greater response to the known language, French, were similar in the adopted subjects and in the French controls. The only difference was that the extent of the activation was larger in the latter. The authors concluded tentatively that the adoptees' native language, Korean, had indeed been lost.

A few years before this study came out, I had gone to interview Noam Chomsky on bilingualism (see Post 15.1) and I had asked him whether a language could be totally lost. He responded that even if a person can no longer use a language, he/she can relearn the language much faster than someone who has never known that language. According to him, "There's got to be a residue of the language somewhere. . . . You can't really erase the system."

Pallier and his group thought this might be the case at the phonetic (sound) level and in a later study they asked a much larger group of Korean adoptees to undertake a phonetic discrimination task. When they compared the results of a subgroup of adoptees that had been reexposed to Korean to one that had not, they only found one small difference. Basically the two subgroups behaved similarly according to them.

The researchers did leave a window open though; phonetic knowledge might be able to be recovered if reexposure to the first language takes place for a longer time than for their own subgroup, and if training is extensive. This is where a research group headed by Kenneth Hyltenstam in Sweden come in. They too studied Korean adoptees but this time the latter, as adults, had spent much more time studying Korean than had the French group. In addition, they had spent some time in Korea as adults. They were compared to a group of Swedish speakers who had also learned Korean and who had lived in Korea.

Even though the two groups did not appear to differ on the two language tests they were given, the results in the phonetic test were more variable for the Korean adoptees, and a third of them actually performed better than the Swedish group. The researchers' conclusion was that if reexposure to the first language takes place over a certain period of time and is intensive, then remnants of a seemingly lost language are more likely to be retrieved. The chances are increased further if the adoption took place towards the end of the first decade of life rather than toward its beginning.

So, to come back to the question asked in the title: "Can a first language be totally forgotten?" Based on the relearning data obtained, and with the use of increasingly sensitive tasks examining specific linguistic levels, the answer may well turn out to be, "No, not totally."

References

Pallier, C., Dehaene, S., Poline, J-B., LeBihan, D., Argenti, A-M., Dupoux, E., and Mehler, J. (2003). Brain imaging of language plasticity in adopted adults: Can a second language replace a first? *Cerebral Cortex*, 13, 155–161.

Hyltenstam, K., Bylund, E., Abrahamsson, N., and Park, H.-S. (2009). Dominant-language replacement: The case of international adoptees. *Bilingualism: Language and Cognition*, 12(2): 121–140.

4.8 CAN A FIRST LANGUAGE BE TOTALLY FORGOTTEN? II

There is additional evidence that the first language that is forgotten is still present in the brain. Neural representations acquired early in life do not seem to be overwritten and can be shown to be present if the right research approach is used.

The fascinating topic of whether a first language can be totally lost will certainly continue to be studied for many years to come. Those who believe that early first language representations are not overwritten, even though the language appears to be lost, can now refer to the results of a very compelling study. Lara Pierce and her coauthors, all based at McGill University and the Université de Montréal in Canada, sought to find neural evidence of a first language in participants who had forgotten it and had no conscious recollection of having known it.

They tested three groups of young people whose mean age was thirteen years. One group was made up of adoptees who had come from China to Quebec when they were one year old. Since then they had grown up speaking French only and had no longer been exposed to Chinese. The second group was composed of Chinese/French bilinguals who had continued speaking Chinese at home and had used French everywhere else. And the third group was made up of monolingual French speakers who knew no Chinese whatsoever.

The brain activation of the participants was examined using functional magnetic resonance imaging (fMRI) while they were doing a Chinese lexical tone discrimination task. In this task, they were asked to listen to pairs of phrases containing three syllables that were either pseudowords (e.g. da-shao-fa) or nonspeech hummed versions of the same syllables. Both pseudowords and their hummed versions contained tone information. The two elements of the pair were either identical, or the final syllable varied on tonal information only. Participants were asked to respond with a button press indicating whether the final syllable was the same or different in the pair.

What is interesting in this study is that it used tone information which is processed differently depending on whether one knows a tonal language or not. Thus, the Mandarin word "ma" can mean "mother," "hemp," "horse," or "scold" to listeners of Chinese depending on the tone used, whereas the meaning remains the same ("mine") for listeners of French despite the change in tone. In the case of French listeners, it is the right hemisphere's frontal and temporal regions that process acoustic frequency information that are activated when listening to lexical tones, whereas it is the left hemisphere language regions that are activated in Chinese listeners since tones are linguistically relevant in their language.

How did the three groups of participants react to the stimuli they heard? In the monolingual French speakers, only the right hemisphere was activated, more precisely the right temporal regions which process complex, but nonlinguistic, auditory signals. In the bilingual participants, who knew and used both Chinese and French, the largest peaks of activation were in the left hemisphere (left temporal regions) showing thereby that they were using their linguistic knowledge of tones to process what they heard. What about the adoptees who had functionally "lost" their Chinese and had no conscious recollection of it? Their neural patterns matched those of the bilinguals showing thereby that they maintained their early neural representations over time even though they had received no Chinese language for some twelve years! The authors concluded that these representations acquired early in life are indeed present and can be revealed if the right procedure is used.

Of course, as more research is conducted in this domain, the story will become more complicated. Other factors will be taken into account and some may be found to have some importance. For example, the Canadian researchers found that the children who were adopted at later ages showed more activation in a part of the left hemisphere, the planum temporale, than those who were adopted earlier. So the amount of input that a language received before being forgotten will probably play a role. Other questions will be asked such as what exactly was acquired linguistically before attrition occurred, how sensitive is the research task used, and is perception restored more quickly than production? To these we must add factors that concern the type of reexposure needed to "reawaken" a language and how long it should last.

This said, the answer to the question in the title of this post, "Can a first language be totally forgotten?," now seems to be clearer than ever before: No, not totally!

Reference

Pierce, L. J., Klein, D., Chen, J.-K., Delcenserie, A., and Genesee, F. (2014). Mapping the unconscious maintenance of a lost first language. *Proceedings of the National Academy of Science (PNAS)*, DOI: 10.1073/pnas.1409411111

4.9 RECOVERING A CHILDHOOD LANGUAGE UNDER HYPNOSIS

In close to sixty years, only three readily available studies have examined whether a forgotten childhood language can reappear under hypnosis. The results are truly fascinating.

The work in progress on whether a language acquired in very early childhood, and then forgotten, is still present mainly examines perception variables such as identification, discrimination, or recognition of speech elements. But what about speech production? Is there a way to help speakers reawaken, or have access to, a forgotten language so that they can actually produce it? This is precisely what three truly fascinating studies that used hypnosis attempted to do at various times since the 1960s. The first was done in 1962 by Arvid Ås, the second in 1970 by Erika Fromm, and the third in 2007 by Rosalie Footnick. I will summarize the second study but will also mention the one by Ås. The study by Footnick would appear to have methodological issues and so will not be described here.

Professor Erika Fromm, the famous German–American psychologist and co-founder of hypnoanalysis, relates how she met a young Japanese–American graduate student – she called him Don – at the University of Chicago in the late sixties. On her return from Japan where she had learned some Japanese, an assistant of hers asked her to watch a hypnotic training session she was giving him. Don had reported that he knew and spoke no Japanese except for a handful of polite words used as a very young child. When Fromm entered the office, he was already in a deep trance, age-regressed to seven years old, which means that he had been mentally taken back in time to that age. Fromm asked him a few questions in Japanese but he did not seem to understand. As she wrote in her article: "None of them seemed to strike a spark."

A few months later, in front of observers, Fromm hypnotized Don herself this time. She age-regressed him to eight years old and they spoke in English. Then, she told him to close his eyes again and to go back further in time, to age three. Here is what happened according to Fromm: "For a few moments there was silence. Then, suddenly, in a high-pitched child's voice, Don broke into a stream of rapid Japanese. . . . He talked on and on in Japanese for about 15 to 20 minutes. He seemed to want to involve me in his Japanese talk, and so again I used any Japanese words I knew. . . . I was more than surprised at his flood of Japanese." Afterward, Don was astonished to hear that apparently fluent Japanese had spurted forth from his lips.

Four months later, Fromm once again age-regressed Don during a psychotherapy session, and tape recorded him this time. When he reached age three, Fromm triggered his Japanese with a homophone (English "hi" and Japanese "hai" meaning "yes") and Don switched over to Japanese and talked happily and excitedly about a puppy he had. Fromm writes, "Apparently he had just received it. He said, 'Thank you, Mother, thank you, Mother,' and asked what the puppy's name was. Over and over he happily reiterated, 'It's mine, it's my dog, it's mine.'"

When he awoke, he said: "It was like my lips all of a sudden would move into these funny shapes. And then I would want to say something and wouldn't know what I was really saying. The words just came out and I wasn't sure whether they were real or not." He listened to the tape and he said that he understood a part of the recording, but by no means all. In the weeks that followed, Don regained progressively more knowledge of his forgotten language.

After each session, Erika Fromm had asked Don about his past and this allowed her to reconstruct his childhood. He was born in San Jose, California, five days before Pearl Harbor, and in 1942 his parents and he were put into a relocation camp. At that time he had spoken Japanese as well as English to his parents. After the war, they had moved to Utah and there he had had trouble communicating with kids on the street so his parents had stopped talking Japanese to him. English became the only language he spoke as of age four, in and out of the house.

Through lack of use, Don had partly forgotten Japanese. But according to Fromm there was also a repression factor at work. He had had a strong desire to be considered fully American upon leaving the relocation camp. Unconsciously, he must have felt at some point that he could better attain his goal if he knew no Japanese and spoke only English.

Is repression of a language always required for it to be recovered during hypnosis? It does not seem to be the case if one examines another case study. Arvid Ås reports on an eighteen-year-old freshman at Stanford University who had spoken Swedish in Finland in his early years. Then, following his emigration to the United States with his mother, and her remarriages, Swedish was no longer spoken in the home. He was about eight years old at the time and from then on, he simply didn't use it since he didn't need it.

When Ås met him and had hypnotic sessions with him, the young man maintained that he had forgotten Swedish entirely except for a couple of words. And yet, when he was age-regressed to first grade, he showed that he still remembered a good deal of Swedish. He also showed clear improvement in a Swedish language test given to him before and after hypnosis.

It would appear therefore that a "lost" language can indeed be recovered under hypnosis. A word of caution is needed though: studies that have produced negative results probably exist but have not been published. In addition, some people are not easily hypnotized, and age-regression may not be used in all situations.

This said, and on a more personal note, were I younger, I'd love for someone to age-regress me to ten years old and record me speaking Italian. I have always regretted having lost this beautiful language I spoke quite fluently as a child!

References

Ås, A. (1962). The recovery of forgotten language knowledge through hypnotic age regression: A case report. *American Journal of Clinical Hypnosis*, 5:1, 24–29.

Fromm, E. (1970). Age regression with unexpected reappearance of a repressed childhood language. *International Journal of Clinical and Experimental Hypnosis,* 18:2, 79–88.

Footnick, R. (2007). A hidden language: Recovery of a "lost" language is triggered by hypnosis. In B. Köpke, M. S. Schmid, M. Keijzer, and S. Dostert, eds., *Language Attrition: Theoretical Perspectives.* Amsterdam: John Benjamins Publishing, pp. 169–187.

5

Becoming Bilingual

INTRODUCTION

One can become bilingual at any time during one's life, as a child, an adolescent, or an adult. This is explained in Post 5.1 and the factors that make bilingualism possible are enumerated. Research, however, has concentrated on childhood bilingualism, and in particular on children who acquire two languages simultaneously. They will be the object of many of the posts in this chapter.

Post 5.2 explains how the main language development milestones are reached within the same age spans in both monolingual and bilingual children. Post 5.3 describes a study that shows that babies with bilingual mothers come to the world already attuned to the two languages they hear before their birth. And Post 5.4 shows that bilingual infants are particularly good at discriminating the sounds of their different languages in their first year, as long as the languages are acquired through live human exposure.

Post 5.5 examines the visual attention bilingual infants pay to faces of people talking to them. They exploit audiovisual speech cues earlier and for a longer period of time than monolingual infants.

One of the most intriguing phenomena in bilingualism is how infants who acquire two or more languages from birth distinguish and differentiate the spoken input they perceive into distinct languages. In Post 5.6, in an interview, Dr. Janet Werker explains this to us.

The post that follows (5.7) is an interview with Dr. Krista Byers-Heinlein who discusses how bilingual infants learn new words in their languages. This is followed by a discussion of a question that many parents ask themselves: Do young bilingual children know as many words as their monolingual peers (Post 5.8).

Older children are covered in Posts 5.9 and 5.10. In the former, we see how a five-year-old came back to bilingualism after having stopped using one of his languages for fifteen months. And in Post 5.10, we learn how two brothers, aged ten and five, became bilingual by being immersed in a totally different language and culture for a year.

Finally, Post 5.11 examines language intermingling in bilingual children and the reasons that explain this behavior.

5.1 ONE CAN BECOME BILINGUAL AT ANY AGE[1]

Even though we associate becoming bilingual with young children, one can become bilingual at any time during one's life.

Some people believe you cannot be a "real" bilingual if you have not acquired your two languages in infancy or at least as a young child. It's true that there is something magical about a toddler who speaks one language to her father and another to her mother. But in fact, one can become bilingual at any time during one's life – as a child, as an adolescent, or as an adult.

Children who acquire two languages simultaneously have been the object of many studies and books. Their parents often adopt an approach that allows them to receive two language inputs, but they are in fact rarer than children who acquire their languages successively.

The majority of child bilinguals start monolingually. They first acquire a home language and then, usually when they start going to school, they learn a second language, most often the majority language. Literally millions of children throughout the world have become bilingual in this manner. Then, depending on the country, they may start learning a third (and even a fourth) language as a school subject.

Older children and young adolescents may also become bilingual. This will happen when they move to another linguistic region or to another country and start to be schooled in their new language. This was my case when I was eight. Writer Eva Hoffman relates vividly in *Lost in Translation* how at age thirteen she arrived in Canada from Poland and was immersed in a new language and culture (see Post 14.10).

---

[1] The original title of this post was, "Becoming bilingual."

Can one become bilingual later on? There is no upper age limit for acquiring a new language and then continuing one's life with two or more languages. Nor is there any limit in the proficiency that one can attain in the new language with the exception of pronunciation skills. Acclaimed novelist Ágota Kristóf fled Hungary at age twenty-one during the events of 1956 and came to the French-speaking part of Switzerland. She acquired French from scratch and many years later published her first novel – in French!

The main factor that leads to the acquisition and development of a language is the need for that language – the need to interact with others, to study or work, to take part in social activities, and so on. If the need for a language is present, then language acquisition will usually take place. This is true of children as it is of adults.

Other factors must also be present: enough language input and use; the help of family, friends, colleagues, and the community in general; formal language learning for some; and positive attitudes toward the language and culture in question, as well as towards bilingualism.

Some might ask: Isn't it better to start becoming bilingual as early as possible? This really depends. For example, as concerns need, a second language may not be needed early in life, hence the fact that bilingualism may develop later on only. If the need for a language is not present, or no longer present, then the language may not be acquired or may become dormant.

There is also the question of language fluency. Some researchers have downplayed the "earlier you start the more fluent you become" argument. It is true that for native-like pronunciation, a sensitive period range is shorter but even then I have known bilinguals who have acquired their second language at age fifteen and have no accent in it. As for other skills, the window is not as clearly marked and acquisition can take place at any time. Admittedly, some underlying listening and speaking mechanisms may not be the same as those of early bilinguals but this does not usually impede communication.

Reference

Grosjean, F. and Byers-Heinlein, K. (2018). Bilingual adults and children: A short introduction. In F. Grosjean and K. Byers-Heinlein, eds., *The Listening Bilingual: Speech Perception, Comprehension, and Bilingualism.* Hoboken, NJ: Wiley, pp. 4–24.

5.2 BILINGUALISM DOES NOT DELAY LANGUAGE DEVELOPMENT[2]

Bilingual infants are not delayed in their language development but they may well be dominant in one language depending on the input they receive.

As we saw in Post 5.1, bilingual infants, that is children who acquire their two languages simultaneously, are far rarer than bilingual children who acquire their languages successively. They have been studied extensively, however, and the findings obtained are both fascinating and reassuring.

To help their children become bilingual from the onset, parents may use a different language with them (for example, the father uses English and the mother Spanish) or they may both use one language and other caretakers (a member of the family, a nanny, the personnel in a day care) use another language (see Post 6.3).

Despite the longstanding concern that infant bilingualism may delay language acquisition in children, the main milestones are reached within the same age spans in both monolingual and bilingual children. For example, researcher D. Kimbrough Oller and his colleagues have found that canonical babbling (that is, babbling using well-formed syllables, such as "da da da") begins at the same age in the two groups.

As concerns the capacity to perceive different sounds, bilingual infants have to discriminate more possibilities but they do so very efficiently. Researcher Janet Werker and her team found that infants raised in a bilingual environment establish the phonetic representations for each of their languages in much the same manner, and on the same time course, as infants establishing representations for one language. However, if there are many similar sounds, bilingual infants may take a bit more time learning to discriminate them appropriately, which only makes sense.

As for when the first word is spoken, we've known for quite some time that monolingual and bilingual children do not differ; this takes place at around eleven months, on average. The development of two vocabularies

---

[2] The original title of this post was, "Bilingual infants".

by bilingual children also seems to follow the pattern found in all children. I contacted a leading expert on the subject, researcher Barbara Zurer Pearson, who confirmed that bilinguals are right on target with onset milestones, on the condition that they don't have just cursory exposure to one of their two languages. All of the children she studied with her colleague, Sylvia Fernandez, showed the traditional "lexical spurt" (when a vocabulary increases suddenly) either alternately, depending on the strength of each language, or when both languages were taken together in the count.

Other researchers working on other aspects of language development have also reported similarities between monolingual and bilingual children: sounds or sound groups that are easier to produce appear sooner than those that are more difficult; some words are overextended (for example, when "doggie" is used to mean small four-legged animals); utterances slowly increase in length; simpler grammatical constructions are used before more complex ones, and so on. Clearly, language development as a human cognitive skill is not delayed in bilingual infants. This is a conclusion that has also been reached by researcher Laura-Ann Petitto and her team who have studied babies acquiring two oral languages as well as one oral and one sign language.

This said, we should keep in mind two factors discussed by researchers Virginia Yip and Stephen Matthews, among others. First, it may happen that certain linguistic constructs are more complex in one language than in the other and hence they can be acquired more quickly in the "simpler" or more transparent language.

Second, if one language receives more input than another, as often happens, then it may take on the role of the dominant language (see Post 1.6): more sounds are isolated, more words are acquired, more grammatical rules are inferred, and so on.

In addition, the dominant language will have a tendency to influence the weaker language in the form of transfers, or the direct use of elements taken from it to fill various language gaps in the weaker language. This is especially prevalent when the children's interlocutors know both languages. It is as if these budding bilinguals were telling themselves that the aim is to communicate after all, and if one language isn't sufficient, then they'll call on the other for help.

Reference

Grosjean, F. and Byers-Heinlein, K. (2018). Bilingual adults and children: A short introduction. In F. Grosjean and K. Byers-Heinlein, eds., *The Listening Bilingual: Speech Perception, Comprehension, and Bilingualism.* Hoboken, NJ: Wiley, pp. 4–24.

5.3 BORN WITH A PREFERENCE FOR TWO LANGUAGES

Babies with bilingual mothers come to the world already attuned to the two languages they hear before their birth.

It has been known for some time that newborn infants with monolingual mothers have become sensitive in utero to some characteristics of the spoken language they are exposed to. Thus, when tested just after birth, they show a preference for their mother's voice as well as their mother's native language over another language that is rhythmically different.

But what about infants who have bilingual mothers? Do they show a preference for their mother's TWO languages? The answer can be found in some fascinating experimental work undertaken by researchers Krista Byers-Heinlein, Tracey Burns, and Janet Werker of the Infant Studies Center at the University of British Columbia.

In a first study, they took newborn infants (zero to five days old) and presented them with speech, alternating each minute between English and Tagalog, a language spoken as a native language or a second language by nearly all Filipinos. Half the infants had mothers with a monolingual English background and half with a bilingual, Tagalog–English, background.

The researchers employed a testing technique that makes use of newborns' sucking reflex. The babies are given a rubber nipple to suck on and the researchers record how often they do so. The greater the amplitude of sucking, the more interested the infants are. The question asked was the following: Would both groups of infants have a high-amplitude sucking behavior when listening to English as well as to Tagalog, or would it only be those infants with bilingual mothers?

What was found was that infants with monolingual mothers marked a clear preference for English over Tagalog (their sucking rate was greater for the former). The infants with bilingual mothers, on the other hand, were interested in both languages – they did not favor one over the other. They had been in contact with their mother's two languages prenatally and hence they responded positively to both.

The researchers then conducted two other studies to make sure that their results couldn't be explained in other ways. One such way, the "insufficient-experience" explanation, ran as follows: because the infants with bilingual mothers had received input *in utero* from the two languages, maybe their experience with each language had been insufficient. Hence the fact that they did not favor one language over the other.

Other newborn infants, this time with mothers who spoke both Chinese and English, were run on the same stimuli. As compared to the previous two groups, they showed an intermediary pattern. They were less interested in Tagalog than were the infants with bilingual mothers, but they were more interested in it than were the infants with English monolingual mothers. Based on the fact that Tagalog shares some characteristics with Chinese but also differs on some others, the researchers took this to mean that the newborns with mothers bilingual in Tagalog and English had indeed been sensitive *in utero* to characteristics of the two languages.

The other follow-up study the researchers undertook was to check that the Tagalog–English newborns had not regrouped their two languages into one broad category of familiar language sounds. Hence, they ran a discrimination study of English and Tagalog. They used a sucking habituation procedure in which the infants were habituated to a language, either English or Tagalog. Habituation was observed when, having heard a language for a period of time, they started to slow down their sucking rate (basically, the language wasn't interesting them anymore). When a preset point was reached, the other language was played to them and the researchers observed whether the infant's interest was revived, as shown by a sudden increase in sucking.

What they found was that the infants with bilingual mothers did react to the other language, in other words, that they did indeed discriminate between the two languages. They had not "lumped" the two into one broad language category.

The authors concluded that the acquired interest in the two languages these infants had been exposed to could help them pay attention to the languages and hence acquire them in their first years of life. . . . IF they were raised in a bilingual environment, of course.

Reference

Byers-Heinlein, K., Burns, T. C., and Werker, J. F. (2010). The roots of bilingualism in newborns. *Psychological Science*, 21(3), 343–348.

5.4 SPEECH DISCRIMINATION IN BILINGUAL INFANTS

Bilingual infants excel at discriminating the sounds of their different languages in their first year as long as the languages are acquired through live human exposure. But this does not mean that bilingualism needs to start at such a precocious age.

Anything that has to do with bilingual infants captures our attention, as it should. One particularly exciting domain pertains to how early and how well they discriminate the sounds of their different languages.

In an interesting study, a team of University of British Columbia researchers led by Janet Werker used a visual fixation procedure to study the development of phonetic representations in English monolingual and English–French bilingual infants. The infants were tested individually. They sat on their caretaker's lap and watched a checkerboard on a monitor. While doing so they heard an intermediate syllable "ba" [pa] which was perceived as "pa" by adult French speakers but as "ba" by adult English speakers. In what follows, we'll refer to it as *intermediate "ba" [pa]*.

The syllable was repeated a number of times through a loudspeaker positioned above the checkerboard until there was habituation (this was seen by the fact that the infants' eyes wandered away from the board). At that point, one of two new syllables was presented. One, [ba], was perceived as a clear "ba" by both English and French adult speakers, and the other, [pʰa], was perceived as a clear "pa" by both groups. If infants could discriminate the new sound, then their interest would be revived and they would start looking at the checkerboard again. Researchers talk of dishabituation when this happens.

The results were fascinating. First, monolingual and bilingual infants behaved in exactly the same way when they were six to eight months old. They dishabituated to the clear "ba" syllable [ba] but not to the clear "pa" [pʰa] syllable. However, when ten- to twelve-month-old infants were tested, the results from the two groups were quite different. The English monolingual infants looked significantly longer at the board when they heard the clear "pa" syllable (this syllable was now heard as different from the intermediate syllable) but not when they heard the clear "ba" syllable (both the intermediate syllable "ba" [pa] and the clear syllable [ba] were now a "ba" for them, hence no dishabituation). Thus, they still had two categories although the boundary between the two had shifted.

What about the bilingual infants? Unlike their monolingual peers, they showed dishabituation to BOTH the clear "ba" and "pa" syllables. The intermediate "ba" [pa] was perceived as different from the clear "pa" [pʰa]. There is an English phonetic boundary between the two, hence the dishabituation. And the intermediate "ba" [pa] was also heard as different from the clear "ba" [ba] as there is a French phonetic boundary between the two. Thus the infants showed the existence of two phonetic boundaries, one for English and one for French. The authors concluded by stating that infants exposed to two languages from birth are equipped to process each language in a native manner, at least at the phonetic level.

Before discussing this further, we can ask ourselves whether any type of exposure to two languages (through human interaction, DVDs, audio input, etc.) will encourage infants to develop the phonetic categories of their languages. University of Washington researcher Patricia Kuhl and her colleagues replied negatively based on a study they undertook. They exposed nine-month-old American infants to twelve sessions with Chinese native speakers who read and played with them in Mandarin. A second group of similar infants received the same amount of Mandarin language exposure but only through DVDs and audio input.

The results were clear. Whereas the live human exposure infants acquired the Mandarin phonetic contrast, the second group did not. This shows that phonetic learning doesn't rely only on raw auditory sensory information. According to the authors, the presence of a live person interacting with an infant generates interpersonal social cues that attract the infant's attention and motivate learning.

What are the lessons to be learned from this type of research? If infants are exposed to two languages through human interaction, they will acquire the phonetic categories of the languages by the end of their first year approximately. If the two languages have many similar sounds, then they may take a bit more time. This said, we should keep in mind that phonetic categories are just some of the building blocks of language. There are many others at all linguistic levels (morphology, syntax, semantics, discourse, etc.) and these will be acquired over several years.

Does all this mean that bilingualism must at all cost start during the first year? The answer is no. In fact, children who acquire their two languages simultaneously are far rarer than bilingual children who acquire their languages successively. As was stated in Post 5.1, there is no upper age limit for acquiring a new language and then continuing one's life with two or more languages. Nor is there any limit in the proficiency that one can attain in the new language with the exception of pronunciation skills. Admittedly, the latter are harder to acquire by the middle teens, but this is still many years after infancy.

References

Burns, T., Yoshida, K., Hill, K., and Werker, J. (2007). The development of phonetic representation in bilingual and monolingual infants. *Applied Psycholinguistics*, 28, 455–474.

Kuhl, P. K., Tsao, F.-M., and Liu, H.-M. (2003). Foreign-language experience in infancy: Effects of short-term exposure and social interaction on phonetic learning. *Proceedings of the National Academy of Sciences of the United States of America*, 100(15), 9096–9101.

5.5 WHEN BILINGUAL INFANTS LOOK AT PEOPLE TALKING

The attention that infants pay to talking faces when learning to speak, and the evolution of their behavior during their first year, is a relatively new topic in the field of child development. The differences, but also the similarities, that are found in the behavior of monolingual and bilingual infants are simply fascinating.

Have you ever observed infants being raised with two languages when they look at someone speaking to them? I have had that opportunity lately and what has struck me is how intense their gaze is, but also the attention they pay to the mouth, and to the eyes of the speaker. But is this simply a figment of my imagination or is there some truth to it?

The attention that infants pay to talking faces when learning to speak, and the evolution of their behavior during their first year, is a relatively new topic in the field of child development. Let's first look at monolingual infants. Researchers David Lewkowicz and Amy Hansen-Tift reported on a study a few years ago that tracked what happened to the infants' eye gaze while they watched and listened to a person reciting a prepared monologue.

The authors looked at several groups of infants as well as one group of adults. The infants either sat in an infant seat or on their parent's lap and watched a person uttering an English monologue on a computer monitor. As they were doing so, the researchers monitored where they looked by using an eye tracker. They were interested in two main areas on the face: one around the eyes and one around the mouth.

In reporting the results they obtained, we will concentrate on the infants who were four, eight, and twelve months old. At four months old, infants looked longer at the eyes, but then a shift took place so that by eight months old, they looked longer at the mouth. Then, during the next few months, a second shift occurred so that infants who were twelve months old looked for an equal amount of time at both the mouth and the eyes.

The researchers explained the first shift toward the mouth by the fact that as they are learning how to speak, infants are attracted by the auditory AND the visual speech signals that are produced by the speaker and that are perceptually salient and redundant. As for the second shift, back to the eyes, the infants' emerging speech output reduces their need to have direct access to both the visual and auditory speech cues, and they can now concentrate on various social cues available in the speaker's eyes (shared meanings, beliefs, and desires).

But what about bilingual infants who are brought up with two languages? A recent study by researchers Ferran Pons and Laura Bosch, along with David Lewkowicz of the monolingual study, gives us the answer. The authors hypothesized that because bilingual infants need to process two languages, and keep them apart, they may well use audiovisual speech cues more than monolingual infants.

Since this study was undertaken in Barcelona, Spain, where different languages are used (Catalan or Spanish), the authors first tested three groups of monolingual infants – four, eight, and twelve months old – who were being brought up with either Catalan or Spanish only. They used the same procedure as in the preceding American study and found similar results: the four-month-old infants looked longer at the eyes, the eight-month-olds longer at the mouth, and the twelve-month-olds equally at the mouth and the eyes.

The next step was to test bilingual infants who belonged to the same three age groups but who were being brought up with a native (dominant) language – it could be either Spanish or Catalan – and who were also exposed to another language for at least 25 percent of the time. For the Spanish native language group, the other language was Catalan, and for the Catalan native language group, the other language was Spanish. Of course, these bilingual infants watched two videos, one in each of their languages.

The results obtained were fascinating. In both their languages, the four-month-old bilingual infants looked equally at the eyes and the mouth (recall that the monolingual infants of that age group looked more at the eyes), the eight-month-olds looked longer at the mouth (as did the monolinguals), and the twelve-month-olds again looked longer at the mouth (whereas the monolinguals looked equally at the mouth and the eyes).

How do the researchers explain the differences between bilingual and monolingual infants? The greater perceptual salience of audiovisual speech cues helps bilingual infants identify distinct language-specific features that keep the languages apart. Four-month-old infants become aware of this, hence their earlier attentional shift to the mouth, even though they also look at the eyes a lot. Attention to the talkers' mouth increases from then on and continues throughout their first year since redundant audiovisual speech cues are of primary importance for these children. In a word, bilingual infants exploit the perceptual information of these cues earlier and for a longer period of time than monolingual infants. (For other cues and strategies during the discrimination and separation of languages, see the next post.)

The authors end their paper with two questions that now need to be studied: Will bilingual children continue to rely on audiovisual speech cues past twelve months of age, and will children who are acquiring more dissimilar languages take even greater advantage of these redundant cues? As we await the answers, let's not forget to continue observing where it is bilingual infants look when we speak to them; it is simply amazing!

References

Lewkowicz, D. J. and Hansen-Tift, A. M. (2012). Infants deploy selective attention to the mouth of a talking face when learning speech. *Proceedings of the National Academy of Sciences of the United States of America*, 109(5), 1431–1436.
Pons, F., Bosch, L., and Lewkowicz, D. J. (2015). Bilingualism modulates infants' selective attention to the mouth of a talking face. *Psychological Science*, 26(4), 490–498.

5.6 HOW DO BILINGUAL INFANTS SEPARATE THEIR LANGUAGES?

(Interview with Janet Werker)

Infants who acquire two or more languages from birth have to distinguish and differentiate the spoken input they receive into distinct languages. Professor Janet Werker who has been at the forefront of research on this topic tells us how they do it.

One of the most intriguing phenomena in bilingualism is how infants who acquire two or more languages from birth manage to discriminate and separate their languages. They have to distinguish and differentiate the spoken input they perceive into distinct languages. How do they do it, we keep asking ourselves. Professor Janet Werker of the University of British Columbia is known the world over for her work on the perception of speech by bilingual infants. She has been one of the pioneers of research on language discrimination and separation, among other domains, and she has very kindly accepted to answer a few of our questions.

In your publications, you write that bilingual infants are more sensitive to the perceptual details of languages than monolingual infants. Can you explain what you mean?
Bilingual infants seem to listen more closely to the actual acoustics of speech sounds, hearing – for example – differences in the strength of the puff of air in one "P" vs. another (put your fingers in front of your mouth when you say "pat" and you'll know what I mean). They also seem to be

more sensitive to visual differences when watching talking faces, and notice, for example, the precise way the mouth or other facial muscles move when a word is being produced.

You also state that bilingual infants are better able to track multiple cues simultaneously. Can you give an example?
The languages of the world have different basic grammars which results in different word orders. In English there are prepositions (e.g. *from* Vancouver) whereas in Japanese there are post-positions (e.g. Tokyo *kara*). Also, in English determiners come before nouns (e.g. *the* house) whereas in Japanese, it is the opposite. Words such as prepositions (*from*) and determiners (*the*) are very common, but are lower in pitch and/or shorter in duration than words like nouns. Monolingual learning infants can use word frequency in a made-up language to figure out the grammar. Bilingual infants can use word frequency PLUS pitch and/or duration!

Languages have phonetic categories with specificities, for example, some languages have short and long vowels, some have nasal vowels, and so on. How does this internal structure help bilingual infants separate their languages?
Some studies suggest that bilingual infants are able to use the existence of different kinds of phonemes to help situate the speech they are hearing within one or another of their native languages. While more work is needed to ensure that this is the case, it seems as if bilingual Japanese-English infants can listen for Japanese grammar and words when they hear, for example, both long and short vowels in speech, but listen for English grammar and English words when they hear clear "r" and "l" sounds in the speech of someone talking to them.

Languages also have allowable sequences of phonemes (sounds) which don't occur in other languages. Can this also help bilingual infants separate their languages and can you give an example?
There is evidence from our colleagues in Spain, Nuria Sebastian-Galles and Laura Bosch, that bilingual Spanish–Catalan infants are sensitive to the allowable sequences of sounds (phonotactics) in their two languages. Catalan allows consonant clusters at the ends of words, whereas Spanish doesn't. Infants were tested on their preference for lists of words that either did or did not contain consonant clusters. Preference was measured by examining looking time to a display while the words were heard. While the monolingual infants listened longer to words that could be in

their native language, the bilingual learning infants showed more mixed preferences, driven by the language they were hearing most at home. As in the example above with phonemes, sensitivity to phonotactics could also help bilinguals separate their two languages.

Bilingual infants are attuned to the prosody (e.g. the rhythm) of their languages. How does this help?
Sensitivity to the rhythm of the two languages helps in two ways. First, it can help bilingual infants keep their two languages apart while simultaneously learning each (but without confusing it with the other). In addition, rhythm correlates with word order, so bilingual infants could use rhythm to help flag where nouns, verbs, prepositions, determiners, and so on, might be in the speech they are hearing.

Infants often look intensely at those who speak to them and pick up on visual cues. Do bilingual infants use this in any way?
All of us can tell, sometimes, whether someone talking is speaking our native language or not just by watching their facial movements. As noted above, bilingual infants seem to watch talking faces more closely than do monolingual infants, and hence may use the visual cues in talking faces to provide another clue as to which language is being spoken. Studies in other laboratories show that bilingual infants look more at the mouth than do monolingual infants (who look mostly at the eyes, particularly by ten months of age), providing even more information that they are tracking "phonetic" properties in facial movements[3]. In current work we are also exploring the hypothesis that bilingual infants who grow up in bi-ethnic homes might be able to use ethnicity in the face as a cue to the language that will be spoken.

In a recent paper with Padmapriya Kandhadai and D. Kyle Danielson you state that bilingual infants may be able to use cultural information in their surroundings to track the properties of each language. What do you mean exactly?
As in the example above with faces of different races, we suggest that bilingual/bicultural infants may be able to use other aspects of their two cultures to keep their languages apart, or to prime them to expect one or the other of their two languages. There is work with bilingual Mandarin–English adults that shows that seeing an iconic image from one culture,

[3] See Post 5.5.

for example, a picture of the Great Wall, speeds up access to Chinese words and slows down, or mixes up, access to English words.

Some bilingual infants get more input in one language than in the other, hence are dominant in that language. What impact does this have in their task of differentiating languages?
This is still an open question, but the research to date would suggest that as long as some threshold level of input is used in each language, the two languages will still be kept distinct.

What current questions concerning language differentiation are of particular interest?
One exciting question that comes from the work of Krista Byers-Heinlein at Concordia University in Montreal, is how language mixing effects language differentiation. Many bilingual children grow up with a lot of intermingled language input (see Post 5.11) but they still separate their languages. Whether mixing has an impact on this process is still not well understood.

References

Werker, J. F. and Byers-Heinlein, K. (2008). Bilingualism in infancy: First steps in perception and comprehension. *Trends in Cognitive Sciences*, 12(4), 144–151.
Kandhadai, P., Danielson, D. K., and Werker, J. F. (2014). Culture as a binder for bilingual acquisition. *Trends in Neuroscience and Education*, 3, 24–27.

5.7 BILINGUAL INFANTS LEARNING NEW WORDS

(Interview with Krista Byers-Heinlein)
Young bilingual infants learn new words in their languages amazingly well. Dr. Krista Byers-Heinlein, an expert on bilingual language development, tells us how they do it.

One of the most amazing phenomena in young children learning a language is how well and how fast they learn new words. There comes a time in their development when we, adults, can hardly keep up with their increasing vocabulary. And yet, this is far from evident, especially when new words only differ from other words by one sound, either a consonant or a vowel. Our amazement increases severalfold when we observe young bilingual children doing the same thing, but in several languages, and doing it well. In this post,

Dr. Krista Byers-Heinlein, of Concordia University in Montreal, a leading expert in language development in bilingual infants, has very kindly accepted to answer a few of our questions. We thank her wholeheartedly.

Can you first tell us what is involved in the learning of new words in infants and notably how they acquire words that sound similar?
Children often seem to learn words effortlessly, but there are actually a lot of different aspects to successfully learning a new word. At a minimum, infants have to identify and remember the sounds of the word, figure out what the word refers to, and associate the word and its meaning. For similar-sounding words, infants have to pay special attention to very subtle differences in sound. For example, "cat" and "cut" differ only in their vowel. If infants only remember the general outline of the word, that it starts with "c" and is one syllable long, for example, they won't be able to tell these two words apart.

In what way is this challenge even greater in bilingual infants?
Every language has different sound distinctions that are meaningful. For example, English has a "th" sound, so "three" has a different meaning from "tree". French does not have a "th" sound, and adult French-speakers often have difficulty with this sound when they try to learn English. Whereas monolingual infants have to figure out what sounds to pay attention to in their single language, bilingual infants have to figure all of this out for two different languages (if not more). This is a lot to keep track of especially while trying to learn a new word.

One approach that is used to study new word acquisition is called the "switch approach." Can you tell us how it works?
When researchers want to study what babies know and how they learn, it can be challenging because babies can't really follow instructions, respond verbally, or press a button. Researchers have to devise clever ways to indirectly figure out what they're thinking.

In the "switch approach," we first teach infants two new words – usually ones we have invented so that we know they haven't heard them before. Sitting on their parent's lap, infants see two different objects presented on a computer screen and hear their labels. Thus, for example, they see a crown moving back and forth and hear "kem," or they see a molecule made of building blocks and hear "gem."

This teaching phase continues for several minutes until infants get bored, and start to look away from the screen. Then we test their learning with a "switch." We show them the first object but accompany it with the second label, that is, the crown and the word "gem," and vice versa. If infants have learned the correct names, they should be surprised by the switch and stare longer at the screen than when we provide a correct label.

With your colleague, Christopher Fennell of the University of Ottawa, you studied whether monolingual and bilingual infants are equally sensitive to new words that differ on the very first consonant. How did you proceed?

In this study, we tested two groups of 1.5-year-old infants: monolingual English learners and bilingual French–English learners. We used the switch approach to teach them two similar-sounding words like the ones above. Half of the infants heard the words spoken by a speaker who was herself bilingual, and the other half heard them spoken by a speaker who was monolingual.

What was the result you obtained and did it surprise you?

We found that both monolingual and bilingual infants were sensitive to a change in sound and could use this difference to successfully learn the two new words. However, they succeeded only when the words were articulated by the speaker of their own language background. That is, bilingual infants could learn from the bilingual speaker, and monolingual infants could learn from the monolingual speaker, but not the other way around. This was surprising because the difference between the two speakers was very subtle – adult listeners could not tell the speaker's background.

Basically, infants are very well adapted to their own language-learning environments. Many bilingual infants have bilingual parents, and many monolingual infants have monolingual parents. However, this doesn't mean that none of the babies could learn from the other speaker. We also found that the bilingual babies who had a monolingual parent did better learning from the monolingual speaker than the ones who didn't.

Keep in mind that our participants were only 1.5 years old, an age when they are just beginning to build their vocabularies. We think that older infants would have done fine learning from either type of speaker.

A more recent study by Leher Singh and her colleagues, at the National University of Singapore, seems to show that bilingual infants might even

have an advantage over monolinguals. Can you first tell us how different their study was to yours?
Their study used a very similar procedure to ours, with three main differences. First, whereas the words in our study differed only in their initial consonant ("kem" and "gem"), theirs differed only in the middle vowel ("min" and "mun"). Second, there were differences in the groups of infants tested. Whereas we only tested English monolinguals, along with the bilinguals, they tested both English and Mandarin monolinguals. Third, our bilingual groups were learning different language pairs: ours French–English, and theirs Mandarin–English.

What results did they obtain?
Once again, bilingual infants learned the words just fine from the bilingual speaker. However, surprisingly, monolingual infants were not able to learn the words, whether they were pronounced by a monolingual or a bilingual speaker. The researchers concluded that bilingual infants might have an overall advantage in learning similar-sounding words that differ only in their vowel.

Where do you see the word-learning research in bilingual infants going in the future?
The studies we have just discussed are inspired by the work of Dr. Janet Werker and her colleagues (see the preceding post), who first observed how challenging learning similar-sounding words can be for monolingual infants. Going forward, word-learning research with bilingual infants is beginning to ask questions that are unique to this population. For example, how do bilingual infants manage to learn words in each of their languages? In challenging word-learning situations, do bilingual infants prioritize one language over the other? And how do they learn words when a speaker switches back and forth between their languages?

References

Fennell, C. and Byers-Heinlein, K. (2014). You sound like Mommy: Bilingual and monolingual infants learn words best from speakers typical of their language environments. *International Journal of Behavioral Development*, 38(4), 309–316.

Singh, L., Fu, C. S. L., Tay, Z. W., and Golinkof, R. M. (2017). Novel word learning in bilingual and monolingual infants: Evidence for a bilingual advantage. *Child Development*, DOI:10.1111/cdev.12747.

5.8 DO THEY KNOW AS MANY WORDS?

It is a constant worry of parents and educators that bilingual children may not know as many words as their monolingual peers. Where do we stand on this issue after two decades of research?

Although the advantages of being bilingual are numerous (see Post 12.6), parents and educators are often worried that bilingual children will not know as many words as their monolingual peers. However much time one spends describing and justifying bilingualism (after all, half the world's population, if not more, is bilingual), the question that keeps coming back is: But do bilingual children know as many words?

Dr. Barbara Zurer Pearson, a pioneering researcher in the field of childhood language acquisition, and her colleague Sylvia Fernández, studied this question in the 1990s. They examined the vocabulary development of English–Spanish bilingual children, aged between eight and thirty months. They found that the rate and pace of development of the bilinguals' lexical knowledge were similar to those of monolingual children. In addition, the total vocabulary count of these children (taking into account both languages) was not different to that of the monolinguals, but their single language vocabularies were somewhat smaller. So we have known for some time that bilingual children do have as many words as their monolingual counterparts when both languages are taken into account, but maybe not so when one examines only one language.

Almost twenty years later, a study by Diane Poulin-Dubois, Ellen Bialystok, Agnes Blaye, Alexandra Polonia, and Jessica Yott confirmed and extended this line of research. They compared the lexical development of two-year-old monolingual and bilingual infants. One of the tasks used was similar to the Pearson and Fernández task; it is based on a vocabulary checklist that parents fill in and that measures a child's expressive vocabulary. They too found that the total vocabulary size obtained for the monolinguals and the bilinguals was not statistically different. As for the vocabulary size in the children's first language, it was once again smaller in the bilinguals than in the monolinguals.

Diane Poulin-Dubois and her colleagues explained the fact that bilingual children have a smaller vocabulary in just one language in the following way: They are exposed to their languages in different environments and hence they may encounter specific items in a context where only one language is used. This decreases the number of words acquired in each language.

This explanation makes a lot of sense. In one of the very first posts in this book (Post 1.5), I have stressed how important the functions of languages are in the life of bilinguals. They usually acquire and use their languages for different purposes, in different domains of life, with different people. Different aspects of life often require different languages. I have called this the Complementarity Principle.

The principle accounts for many interesting phenomena in bilingualism such as the ultimate proficiency one attains in a language (at least at the lexical level), automatic language behaviors such as counting and praying (often done in just one language), the need to switch languages when the "wrong language" is used, the difficulty bilinguals have with translating, and so on.

It would seem that the Complementarity Principle is also at work in very young bilingual children. The above research points in this direction as does work undertaken by York University researcher and bilingualism specialist, Ellen Bialystok, along with her colleagues Gigi Luk, Kathleen Peets, and Sujin Yang. They tested the English receptive vocabulary of a very large number of monolingual and bilingual children, between the ages of three and ten years, whose school language was English. Once again, they found that monolingual children outperformed bilingual children when tested in just one language. To try to understand this finding, they took the step of examining the results by domain: the school domain (with words like "writing," "rectangle," "astronaut," etc.) and the home domain (with words like "squash" and "camper," for example).

The results they obtained confirm the presence of the Complementarity Principle. The difference that had been found between monolinguals and bilinguals was maintained in the home domain. This is normal as the bilingual children used their other language at home and hence didn't know English home words as well. However, in the school domain, a domain where English is used by both groups, the monolingual and bilingual children showed similar

LIFE AS A BILINGUAL

results. The authors concluded that bilingual children are not disadvantaged in academic uses of English.

In sum, the vocabulary of bilingual children will be in a given language for certain domains, in the other language for other domains, and in both languages for some shared domains. Concerning shared domains, back in the 1990s already, Barbara Zurer Pearson and her colleagues had found that a bit more than 30 percent of words in bilingual children were doublets or translation equivalents (i.e. a particular concept had a label in both languages), and more recently Diane Poulin-Dubois and her colleagues report a very similar percentage (37 percent).

All these results make perfect sense and reflect the fact that different aspects of life in bilingual children and adults often require different languages. Increasingly, sociolinguistic aspects of bilingual language knowledge and use are being taken into account in psycholinguistics research and this can only be applauded.

References

Bialystok, E., Luk, G., Peets, K. F., and Yang, S. (2010). Receptive vocabulary differences in monolingual and bilingual children. *Bilingualism: Language and Cognition*, 13(4), 525–531.

Pearson, B. Z. and Fernández, S. (1994). Patterns of interaction in the lexical growth in two languages of bilingual infants and toddlers. *Language Learning*, 44, 617–653.

Poulin-Dubois, D., Bialystok, E., Blaye, A., Polonia, A., and Yott, J. (2013). Lexical access and vocabulary development in very young bilinguals. *International Journal of Bilingualism*, 17(1), 57–70.

5.9 COMING BACK TO BILINGUALISM

A young bilingual child stopped speaking one of his languages when he came to the United States for some fifteen months. The linguistic and social strategies he adopted when he returned to his home country and once again became bilingual make for some fascinating reading.

It is not rare for bilinguals to go from being active, regular bilinguals, interacting with the world around them using their different languages, to being single language users. This can happen at any time and is usually due to a major life change. The language no longer being used on a regular basis will become dormant (see Post 4.2) and even start to be forgotten.

The wax and wane of languages takes place particularly quickly in children. As we saw in an earlier post based on a case study, three-year-old Stephen who was bilingual in English and Garo (a language from the district of Assam in India), stopped using Garo when he went back to the United States with his parents, and within six months he was having problems with the simplest of Garo words (see Post 4.5).

Of course, the movement can go both ways: from bilingualism to monolingualism as with Stephen but also from monolingualism to bilingualism. In a recent case study, University of Tromsø researchers Tove Dahl, Curt Rice, Marie Steffensen, and Ludmila Amundsen show how a little Norwegian–American boy, Per, reverted to bilingualism in English and Norwegian after some fifteen months of solely using English.

Per grew up with both English and Norwegian and was a balanced bilingual when, at age three, he left with his parents for the United States. They stayed there for some fifteen months and during that time Norwegian was not actively used either in his home or in his preschool. When the family came back to Norway, Per had to reacquire Norwegian and hence become bilingual once again.

The researchers recorded him in his Norwegian preschool for a number of weeks starting five weeks after Per's return. Before the recordings started, they noticed that Per spent less time speaking and more time listening. He was busy assessing the language skills of those around him while reactivating his Norwegian. When they did start recording, they found that Per kept to English, even though only his teachers spoke it, but within a few weeks it stopped being his sole language. It was replaced by a mixture of English and Norwegian (he code-switched and borrowed), and increasingly by Norwegian only. Some eleven weeks after his return, Per was basically only using Norwegian in his preschool.

What was especially interesting was how during this very short time span, Per adopted a number of linguistic and social strategies to communicate. Per quickly learned which interlocutors were bilingual (the teachers) and which were monolingual (his peers). Since he struggled with Norwegian at first, he interacted primarily with the adults to whom he would speak English, with or without code-switches and borrowings.

He avoided the situations where it was required of him to speak Norwegian only, that is, with his peers. He waited until the ninth week before communicating with them by themselves. And when he did so, he borrowed from English sparingly as he realized they did not know that language. Thus, little Per (recall that he was not yet five then) showed great sensitivity to social and community norms, matching his communication to the preference and ability of his interlocutors and seeking out situations that he could manage linguistically.

The authors raise an interesting theoretical question in their paper: Was Per reacquiring Norwegian during his first weeks back in Norway, particularly in his preschool setting, or was he basically reactivating his Norwegian? A similar question can be asked of adoptees who come back into contact with their first language many years after their adoption (see Post 4.7). As concerns Per, the authors feel that his use of strategies common to both language learners and bilinguals make it difficult to state that he was in the process of reacquiring the language he was once proficient in. They opt for reactivating a once fluent language.

Whatever the answer to this fascinating question may be, Per (or Espen as he is usually known) is doing very well. His father sent me a message stating, "Our bilingual son is as balanced as one can be, spending school years in Norway and summers in the US."

References

Dahl, T. I., Rice, C., Steffensen, M., and Amundsen, L. (2010). Is it language relearning or language reacquisition? Hints from a young boy's code-switching during his journey back to his native language. *International Journal of Bilingualism*, 14(4), 490–510.

Grosjean, F. (2010). In and out of bilingualism. Chapter 14 of *Bilingual: Life and Reality*. Cambridge, MA: Harvard University Press.

5.10 TWO AMERICAN KIDS IN A SMALL SWISS VILLAGE

One of the finest ways of acquiring a language is to go and live in a country or region where the language is used. This is what happened to two American kids when they came to live in a small Swiss village for a year.

It is often said that the best way of acquiring a language is to be immersed in it. This is what happened to two boys, Cyril (ten) and

Pierre (five) when their parents moved from Cambridge, MA, to a small Swiss village in the French speaking part of Switzerland for a year.

Although the parents had originally come from France, their boys only spoke English and they did not understand the simplest of French utterances. In addition, they were culturally American; for example, Cyril had just finished his second year in Little League and was getting ready for another hockey season.

A month after their arrival in Switzerland, both boys were enrolled in the village schools – Cyril in the primary school and Pierre in kindergarten. Their teachers spoke very little English but were welcoming. Cyril's teacher even told him, "You'll learn French and I'll learn English!"

What was striking from the start was the approach adopted by each child to acquire French. Cyril threw himself into the language and communicated as best as he could, using set expressions, body language, a bit of English here and there – and a big smile! His new friends, in turn, did all they could to help him out. One of the ways was by simplifying their French considerably. Thus, concerning an animal toy Cyril wanted, one of his Swiss friends was overheard telling him in broken French, "Moi avoir alligator, te donner" (literally, "Me get alligator, I give you") when he would have used a much more complicated utterance normally.

Cyril was a perfect fit to the natural second-language learning model proposed by Berkeley Education Professor Lily Wong Fillmore. She stresses the importance of social processes whereby, among other things, language learners have to make the speakers of the language aware of their needs, and get them to make accommodations and adjustments so that they can acquire the language. Cyril was a master at this. For example, his teacher would regularly give him, in advance, the text of the weekly dictation (the infamous French "dictée") which Cyril simply learned by heart the evening before. He would then come home the next day proudly stating that he had got full marks once again!

Pierre's approach to French was quite different. He was much more reserved than his older brother and, at first, he did not talk to his schoolmates or his teacher. Instead, he used a lot of body language. He was busy acquiring the language, however, and he would show his parents what he knew (songs, rhymes, set expressions, etc.) when he came back from school.

When Pierre did start speaking French spontaneously, the language he produced was much more grammatical than Cyril's. He even had the nerve to correct his older brother at times. For example, the latter said "formage" one day instead of "fromage" (cheese). Pierre corrected him, "C'est fromage, Cyril," much to the latter's annoyance.

Both children would reflect, from time to time, on their languages, a well-known effect of childhood bilingualism. Pierre one day told his parents, "I can't speak Chinese yet, because I've never been to China, but I could speak all the languages in the world ... (pause) ... but it would take a long time to travel around the world!"

Of course, both Cyril and Pierre intermingled their two languages a lot, both with their parents and among themselves (see the next post). This said, they remained as happy and as mischievous as before; the only difference was that they talked and teased one another in "Franglais" and no longer only in English.

At the end of their year in Switzerland, Cyril spoke very fluent French but still controlled English quite well, although hesitantly. (The family language had switched over to French some eight months after their arrival.) Pierre, on the other hand, was on the verge of becoming a French monolingual; he never spoke English and had a hard time repeating simple English sentences.

The family returned to Cambridge, MA, at the end of the school year and very quickly English took over again as the dominant language although the family remained bilingual in English and French. The strategies adopted by the parents to keep French alive the following years are discussed in Post 4.4.

As the years went by, both Cyril and Pierre were to acquire other languages. As adults now, Cyril is trilingual and Pierre regularly uses five different languages, but not Chinese ... yet!

References

Wong Fillmore, L. (1991). Second-language learning in children: A model of language learning in context. In E. Bialystok, ed., *Language Processing in Bilingual Children*. Cambridge: Cambridge University Press, pp. 49–69.

Grosjean, F. (2010). Acquiring two languages. Chapter 2 of *Bilingual: Life and Reality*. Cambridge, MA: Harvard University Press.

5.11 INTERMINGLING LANGUAGES IN CHILDREN

When bilingual children intermingle their languages, the comments one over-hears can be quite negative. And yet, there are very good reasons for their behavior. In addition, there are ways of helping them restrict language inter-mingling to bilingual situations.

"Susana keeps mixing her two languages; she's semilingual!"
"Pierre doesn't know either language well; he combines them all the time!"

I cringe, as do other language specialists, when I hear comments such as these concerning children who know and use two or more languages. In fact, there are a number of factors that can account for the active presence of the other language when children are speaking a particular language.

First, children may simply be in the process of becoming bilingual. When that is the case, their first language may well intrude upon their new language in the form of interferences, that is, deviations from the language being spoken due to the influence of the other language (see Post 3.7). In addition, even when they are speaking to monolinguals, they may well call on their other language through code-switching, that is they will bring in a word, a phrase, or a sentence from the language not being used (see Post 3.4). After all, their interlocutors might just understand parts of what they say in the other language and since communication is crucial, why not try?

A second factor is that even when the acquisition of the other language has stabilized, children are often dominant in one of their languages. This is true of very young bilinguals as well as of older ones. For instance, it is relatively rare that children acquiring two languages simultaneously receive just as much input in each of their two languages. One language is usually the stronger one and it has a tendency to influence the weaker language. With time, stop-gap elements such as code-switches will diminish in number as the non-dominant language is heard more, is used increasingly, and is better known.

A third factor concerns the language mode – monolingual or bilingual – children are in when they are communicating (see Post 3.1). It is still not totally clear when very young children who are acquiring their two languages simultaneously start controlling language choice, that is, which language to use with whom and for what, as well as code-switching. It happens quite early on, and they become adept at it, but there seems to be a short period of adjustment for the appropriate mechanisms to be in place. Slippage can take place during this period, hence the intermingling of languages.

For slightly older children, the crucial question will be whether they are with interlocutors (parents, siblings, friends) who understand their languages, even if incompletely. Children are quite pragmatic: if they know the person with whom they should be using a particular language has some knowledge of the other language, then they may well bring it in if they need it. Getting the message across is their foremost concern. And more generally, if children are raised in bilingual families where code-switching is frequent, then they too will intermingle their languages.

As children come into increasing contact with speakers of just one language, the amount of intermingling will be reduced. In addition, caretakers can influence the course of things by putting their children in monolingual environments, whenever possible, where people know and use just one language. This will allow the children to receive language input that does not contain elements of the other language, and it will increase their knowledge of the language.

With time, bilingual children will learn how to adapt their language mode to the situation they are in and the person they are speaking to. They will become proficient at navigating between a monolingual mode, where just one language is used, and a bilingual mode, where the intermingling of languages is possible . . . and is accepted.

Reference

Grosjean, F. (2010). Linguistic aspects of childhood bilingualism. Chapter 16 of *Bilingual: Life and Reality*. Cambridge, MA: Harvard University Press.

6

Bilingualism in the Family

INTRODUCTION

Post 6.1 sets the stage for many of the posts in this chapter. It proposes five factors that parents want to consider when planning the bilingualism of their children. They relate to when the second language should be introduced, which bilingual strategy to use with them, whether there will be a real need for each language, what the type and amount of input will be for each language, and what other support parents will be able to count on.

Post 6.2 examines the myth that you cannot be a "real" bilingual if you have not acquired your two languages in infancy or as a very young child. In fact, there is no age limit to entering the world of bilingualism. Posts 6.3 and 6.4 discuss the strategies families use to ensure that their children become bilingual. In the first, the main ones are evoked, and the importance of varying the language mode is stressed. In Post 6.4, the principal aspects of the "one person–one language" strategy, along with its advantages and inconveniences, and its beginnings, are discussed in detail.

Post 6.5 concentrates on the types of language input children get from their parents and from other sources. Different input patterns have different effects on childhood bilingualism. Examples from families with two, and also three, languages are discussed.

Post 6.6 is the interview of Keith Gessen, a father who is his son's only second-language source. His honest testimony shows how challenging it can be to bring up a child bilingual under those circumstances.

In Post 6.7, Dr. Aneta Pavlenko relates how she started her journey in languages and cultures in Ukraine. Her mother's attempts to have her learn English failed at first. Discovering the outside world through written Polish was much more exciting for the young girl that she was.

Post 6.8 relates how a French bilingual couple resigned themselves to the English monolingualism of their children. Parents rarely evoke in testimonies how this happens and the disappointment they feel.

Finally, the last two posts, Posts 6.9 and 6.10, concentrate on the person–language bond in children. Bilinguals often have a preferred language they use with the bilinguals they know well, but this attachment can be particularly strong in the very young. Why the bond exists, its evolution over time, and why it is less strong in certain bilingual societies are considered in turn.

6.1 QUESTIONS TO ASK WHEN DECIDING TO BRING UP A CHILD BILINGUAL[1]

An increasing number of families plan the bilingualism of their children. Five important factors they may want to consider are discussed here.

Most bilingual children acquire their languages "naturally" in the sense that they are brought up in a home and/or an environment which require the use of two or more languages. Usually no planning takes place but because a number of factors are favorable, these children end up becoming bilingual.

However, an increasing number of families plan the bilingualism of their children, and parents spend a lot of time and energy thinking about how best to go about it. Many read articles and books on the subject, join support groups, as well as visit the many websites dedicated to the topic.

Among the questions that parents may want to consider, here are five that are important:

1. When should the languages be acquired? Some people still believe that you cannot be a "real" bilingual if you have not acquired your two languages in infancy or as a young child. In fact, one can become bilingual at any time during one's life – as a child, as an adolescent, or as an adult. As we saw in Post 5.1, the majority of child bilinguals start monolingually; they acquire a home language first and then, usually when they start going to school, they learn a second language (and then maybe other languages). There is no age limit to entering the world of bilingualism as we will discuss in Post 6.2. Parents may want to keep this in mind when deciding which languages to introduce and

---

[1] The original title of this post was, "Planned bilingualism: Five questions to consider."

when. They should also factor in the answers they give to the four remaining questions.

2. Which bilingual strategy should be used? Parents who plan to make their children bilingual usually adopt a strategy: for example, the "one person–one language" strategy (each parent speaks his or her language exclusively to the child), the "one language at home, the other language outside the home" strategy (usually the minority language is spoken in the home exclusively and the other language is used outside the home), the "one language first followed by a second language later" strategy (the acquisition of each language is staggered), and so on. All these strategies have advantages as well as some inconveniences (see Posts 6.3 and 6.4), which are well covered by books on bilingualism as well as by many support group websites.

3. Will the child have a real need for each language? It has long been known that children acquire languages, but also forget them, in a very short time depending on the need they have for each language: the need to communicate with family members, caretakers, or friends, to participate in the activities of a day care or a school, to interact with people in the community, etc. If children feel that they really need a particular language, and other psychosocial factors are favorable, then they will develop that language. If the need disappears or isn't really there (e.g. the parents also speak the other language but pretend they don't), then the language may no longer be used and, over time, it may be forgotten. In Post 6.7, we give an example of a young girl coldshouldering a language and embracing another largely based on interest and need.

4. What will be the type and amount of input from each language? To develop a language, children require a certain amount of input, in a variety of situations, from people who matter to them – parents, caretakers, members of the extended family, friends, and so on. Research has shown that children need the presence of a live person interacting with them to acquire a language (e.g. its phonetic categories) and this cannot be done simply by watching television or listening to DVDs and audio input (see Post 5.4). In addition, the input should not only be made up of speech spoken by bilinguals and hence contain code-switches and borrowings as invariably happens in a bilingual household; it should also be composed of

monolingual speech as spoken, for example, by family members who do not know the other language or by monolingual caretakers. Later on, written language input will be an excellent source of vocabulary and of cultural information.

5. <u>What other support can parents count on?</u> The presence of extended family members and friends who speak the children's languages, most notably the minority language, is precious as input is increased and it shows children that using those languages is quite natural. In addition, if the minority language is reinforced in school, in the community or, at the very least, in support groups, then it will be acquired more easily. Children are extremely receptive to the linguistic attitudes of their parents, teachers, and peers, and hence positive attitudes toward both languages, as well as toward bilingualism, will be a real advantage. Another source of support will be professionals such as linguists, educators, psychologists, speech therapists, and so on, who hopefully will be able to discuss bilingualism with parents and help them differentiate between its myths and its reality.

Making children bilingual, and sometimes even bicultural, is a way of giving them an additional asset in life. Some family planning can help prepare this journey into languages and cultures and, hopefully, make it a joyful one for both parents and children.

References

Grosjean, F. (2010). In and out of bilingualism and Family strategies and support. Chapters 14 and 17 of *Bilingual: Life and Reality*. Cambridge, MA: Harvard University Press.

Bigelow, M. and Collins, P. (2019). Bilingualism from childhood through adolescence. In Annick De Houwer and Lourdes Ortega, eds., *The Cambridge Handbook of Bilingualism*. Cambridge: Cambridge University Press, pp. 36–58.

6.2 HOW EARLY A SECOND LANGUAGE?

There is a common belief that the earlier a second language is acquired, the more fluent a child will be in it. But how true is this?

As we saw above, some people still believe that you cannot be a "real," totally fluent, bilingual if you have not acquired your two languages in infancy or as a very young child. And yet when we examine the scientific foundation this belief is based on, we find that it is not as strong as we could imagine.

In a paper entitled, "Three misconceptions about age and L2 learning," University of British Columbia researcher Stefka Marinova-Todd and her two coauthors argue convincingly against the fact that there is a critical (or sensitive) period for second-language acquisition beyond which the language will not be acquired adequately.

They claim that some researchers, as well as the lay public, have fallen prey to three fallacies. The first is based on a misinterpretation of observations of learners of different ages which tend to suggest that children, especially young ones, are fast and efficient at picking up a second language. In fact, it has been shown repeatedly that young children are rather unsophisticated and immature learners in that they have not yet fully acquired certain cognitive skills, such as the capacity to abstract, generalize, infer, and classify, that could help them in second-language acquisition.

In an often-cited study, Harvard professor Catherine Snow and her coauthor, Marianne Hoefnagel-Hohle, examined the learning of Dutch by speakers of English in different age groups. They showed that twelve- to fifteen-year-olds did better than younger learners. This has been confirmed since then in other studies such as those that examined late immersion as opposed to early immersion children. Older children were simply more efficient learners than younger children. Of course, beyond a certain age (most situate it at around age twelve or even later), it might be difficult to acquire the right pronunciation in a second language, but this still leaves many years between infancy and adolescence.

The second fallacy Stefka Marinova-Todd and her coauthors point out is the fact that some researchers report differences in the brain organization of early and late second-language learners and then misattribute presumed language proficiency differences to this factor. In fact, as expounded by neuropsycholinguist Jubin Abutalebi, a second language is acquired through the same neural structures responsible for first-language acquisition. This is true for the acquisition of grammar in late second-language learners contrary to what one might expect from the notion of a critical (or sensitive) period.

The third fallacy is based on taking frequent failure in second-language acquisition and extending it to the impossibility of success. Many older learners (adolescents and adults) do admittedly end up with low levels of proficiency but this is not due primarily to the age they started learning their second language as such but to other factors such as motivation, time, energy, language input, support from the environment, etc. This misemphasis on poor older learners has distracted researchers from focusing on the truly informative cases, that is successful older learners who spend sufficient time on second-language learning, give it their full attention, and who benefit from high motivation and from supportive language-learning environments.

The authors conclude their analysis by stating that older learners have the potential to learn a second language to a very high level of competency and that introducing a second language to very young learners cannot be justified on grounds of biological readiness to learn languages.

And so the next time we read or hear that to reap the full benefits of bilingualism, the earlier you start the child's exposure to a second language, such as in infancy, the better it is, let's keep in mind that the majority of bilingual children start monolingually, and only begin acquiring their second language when they enter school or, later, in their adolescence. And yet they become fully functioning bilinguals. There is no age limit to entering the world of bilingualism; it can take place at any time.

References

Marinova-Todd, S. H., Marshall, S. D., and Snow, C. E. (2000). Three misconceptions about age and L2 learning. *TESOL Quarterly*, 34(1), 9–34.

Abutalebi, J. (2008). Neural aspects of second language representation and language control. *Acta Psychologica*, 128(3), 466–478.

Snow, C. and Hoefnagel-Hohle, M. (1978). The critical period for language acquisition: Evidence from second language learning. *Child Development*, 49, 1114–1128.

6.3 THE USE OF STRATEGIES IN THE NURTURING OF
BILINGUALISM IN CHILDREN[2]

Even though many children "just become bilingual," an increasing number of families develop strategies to ensure that their children become bilingual. They also consciously nurture their children's languages over time.

Of the three most used strategies by families, the first, and probably the best known, is the "one person–one language" strategy. The child becomes bilingual because each parent speaks his or her language exclusively to the child. The approach has many advantages, one of which is that parents can use their dominant language with their child. A problem that can arise with time, however, is that the minority language (e.g. Chinese in the United States) may suffer as the child interacts increasingly with the outside world where the other, stronger, language is used. Post 6.4 discusses this strategy in more depth and talks about its onset.

In the second strategy, only one language is used at home, usually the minority language, and the other language is used outside the home. This guarantees that the home language receives a lot of support as the parents use it exclusively, as do other family members. The other language (usually the majority language) is acquired when the child ventures outside the home. It is a very successful strategy but it does mean that one parent has to agree to speak his or her second (or third) language to the child.

The third strategy – a variant of the second – is to use solely one language, inside and outside the home, and then, at age four or five only, to introduce the other language. This was the strategy used by the parents of Einar Haugen, a well-known bilingualism specialist who was brought up in Norwegian first. He wrote many years later: "[My parents] took the position that I would learn all the English I needed from my playmates and my teachers, and that only by learning and using Norwegian in the home could I maintain a fruitful contact with them and their friends and their culture."

To these home strategies, we should add an educational strategy that is used with older children and that is increasingly popular. It is

---

[2] The original title was, "Nurturing bilingualism in children."

to enroll one's child in a bilingual program (immersion, dual language, etc.) where the language of instruction is at first, in part or in whole, in the other language (e.g. Spanish for English-speaking children).

Of course, as the child grows up, the strategies evolve and parents have to keep monitoring matters to make sure that the child continues to have a real need for the two (or more) languages.

As time goes by and children stabilize their bilingualism, it is important that they find themselves, occasionally, in a monolingual mode in each of their languages, that is, in contact with monolingual speakers who do not know their other language(s). This is because it is simply too easy to only use the stronger language in a bilingual environment where parents and caretakers are themselves bilingual. When this happens, the weaker (usually minority) language will slowly be replaced by the stronger language, most often the language outside the home.

An additional challenge for families concerns the cultural changes that children or adolescents go through when they have moved from one country or region to another. Many of them experience culture shock, as do their parents, and they need to be helped and advised during this transition phase.

It is comforting to see just how seriously some parents take the nurturing of bilingualism in their children. Many read articles and books on the subject, join support groups, as well as visit websites that offer posts on the topic. They are present when the going gets difficult and frustration occurs due to such things as a communication problem, an unkind remark by an adult or a child, a bad grade in the weaker language, and so on.

With this kind of support, there is every chance that bilingual children will retain their bilingualism and become adults who know and use two or more languages.

References

Pearson, B. Z. (2008). *Raising a Bilingual Child.* New York: Random House.
Grosjean, F. (2010). Family strategies and support. Chapter 17 of *Bilingual: Life and Reality.* Cambridge, MA: Harvard University Press.

6.4 THE ONE PERSON–ONE LANGUAGE STRATEGY: ADVANTAGES AND INCONVENIENCES[3]

A well-known approach used with children who are acquiring two languages simultaneously is for each parent to use his or her own language with their child. It is an appealing strategy with advantages but also some inconveniences. Researching into its modern onset a bit more than 100 years ago has revealed a surprising finding.

As we saw in the preceding post, a well-known approach used with children who are acquiring two languages simultaneously is for each parent to use his or her own language with their child. Thus, for example, parent 1 will use Spanish and parent 2 English. This is known as the one person–one language strategy or OPOL.

The strategy has probably been around since the beginning of intermarriages between people belonging to different language groups. In recent times, however, its onset has a precise date: 1908. It was in that year that a baby boy, Louis, was born to the Ronjat family in France. Jules Ronjat was a French linguist who had a German wife and they wanted to bring up their son bilingual. So Jules asked a colleague, Maurice Grammont, who had done some research on language development, for his advice.

Grammont replied soon after Louis' birth and Jules Ronjat cites ten lines of his letter in a book he was to write about Louis' bilingualism in 1913. Grammont told Jules that each language must be represented by a different person. Thus, Jules would always speak French to Louis, and his wife German, without ever reversing the pattern.

Jules Ronjat's book was read by many linguists, among them Werner Leopold in the United States in the 1930s who decided, with his wife, Marguerite, to use this approach with their own child, Hildegard. Leopold spoke German to her and Marguerite, English, and Hildegard did grow up bilingual, although dominant in English. Hildegard's bilingual development is well known in the linguistic world as her father, himself a linguist, wrote four volumes in English on her dual language acquisition. Since then, the OPOL approach has been used continuously and is reported on in the majority of books dealing with the simultaneous acquisition of two languages.

[3] The original title was, "One person–one language and bilingual children."

The approach is very appealing to parents who wish to nurture bilingualism in their children from the start, to the point that some people talk of the one parent (not person)–one language rule or principle. It allows parents to use their dominant language with their child which may also be their language of emotion (see Post 10.1). With this dual input, children very quickly produce sounds, syllables, and words in each language, and are remarkably good at knowing which language to use with which parent.

However, as time goes by, problems often start appearing. Since exposure to the two languages is rarely equal, especially when the child starts interacting with the outside world, the language with less input, often the minority language, suffers. If, in addition, the parent who speaks it is bilingual, then the child may well start responding in the other, stronger, language. In the end, the child may only retain receptive skills in the weaker language.

The success rate of the approach has been studied, most notably by researcher Annick De Houwer who reports in her study of 2,000 families that a full quarter of the children brought up with the approach did not become bilingual (see Post 6.5). When both parents spoke both languages to their children – something Grammont insisted they not do – the percentage of children who ended up bilingual was not significantly different!

I have often talked to parents who use the approach and many find it stressful to have to keep to one language with their child, as well as insist on getting a response in the weaker language, and others worry about what to do when the context calls for the other language (e.g. when they are outside the home). Parents often end up adapting the strategy to their own needs or simply shifting to another approach.

Over the years, researchers who discuss Grammont's approach have often referred to his 1902 book, *Observations sur le langage des enfants* (Observations on Children's Language). In my attempt to understand the underpinnings of his proposal, I looked for the book and, to my astonishment, found that it did not exist! Instead, there is a Festschrift, with a different title, honoring the French linguist, Antoine Meillet, which contains a chapter by Grammont with that title. So I went to the archives of the University of Geneva library and took it out. Grammont's contribution does indeed discuss the language development of two French-speaking children but it has nothing on bilingualism, and nothing on the OPOL approach! In sum, his original proposal had no theoretical or scientific underpinning, at least published, and was stated in just ten lines in his letter to Ronjat!

Of course, the OPOL approach deserves to continue being an option for parents. But at the very least, it should be adapted (when that is not already the case) and a family plan should be set up which takes into account important considerations such as what is the best strategy for that particular family, when should the languages be acquired, will the child have a real need for each language, what will be the type and amount of input from each language, and what other support can the parents count on (see Post 6.1). Parents also have to work out how much of the other language each can use with their child (Hildegard often heard her father speak English!) and how much switching between languages can take place (there is no proof that intermingling languages affects language learning in the long run).

The final word goes to Suzanne Barron-Hauwaert who has written a book on the approach and has used it with her own children: "I do wonder sometimes if it is the best method. Perhaps being able to switch effectively and know when to use each language in context is really the best tool we can give our children in the long term."

References

De Houwer, A. (2007). Parental language input patterns and children's bilingual use. *Applied Psycholinguistics*, 28, 411–424.

Ronjat, J. (1913). *Le développement du langage observé chez un enfant bilingue.* Paris: Edouard Champion.

Barron-Hauwaert, S. (2004). *Language Strategies for Bilingual Families: The One-Parent-One-Language Approach.* Bristol: Multilingual Matters.

6.5 PARENTAL LANGUAGE INPUT AND CHILDHOOD BILINGUALISM[4]

Children who are being brought up with two or more languages need as much input as they can get from each language. Parents can play a major role in this by choosing which language(s) they speak to them in the home.

---

[4] The original title was, "The languages you speak to your bilingual child."

Lauren is a little Dutch–English bilingual girl whom Belgian psycholinguist Annick De Houwer tells us about in one of her publications. Her father spoke English to her and her mother Dutch. But because her father worked hard, and saw her rarely – mainly on weekends – Lauren only heard English about three hours a week. When she was three years old, she could only say "yes" and "no" and this upset her father no end. He thought she was rejecting him.

Situations such as this one can be avoided in part if parents take the time to consider a number of factors I presented in Post 6.1 and have been looking at in this chapter. A question of primary importance concerns the type and amount of language input the child will receive, mainly from his/her parents but also from other sources.

Annick De Houwer has spent many years researching this precise point. Using a questionnaire approach, she examined the language behavior of close to 2,000 families in Dutch-speaking Flanders, Belgium, where at least one parent spoke a language other than Dutch in the home. The first thing she found was that despite the presence of both Dutch and another language in the lives of these families, nearly one-quarter of the families had no children who spoke the other language.

But what is perhaps even more interesting is that different parental input patterns had different effects on whether the children became bilingual or not. For example, when both parents only used the other language in the home, its transmission rate was quasi perfect (97 percent). The success rate only decreased by three percentage points when one of the two parents also spoke Dutch in the home. As for the "one person, one language" strategy, and contrary to general belief, it only produced a 74 percent success rate. In other words, a quarter of the children to whom the father spoke one language and the mother the other, simply did not become bilingual.

It is interesting to note that both parents speaking both languages to their children obtained a score that is not significantly different (79 percent). As for the situation where one parent spoke both Dutch and the other language, and the other parent only spoke Dutch, then only 36 percent of the children spoke the other language.

Studies are still trying to isolate the reasons that underlie results such as these but what seems clear is that when the minority language is used exclusively, or at least extensively, in the home, it will be acquired by the child. Not only is there more parental input of that language but the home environment is conducive to using it. Thus there is every chance that the child will grow up speaking it. As for the majority language, it will be picked up very quickly, but mainly outside the home.

To better understand what is taking place in bilingual homes, researchers are turning more and more toward large databases of natural conversations in bilingual families. One of these was obtained by Canadian psycholinguist Shanley Allen in five families who, at home, speak both English and Inuktitut, one of the main Inuit languages in Canada. Annick de Houwer used it to examine the amount of dual language input the children received and the outcome of this on their bilingual language production. What she found was that caregivers who spoke more English had children who also spoke more English and, conversely, those who spoke more Inuktitut had children who used that language more. This simply substantiates the fact that the length of time a language is heard and used is a crucial factor in its acquisition by children.

In another study, Annick De Houwer examined trilingual families in Flanders. They used two minority languages in the home and some also used Dutch whereas others did not. In the latter case, Dutch was picked up outside the home, primarily at school. Once again, she found that despite this trilingual input, not all children actually spoke the three languages – two fifths were trilingual, more than a third were bilingual and more than a fifth spoke only one language. Thus trilingual input is no guarantee to actually developing three languages.

Two factors played an important role in accounting for these results. The first is that when no Dutch was spoken in the family, and only the two minority languages were used, then the probability of becoming trilingual was higher. Three quarters of the families in that case had children who were actively trilingual. The other factor was that when both parents (and not just one parent) used both minority languages with their children, then the chance of having trilingual children was higher.

In sum, children being brought up with two or more languages will need as much language input as they can from each of their languages, but primarily the minority language(s). The majority language is in less danger and will get its input in varying ways, outside and inside the home.

To end, let's go back to the example given at the beginning of this post. Little Lauren's lack of English was not a sign that she was rejecting her father. She simply had not received enough English input from him in the very restricted amount of time she spent interacting with him in their common language!

References

De Houwer, A. (2007). Parental language input patterns and children's bilingual use. *Applied Psycholinguistics*, 28, 411–424.
De Houwer, A. (2009). *Bilingual First Language Acquisition*. Bristol: Multilingual Matters.
Allen, S. (2007). The future of Inuktitut in the face of majority languages: Bilingualism or language shift? *Applied Psycholinguistics*, 28(3), 515–536.
Armon-Lotem, S. and Meir, N. (2019). The Nature of Exposure and Input in Early Bilingualism. In Annick De Houwer and Lourdes Ortega, eds., *The Cambridge Handbook of Bilingualism*. Cambridge: Cambridge University Press, pp. 193–212.

6.6 WHEN A PARENT IS A CHILD'S ONLY LANGUAGE SOURCE

(Interview with Keith Gessen)

Raising a bilingual child is full of challenges when one parent is the only source of the second language. A father tells us how he is going about it with his three-year-old son.

A few years ago, the title of an article in *The New Yorker* caught my attention, "Why did I teach my son to speak Russian?" The story the author tells is both captivating for a psycholinguist who specializes in bilingualism, but also very touching for the father and grandfather that I am. Keith Gessen, novelist, journalist, and academic, relates how he started speaking his native language, Russian, to his English-speaking little boy, Raffi, whose mother knows no Russian.

As he carried him through the neighborhood or pushed him in his stroller, "(he) liked the feeling ... of having our own private language. ... Before I knew it, I was speaking to Raffi in Russian all the time, even in front of his mother." Raffi is now three and Keith Gessen has kindly accepted to answer a few questions about how his son is acquiring Russian. His honest testimony shows how challenging it can be to bring up a child bilingual when a working parent is his child's only language source.

You write that you had doubts, and still do, about teaching Raffi Russian. Can you explain?
I have two main doubts. The first is that my Russian is imperfect. We came to the US when I was six, and though I grew up speaking Russian with my parents, I do not have access to the full range of verbal possibilities – I have fewer words and run out of them faster. I find myself being more impatient and more quickly upset than I would like. This makes me a less than ideal father.

The second doubt is specific to Russia. The best way to teach Raffi Russian would be to take him to Moscow, where I still have some family. But the political situation there is deteriorating; there is more xenophobia and more aggression. It's not something I necessarily want to expose my family to. I'd be worried about Raffi going to Russia – as I remember my father being worried about me going.

Do you see yourself polishing your Russian up in order to enrich Raffi's own Russian?
My Russian is already improving in that I have to speak in it all the time to Raffi. And as he starts asking more sophisticated questions about the world, I have to try to produce more sophisticated answers. Or at least sensible ones.

I'm impressed by the extensive reading you have done about young bilingual children, including Werner Leopold's four volumes on his own daughter, Hildegard. You recognize that a bilingual child has to have a real need for a language if he/she is to develop it. Can you explain how you are creating this need?
Reading Leopold's book (which I first learned about in your book, *Bilingual: Life and Reality*) was a delight – there was so much that was recognizable to me, and Hildegard is so adorable! I laughed when Leopold recounted his frustration with his polite German émigré friends who immediately switched to English when Hildegard addressed them in English, instead of insisting on German as Leopold himself did.

I've found that recently I've been able to convince my Russian-speaking family members to switch less often to English with Raffi. I think it feels strange to them at first, because for now he only ever answers in English, but once they see that he understands their Russian perfectly well, they will be able to keep it up.

Another important factor is input, a lot of input, as well as a diversified input. How will you make sure that Raffi gets it in the years to come?

I read to him in Russian a lot, and will continue to do so. Despite a somewhat exalted reputation, Russian literature for little kids is not as rich as American literature for that age group. But there are some wonderful things, especially the poems of Korney Chukovsky, which Raffi really loves, and there are also translations.

Speaking of translations, we've recently discovered a rich treasure trove of Russian-language versions of Western cartoons. On YouTube you can get "Peppa Pig" in Russian, "Ninja Turtles" in Russian, and even the awful "Paw Patrol" series in Russian. There are also some excellent Soviet-era cartoons on YouTube, but on the whole they're a little too slow-moving for someone who's been exposed to the speed of American cartoons.

Will Raffi soon be going to daycare? If so, were you thinking of finding a Russian-speaking one in New York?

There are many Russian-language daycares in south Brooklyn. Unfortunately, we live in central Brooklyn, and the closest one to us is about a forty-minute train ride away, and in the opposite direction from where I work. In general there are many opportunities in New York for Russian enrichment that I know I'm not taking advantage of – because I don't have the time, or the energy, or we've got other commitments. But parenting is like that, I am finding. In truth, if I had to choose between teaching Raffi Russian and teaching him to play hockey, I think I'd choose hockey! But maybe I can manage both.

What other strategies were you thinking of to make Russian an important part of Raffi's life and anchoring the language in his mind?

The closest thing to a Russian-only environment within driving distance of us is my father's house in Massachusetts, and I hope to continue getting Raffi (and now his younger brother, Ilya) there as much as possible. But I must say, even in the past couple of months (approxi-mately since Raffi turned three), he has been finding his Russian to be a source of pride. "Mama," he now tells his monolingual mother, "I speak Russian *and* English." It's not strictly true that he *speaks* Russian. His passive vocabulary is large but his active vocabulary is currently about ten words. But the other day we had a Russian-speaking friend over and Raffi started showing off by giving the Russian names for various objects.

So he clearly has, at least for the moment, an aspiration to learn Russian better. That seems to me a good start[5].

References

Gessen, K. (2018). Why did I teach my son to speak Russian. *The New Yorker*, June 16.

Leopold, W. (1948). The study of child language and infant bilingualism. *Word*, 4(1), 1–17.

6.7 HOW MY MOTHER LURED ME INTO MULTILINGUALISM

Once upon a time, in a land far away, a mother convinced her daughter that foreign languages would open a window in the Iron Curtain.

Post written by Aneta Pavlenko.

For as long as I remember, my life has been multilingual, even if I didn't think of it that way. Born in Kiev, capital of Soviet Ukraine, I grew up hearing three tongues. Russian was the language of daily life. Ukrainian was used alongside it in the media and in education. Parents had a choice between Ukrainian schools that taught Russian as a second language, and Russian ones that did the same with Ukrainian. The third language I was in contact with, Yiddish, had been outlawed in schools and was dying out. My grandparents used it as a secret code. My mom understood some and I got the gist from individual words: *naches* [pride, joy] and *sheyne punim* [pretty face] meant they were talking about their beloved granddaughter, and *tuches* [derrière] and *meshuggeneh* [batshit crazy] referred to downstairs neighbors.

As it happens, I also got an earful of English as a kid, because my mother Bella – a teacher of English in an evening school for adults with an interest in foreign tongues – used to bring me with her to work. An ardent believer that foreign languages were the key to the world beyond the Iron Curtain, she hoped I would soak the language in, but she couldn't have been more

---

[5] As I am preparing this book, practically two years have passed since I interviewed Keith Gessen. In a recent email he wrote, "Raffi continues to understand most everything I say, even as we get into more and more complex terrain, though I do feel the gap between his Russian and English increasing as his English vocabulary becomes really immense (and the limits in my own Russian vocabulary start showing)."

wrong. The lifeless *boy and girl* and their dull possessions, *ball, pen, and book*, made me yawn, and as a seven-year-old I was already resistant to useless knowledge. Bella, however, had more tricks up her sleeve.

Figuring that a Slavic language made for an easier start, she asked a colleague from her evening school to come to our home once a week to teach me Polish. Soon, I was hooked. There was no one I could speak Polish to besides my teacher but that wasn't the point. Polish was the language of cult pop songs and of glossy women's magazines sold "under the counter" in our newspaper kiosks, whose gossip and glamor were a welcome respite from the drabness of their Soviet counterparts, *Rabotnitsa* [Female factory worker] and *Krestianka* [Female peasant]. Most importantly, I could read Polish books from *Druzhba* [Friendship], a magnificent bookstore at the heart of Kiev that specialized in titles from the socialist block, including translations of works unavailable in Russian. The first time I read *Godfather* and *Gone with the wind* was in Polish.

By fifth grade I was ready to give English another try. On the first day, our English teacher welcomed us with a passionate speech: "My dear fifth graders, today is a very important day in your life – you are starting to study English. Your knowledge will prove crucial when we are at war with imperialist Britain and the United States and you will have to decode and translate intercepted messages." This was a novel idea, since Bella had conveniently forgotten to inform me that one day we would have to confront capitalist powers and interview their spies. The mission didn't appeal to me one bit, and English was put once again on the back burner as I transferred to French. The move didn't free me completely from ideological onslaught – our classes still revolved around Lenin's activities in Geneva – but now I could sing along with Mireille Mathieu and Joe Dassin.

And then the unthinkable happened. One day I picked up an Agatha Christie novel my mother was reading with her students and realized I had soaked in enough English to be intrigued. I don't know if she left the book on my desk on purpose, feeling smug to see me plow through it, nor did I care – I was too busy trying to figure out who had killed Roger Ackroyd. Reluctantly, I acknowledged that she was right: one could learn from osmosis. Ever since I have hidden a sordid secret – I have never had any formal instruction in English. My only teachers were the Grand Dame of Mystery and my own mother, whom I apparently failed to ignore, while doodling at the back of her class.

By high school, I was avidly reading whatever Polish, French, and English novels I could get my hands on, listened, clandestinely, to broadcasts from abroad and was always on the lookout for left-leaning foreign dailies that squeaked by Soviet censors, like the English *Morning Star* and the French *L'Humanité*. The latter taught me the difference between us and the French: no self-respecting Soviet newspaper would feature cartoon adventures of a puppy named Pif.

Today, I live in a world vastly different from the tightly controlled universe of my youth, a world where the 24/7 news cycle connects us to the rapidly shrinking – and increasingly fragmented – universe, where everyone has a sense of unlimited access through their favorite news "provider." Yet as I start my day with sites in several tongues, I find that many events in Russia, Ukraine, and Poland never find their way to English-language news, while others acquire new facets through the lens of *Le Monde* or *El País*. These differences, familiar to every bilingual, make me wonder: Was my mother right? Does monolingualism constrain the way we see the world? Is our sense of unlimited access only an illusion, fed by "providers" that preselect and translate second-hand news from the around the world?

And if so, why do some foreign language programs still insist on teaching students how to order rooms and meals from people who speak perfectly serviceable English? Wouldn't it be more productive to get students in the habit of reading, comparing, and contrasting the coverage of 'the same' events on different sites and in different languages? My mother certainly thought so. In a world bent on information control, she opened a window her daughter could look through, even if all I did, for the longest time, was to stare at Scarlett O'Hara, Roger Ackroyd, and Pif!

6.8 GIVING UP ON BILINGUALISM ... FOR A WHILE AT LEAST

Making sure that children in a family become bilingual and stay that way can be hard work. This tale started with linguistic disappointment and ended with linguistic success.

One of the least talked about aspects of family bilingualism is how and when parents resign themselves to the monolingualism of their children despite all the efforts they made to bring them up bilingual. Some are sad, some frustrated, some resigned ... and almost all, outside the family circle, do not easily talk about what happened.

I have real empathy for their feelings, and what they are going through, as the very same thing happened to my French-speaking wife and me. When we arrived in the United States for what turned out to be a twelve-year stay, our son, Cyril, was a twenty-two-month-old French-speaking toddler. Since we both had to work, we found him a daycare in the city we lived in, Cambridge, MA, and within weeks he was making headway in his second language, English. He also watched his favorite shows on television, and he would repeat all kinds of expressions he heard.

In a matter of months, and without us quite realizing it, our little French boy was becoming bilingual, and was using more and more English with us. At first we would only speak to him in French, and try to get him to answer back in that language, but enforcing French became difficult. With time, he used less French with us especially in front of other children.

I personally recall the day he told me outside, "Dad, speak like all the other dads," by which he meant something like, "Since you also speak English, and English is the language used here, and I don't want to be different from the others, then let's speak English together instead of French." Cyril became a dormant bilingual (see Post 4.2) and we sometimes wondered how much French he continued to understand.

We didn't worry too much as we thought we wouldn't be staying that long in the States – we were on a two-year exchange program – and his French would be reactivated in no time once we got back to France.

But we stayed on, and our little Cyril never went back to French. Four years after our arrival, our second son, Pierre, was born and we hoped that with him we would do things right and make a real bilingual out of him. We made sure to speak French to him and we read him stories in French. However, from birth, he was also in contact with English through his brother, his brother's friends, his brother's TV programs, and finally at daycare.

For the first few months of language learning, Pierre spoke both French and English and I remember proudly posting his new words in each language on my lab's notice board. But Pierre quickly realized, like his brother four years before, that he really only needed to use one language and that, for reasons related to school and to life outside the home, it had to be English. So he too slowly became monolingual in English.

All this happened more than forty years ago when there was very little literature on bringing up bilingual children. Had we known back then what we know now – see for example my *Bilingual: Life and Reality* – we would certainly have done things differently. There are a number of strategies parents can use, and there are ways of creating a real need for each language.

As I write in Post 6.1, children acquire languages, but also forget them, in a very short time depending on the need they have for each language. If they feel that they really need a language, and other psychosocial factors are favorable, then they will develop that language. If the need disappears or isn't really there (e.g. the parents also speak the other language but pretend they don't), then the language may no longer be used and, over time, it may be forgotten.

One lesson I learned firsthand is that bilingual parents are not a guarantee that their children will be bilingual. The latter are very pragmatic and will not acquire, or maintain, a language, unless the conditions are right. In addition, our own boys simply didn't receive enough French input either from us or from other French-speaking caretakers, friends, family members, etc. to foster their bilingualism.

We had become a bilingual family in that two languages were spoken in the home, English and French. But only we, the parents, were in fact bilingual; the two children were monolingual in English. I reflected this when I dedicated my first book on bilingualism in 1982 to my wife and to our two sons, "for their monolingualism, so categorical and yet so natural."

Fortunately, after eight years in the United States, we spent a sabbatical year in the French-speaking part of Switzerland. This was our chance to make Cyril and Pierre bilingual and everything worked out perfectly. I relate in two posts how they acquired their French in a small

Swiss village (see Post 5.10) and how we used various strategies to maintain their bilingualism when we came back to the United States (see Post 4.4).

We finally returned to Europe for good after twelve years, and the boys then added other languages to the two they already had. As adults, Cyril is trilingual and Pierre uses five different languages regularly. We feel grateful that we were given a second chance to allow them to live with several languages. May this also be the case, if at all possible, for other parents who are in the same predicament we were in back then!

Reference

Grosjean, F. (2019). *A Journey in Languages and Cultures: The Life of a Bicultural Bilingual.* Oxford: Oxford University Press.

6.9 THE PERSON–LANGUAGE BOND I

Bilinguals often have a preferred language they use with bilinguals they know well. The person–language bond is particularly strong in very young bilingual children; it helps them acquire and differentiate their languages.

Juliette, a two-and-a-half-year-old French–English bilingual, was playing with Marc, a five-year-old English-speaking boy. Their usual language of communication was English, but to please and surprise her, Marc decided to speak to her in French. He asked his mother for the equivalent of "come" in French and then returned to Juliette and said, "Viens, viens." Much to his surprise, Juliette was far from pleased; instead of smiling, she said angrily, "Don't *do* that, Marc," and repeated this several times.

Through her reaction, Juliette was showing the importance of the person–language bond that exists between bilinguals, be they adults or children. In Post 3.1, we noted that bilinguals often have an agreed upon language they customarily use with bilinguals they know well. Violation of this "agreement" is likely to create an unnatural or even embarrassing situation, which may end with the question, "Why are you speaking language X to me?"

As a bilingual friend once told me, "I never speak English to my French friends, even if they are fluent in English. I find it unnatural, and I hate it when close friends suggest I speak to them in English ..."

Of course, if a third person enters the room, or if the location of the interaction changes, or the participants want to exclude someone, speaking the other language is considered perfectly natural. But as soon as the situation permits it, the participants will revert to their customary language of interaction. This does not exclude bringing the other language into the interaction for a word, a phrase, or a sentence (see Post 3.4), but the base language is usually firmly established.

Sometimes, the agreed-upon language is changed for good and this may create some distress. Concert pianist Kenneth van Barthold told me how as a boy he would speak Dutch to his mother. Over dinner one evening, at the onset of World War II, his British father announced that since there was a war on, and consequently they could not have any further contact with The Netherlands, the language of the family was henceforth to be English! His mother burst into tears and left the room. Kenneth van Barthold reassured me that he continued speaking Dutch to his mother until he was an adult ... but he most probably did so in the absence of his father.

The person–language bond is particularly strong in very young bilingual children. Juliette's reaction above is not unique. Here is another example. Little Luca, bilingual in French and Croatian, was speaking to his paternal grandmother. Their language of communication is French but since they were in Croatia, his grandmother asked him to name a few things in Croatian. He refused to do so and then said, in French, "It's mummy who asks that" (Luca speaks Croatian only to his mother and her parents). Luca's reaction was in fact rather mild compared to that of other children who can get quite upset when the wrong language is used.

Psycholinguists have asked themselves why the person–language bond is so strong in very young bilinguals. Some have proposed that it helps them differentiate their languages. In order to do so, young bilingual children rely on different factors: the phonetic and prosodic cues (e.g. the rhythm) of each language, other structural aspects, the context the language is used in, and, very importantly, the language spoken by a given person. (For a discussion of this very issue, see Post 5.6.)

As a consequence of this bond, bilingual children are often ready to correct and help out the adult. For example, when Juliette's mother switched over to English, little Juliette translated what she said into

French, the language they always spoke together, thus reestablishing the person–language bond. Only when her mother failed to understand something her daughter was telling her in French did Juliette agree to use English, but she switched back to French as soon as possible.

So the next time a very young bilingual child refuses to speak to you in a language you don't usually use with her, don't be surprised. She is simply busy acquiring and differentiating her languages as well as working out the social constraints of language choice.

Reference

Grosjean, F. (2010). Acquiring two languages. Chapter 15 of *Bilingual: Life and Reality*. Cambridge, MA: Harvard University Press.

6.10 THE PERSON–LANGUAGE BOND II

The person–language bond is well documented in very young bilingual children. But how does it evolve over time? And do all bilingual children show it?

As we saw above, examples abound that show how children can refuse to answer in the "wrong language" or even become upset when it is used with them. Psycholinguist Annick de Houwer illustrates it in her book, *Bilingual First Language Acquisition*, concerning her Dutch–English bilingual daughter Susan who was three and a half years old at the time and with whom she always spoke Dutch. She had just got off the phone where she had spoken English and without realizing it she asked Susan a question in English and not in Dutch. Susan started to cry and said, in Dutch: "Nee mama, nee! Niet Engels mama!' (No mommy, no! No English, mommy!).

I have become aware, once again, of the person–language bond with a little French–English bilingual boy I know well. I speak French to him and whenever I try to switch over to English, he turns away or shows he doesn't like it. One day, getting ready to read a Bill Peete story to him, written in English, I asked, "Do you want the story in English or in French?" He immediately replied, "In French," forcing me to translate the story even though it would have been easier for me to read it in English. I've tried since then to read him other books in English but he always balks at this.

Does the person–language bond remain as strong as the child grows older? Sometimes it can but it will be expressed in a different way. One parent, Nayr, who commented on my earlier post, relates how her son has tagged her as a speaker of English. In his earlier years he was bilingual in Portuguese and English but refused that she speak to him in Portuguese. Then, later when they moved to France, he became predominantly a speaker of French and English but still insisted that English be his mother's language (although she also speaks French). She writes that her son is now seventeen and still insists that she "act" English, both linguistically and culturally.

Another comment came from Noemie who was raised in an English–French bilingual family. The family mainly spoke English at home but when French guests came over, her parents insisted that they speak French. She reports that she simply couldn't do it when members of her family were there: "... I would rather leave the room than speak French with my family." She continues, " ... it has lasted into my adulthood. I am still today completely unable to address my family members in French ... "

Most often though, the person–language bond evolves into a "preferred language" or "agreed-upon" language that bilinguals have with other bilinguals that they know well such as parents, brothers and sisters, other relatives, close friends, etc. Violation of this "agreement," when there is no good reason to use the other language (such as the presence of a monolingual, or a topic that is usually dealt with in the other language) is likely to create an unnatural or even embarrassing situation, and may end with the question, "Why are you speaking language X to me?"

Is the person–language bond found in all societies among bilingual children? For a long time, I thought this was the case, to a greater or lesser extent. But then I reread the writings of Abdelali Bentahila and Eirlys Davies, both researchers on bilingualism based in Morocco, and realized that this was not the case. They report on Arabic–French bilingualism which is prevalent in the middle and upper classes in their country. The children hear both languages at home and are addressed in both languages by their parents. Later, they are placed in nursery schools where the two languages are present.

Abdelali Bentahila and Eirlys Davies stress that these young bilinguals are used to hearing their parents and other adults use the two languages –

sometimes the one, sometimes the other, and very often intermingling both languages substantially. As a result, children do not "tag" adults with a particular language and do not develop the strong person–language bond that other children do.

For these authors, whether such a bond develops or not depends on the way children are brought up bilingual. If the languages are clearly separated during childhood, by person (e.g. with the one person–one language approach) or by environment (one language at home, one outside the home), then a bond might develop. If the use of one or the other language by individuals is freer, and the languages are interchangeable, then it probably will not.

The good news for parents who do use both languages interchangeably in the home is that the probability that their children will become bilingual will be as high as it is for those who use a more restricted approach (see Post 6.5). In addition, their children will not notice, to the point of sometimes being upset, if they hear their parents use the other language!

References

De Houwer, A. (2009). *Bilingual First Language Acquisition*. Bristol: Multilingual Matters.
Bentahila, A. and Davies, E. E. (1995). Patterns of code-switching and patterns of language contact. *Lingua*, 96, 75–93.

7

Children with Additional Needs

INTRODUCTION

Parents of children with additional or special needs often want guidance on whether their children can become bilingual, or remain bilingual, despite the challenges they have. They often consult professionals such as doctors, psychologists, speech and language pathologists, educators, and so on and many come away with words of warning. Bilingualism might have consequences on the development of their child they are told erroneously: it may delay the acquisition of the majority language, cause a burden for the child, create language confusion, and so on. And sometimes, they are encouraged to concentrate on just one language, the majority language, and give up the minority or home language. One can only be extremely concerned by this kind of feedback and over the years I have prepared posts on the topic, very often with the help of specialists. They are the object of this chapter.

Post 7.1 concentrates on children who have developmental disabilities. Dr. Elizabeth Kay-Raining Bird answers questions on children with Specific (or Primary) Language Impairment (SLI), Down syndrome (DS), or Autism Spectrum Disorder (ASD). She stresses that the real issue is not whether these children should become bilingual – many are or will be – but how best to support them in their life with two or more languages.

Posts 7.2 and 7.3 concern children who are deaf or have hearing loss. In 7.2, it is shown that neither bilingual children who follow the oral approach (speech only) or the manual approach (sign language primarily) are hindered or delayed in the development of the majority language. On the contrary, bilingualism brings benefits to both children and caretakers. In Post 7.3, bilingualism in a sign language and an oral language is described, the similarities and differences with bilingualism in two oral languages are enumerated, and the many advantages of allowing deaf children to know and use both a sign language and an oral language, at least in its written modality, are presented.

Post 7.4 turns to dyslexia, a very common learning difficulty. Dr. Fred Genesee talks about it as it pertains to bilingual children and second-language learners. He underlines the fact that bilingualism does not cause dyslexia, and that giving up the home language(s), or not learning second languages, will not make it easier for the child to over-come their dyslexia. On the contrary, they should continue using them or learning them.

Finally, Post 7.5 is an interview with Dr. Valerie Lim on stuttering in bilinguals. She states that there is no support for the notion that bilingual families should only focus on using one language so as to avoid stuttering. Quite the reverse, parents should be encouraged to continue promoting both languages in their children.

7.1 SUPPORTING BILINGUAL CHILDREN WITH SPECIAL EDUCATION NEEDS

(Interview with Elizabeth Kay-Raining Bird)

Despite what has been maintained for too long, children with developmental disabilities can indeed become bilingual, or remain bilingual, if they have grown up with two languages.

One of the longest-lasting myths that concerns bilingualism is that children with developmental disabilities should not become bilingual, or if they already are using a minority language in the home, should stop using it. Thanks to new research in the field, this view is slowly being replaced by one that states that these children can indeed become bilin-gual, or remain bilingual. A 2016 special issue of the *Journal of Communication Disorders* presents research that examines bilingual access and participation for children with developmental disabilities, con-ducted by an international team of researchers. The principal investiga-tor on the study was Professor Elizabeth Kay-Raining Bird of Dalhousie University in Canada. She has very kindly accepted to answer some of our questions and we wish to thank her wholeheartedly.

In your review of the field with Fred Genesee and Ludo Verhoeven, you concentrate on three groups of children with developmental disabilities. Which are they?

The three groups we focused upon were children with Specific (or Primary) Language Impairment (SLI), Down syndrome (DS), or Autism Spectrum Disorder (ASD) because these are the ones who have been studied to any real degree with the emphasis having been put on bilingual children with SLI. Almost no research exists on bilingualism in other populations of children with developmental disabilities such as children with cerebral palsy or intellectual disabilities of other etiologies.

Why has there been such opposition to bilingualism for children with developmental disabilities over the years?

A prevalent fear, expressed by families and professionals alike, is that learning one language is already difficult for these children, therefore learning two or more languages would be just too difficult. Exposing a child with developmental disabilities to two languages, the argument goes, might result in no language being learned well. This is a myth and it has been debunked through studies of typically developing children, and children from our three groups. Children with developmental disabilities, regardless of diagnosis, can and do become bilingual but, unfortunately, many professionals and families are not aware of these research findings.

Since we know many children with developmental disabilities need or want to be bilingual, and that many are indeed bilingual, the real issue is not whether they should become bilingual, but how to best support them in their life with two or more languages.

Are simultaneous bilinguals with developmental disabilities any different from their similarly affected monolingual peers?

All the available evidence says no, there are no differences in the language skills of children with developmental disabilities and their similarly affected monolingual peers, as long as bilinguals are compared to monolinguals in an appropriate way. By appropriate I mean that if a simultaneous bilingual child with a developmental disability has relatively equal abilities in both languages, then research shows their ability in each language does not differ from that of monolingual similarly affected peers.

However, many simultaneous bilingual children do not have equal abilities in both their languages because they hear and use one language more often than the other. In that case, their stronger language should be the language that is compared to that of monolingual children. When that happens, they are no different from their similarly affected peers.

How do sequential bilinguals with disorders fare?

They fare somewhat differently. As you know, these children have one language they are exposed to from birth and a second language they begin to learn somewhat later. Often, their first exposure to a second language occurs when they enter school and they are taught in this second (majority) language. Research shows that children with Specific Language Impairment (SLI) will often take a number of years to "catch up" to monolinguals who are similarly affected in their second-language skills. Research on typically developing children has reported similar lags in second-language development. This is not surprising – learning a second language takes time.

The story for children with Down Syndrome (DS) or Autism Spectrum Disorder (ASD) is not clear, but currently the evidence shows no detrimental effects of sequential bilingualism if you take into account both languages of the bilingual child when making comparisons.

Why is it so crucial not to abandon a home language in favor of the majority language?

The impact of abandoning a home language has been studied by interviewing parents of children with Autism Spectrum Disorder (ASD). Many families in these studies were advised to speak only the majority language to their children even though the parent was not fluent in it. Parents often talked about feeling less comfortable and less natural interacting with their child, and some reported that they actually avoided talking to him/her because of their discomfort. This has a detrimental effect on the child's language development and is particularly problematic for children who have difficulty with communication, such as those with ASD.

Even if parents reported feeling comfortable speaking the majority language to their child with ASD, they expressed feelings of sadness and guilt at not passing their language (and culture) on to their children. When the majority language was the only language of input to a child with ASD in the home, other family members continued to use the home language(s), which effectively isolated the child with ASD from various family conversations.

How important is everyday exposure to both languages, in particular the weaker one, in children with developmental disabilities?
By definition, children with developmental disabilities have difficulty learning, and this includes learning language. To become and stay bilingual, children with developmental disabilities, just like typically developing children, need to be exposed to and use both their languages on a frequent and ongoing basis. It has been shown that frequent input in a language is highly and positively related to proficiency in that language. This is particularly true for the weaker language.

Quantity is not all that is needed; however, as we saw in the interviews of parents with ASD – quality is also important. Children with developmental disabilities, because of their language-learning difficulties, need to experience both their languages in functional interactive contexts designed to facilitate their language learning.

Do children with developmental disabilities have equal access to bilingual programs (immersion, dual language) and, if not, what should be done?
No, they do not have equal access to bilingual programs and to services as shown in our survey in six sites and four countries. Our respondents reported that both sequential and simultaneous bilinguals with disabilities were taught only in the majority language and were assessed and treated only in that language more often than they should be. In general, the more severe the disability, the less likely children with developmental disabilities have access to bilingual supports and services.

Our team also interviewed practitioners and administrators to identify barriers that prevent children with developmental disabilities from accessing and/or participating fully in bilingual services and supports. We found both systemic barriers (e.g. limits in funding, service availability varying by geographic location, etc.) and barriers specific to children with developmental disabilities such as a tendency to prioritize special education services over bilingual services, a lack of integration of special education and bilingual services, and so on.

What are some of the suggestions that come out of your research project?
We feel that a number of changes should be made such as: all those involved with children with developmental disabilities need to know that

these children can and do become bilingual; their families should be encouraged to enroll them in bilingual programs and services available to other children; special education and bilingual education programs and services should be integrated; staff who work with them should be provided with training and supports, and so on.

What are your hopes for the future?
My hope is that our societies will value and support people from diverse cultural and linguistic backgrounds. After all, we know a lot about how we can help children become bilingual and remain bilingual and we also know a lot about how to appropriately assess and treat bilingual children with developmental disabilities. I hope that in the future we will continue to study these issues and make bilingual programs accessible to, and supportive of, the needs of children of all ability levels.

References

Bedore, L., Kay-Raining Bird, E., and Genesee, F. (2016; eds.). The road to bilingualism: Access, participation and supports for children with developmental disabilities across contexts. *Journal of Communication Disorders*, 63, 1–92.
Kay-Raining Bird, E., Genesee, F., and Verhoeven, L. (2016). Bilingualism in children with developmental disorders: A narrative review. *Journal of Communicative Disorders*, 63, 1–14.
de Valenzuela, J., Kay-Raining Bird, E., Parkington, K., Mirenda, P., Cain, K., MacLeod, A. A., and Segers, E. (2016). Access to opportunities for bilingualism for individuals with developmental disabilities: Key informant interviews. *Journal of Communication Disorders*, 63, 32–46.

7.2 BILINGUAL CHILDREN WITH HEARING LOSS[1]

Recent studies have put to rest claims that bilingualism hinders the acquisition of the majority language in children with hearing loss.

Some 1 to 3 children per 1,000 suffer from hearing loss, many of whom are bilingual. Knowing and using two or more languages is a perfectly natural phenomenon but it is often perceived negatively

[1] This post is not about the educational approaches as such used with deaf children – the author has always defended a bimodal approach (see Post 7.3) – but about whether bilingualism, in two oral languages, or in an oral language and a sign language, has a negative impact on the acquisition of the majority language in children with hearing loss.

by some clinicians and educators when it involves children with hearing loss. They state that bilingualism will delay the acquisition of the majority language, burden the child unduly, dilute his/her linguistic resources, even create language confusion. They therefore encourage parents to use just one language, the majority language, and to give up, or not start using, a second language, most often the minority language.

The counter arguments of those who defend bilingualism, and the minority language in particular, are many: parents and children can communicate in the home language (some minority language parents don't speak the majority language well), the bonds between parents and children are strengthened, as are those with the local community, there are long-term benefits to being bilingual, and so on. Their position is now strengthened by recent studies that show that being bilingual is not detrimental to children with hearing loss. We will cover three in what follows.

In a first study, Dr. Ferenc Bunta of the University of Houston and his colleagues compared the English language skills of two groups of young children with hearing loss: English–Spanish bilingual children, and English-speaking monolinguals. All children had received their cochlear implants and/or hearing aids before the age of five and all were given instruction and therapy at the Center for Hearing and Speech in Houston. The bilingual children also received auditory-based therapy in Spanish and their parents were given linguistic goals and strategies so that they could implement them at home in their daily activities in Spanish.

The children were given a well-known language test, the Preschool Language Scales (PLS-4), which assesses the developing child's ability to understand and use spoken language. The bilingual children were also given a Spanish version of the test. The results were clear: the English scores of the bilingual children were not significantly different from those of their monolingual peers. In addition, no difference was found between the English and Spanish results obtained by the bilinguals. The authors concluded that dual-language use is not detrimental to overall speech and language development in bilingual children with hearing loss. In their words, "Our data provide evidence that children and their families should not abandon using their home language; rather, they can and should encourage speech and language development in both languages if they choose to do so."

In a second study, published three years later, Ferenc Bunta and his colleagues wanted to find out if the bilingual children who were given support in their two languages did better than other bilingual children, also with hearing loss, who only received support in English. They matched the children on a range of demographic and socio-economic variables and gave them the English version of the Preschool Language Scale test. What they found was that the bilingual children with dual-support obtained similar results as their English-only peers on auditory comprehension but outperformed them on the overall measure as well as expressive communication. They concluded that encouraging home language use and providing treatment support in the first language may help develop both English and the home language.

The studies mentioned so far have dealt with bilingualism in children who have two oral languages. What about bimodal bilinguals, that is children who are brought up with a sign language, such as American Sign Language, and with a spoken, majority, language, in this case English? Here too some health professionals have expressed reserve, if not outright rejection, of a bilingual approach for children with cochlear implants and/or hearing aids despite everything that sign language brings to the child and to his caretakers. For example, it can be used to communicate early on while the oral language is being acquired – a difficult and lengthy process in deaf children –, it helps them develop their cognitive abilities and acquire knowledge of the world, and it allows for normal parent–child bonding which otherwise can be very difficult. Post 7.3 reviews the many benefits of bimodal bilingualism for these children.

Dr. Elizabeth Fitzpatrick, at the University of Ottawa, and her colleagues have published a systematic review of the effectiveness of early sign and oral language intervention compared to oral intervention only. They took eleven studies published in the last twenty years that had between thirteen and ninety participants each, most of them with severe to profound deafness. Their conclusion was clear: They found no evidence that adding sign language interfered with spoken language development, contrary to what some have maintained for years.

Thus, in the span of three years, researchers who have examined two very different approaches used with children with hearing loss – the oral approach and the manual approach – have come to similar conclusions. Bilingualism does not hinder or delay the development of the majority language. On the contrary, it brings many benefits to both the child and to his/her caretakers!

References

Bunta, F. and Douglas, M. (2013). The effects of dual-language support on the language skills of bilingual children with hearing loss who use listening devices relative to their monolingual peers. *Language, Speech, and Hearing Services in Schools*, 44, 281–290.

Bunta, F., Douglas, M., Dickson, H., Cantu, A., Wickesberg, J., and Gifford, R. H. (2016). Dual language versus English-only support for bilingual children with hearing loss who use cochlear implants and hearing aids. *International Journal of Language and Communication Disorders*, 51 (4), 460–472.

Fitzpatrick, E. M., Hamel, C., Stevens, A., Pratt, M., Moher, D., Doucet, S. P., Neuss, D., Bernstein, A., and Na, E. (2016). Sign language and spoken language for children with hearing loss: A systematic review. *Pediatrics*, 137 (1): e20151974.

7.3 SIGN LANGUAGE AND BILINGUALISM

Bilingualism in a sign language and an oral language, in its spoken or written modality, is relatively frequent but is still not fully accepted. Thus, children who are deaf [2] or hard of hearing are not systematically brought up knowing and using a sign language and an oral language.

All language scientists have a wow moment in their profession. Mine was when I was introduced to sign language and to the world of the Deaf. I was simply overwhelmed by the beauty of this visual gestural language as well as by the history of deaf people.

Many myths still surround sign language such as that it is universal (in fact, there are as many sign languages as there are deaf communities), that it is speech on the hands (as a visual gestural linguistic system it is in

---

[2] After an exchange with Professor Carol Padden (August 12, 2018), I no longer differentiate between "deaf" and "Deaf" in my spelling but continue to do so in my thinking of the cultural issues. As she writes, "Once you leave American culture, or Western culture, the distinction becomes hard to use."

many ways very different from a spoken language), that it only expresses concrete notions (one simply needs to look at sign poetry to understand how very rich and symbolic it can be), and so on.

The users of sign language are often bilingual – one language is sign language (e.g. American Sign Language) and the other is the language of the hearing majority (e.g. English), often in its written form. This is termed bimodal bilingualism. These bilinguals share many similarities with bilinguals of two or more oral languages: they are diverse (some are deaf, some are hard of hearing, some even are hearing), many do not consider themselves to be bilingual (see Post 1.1), they use their languages for different purposes, in different domains of life, with different people (as explained in Post 1.5), and they communicate differently depending on whether they are addressing monolinguals or bilinguals.

There are also aspects that are specific to the bilingualism of the deaf one of which is that there is still no widespread acceptance that they have the right to be bilingual. Thus, many deaf children in the world are not given the chance of mastering both a sign language and an oral language from their earliest years on. A purely oral language education is preferred for them even though many of them may not adequately master the oral language. As a consequence, they will have problems communicating with many of those who matter most in their lives.

And yet, recent research has shown the many advantages of allowing deaf children to know and use both a sign language and an oral language. It is the optimal combination that will allow these children to meet their many needs, that is, communicate early with their parents (first in sign and then, with time, also in the oral language), develop their cognitive abilities, acquire knowledge of the world, communicate fully with the surrounding world, and acculturate into their two worlds.

Depending on the child, the two languages will play different roles: some children will be dominant in sign language, others will be dominant in the oral language, and some will be balanced in their two languages. Just like other bilingual children, they will use their languages in their everyday lives and they will belong, to varying degrees, to two worlds – in this case, the hearing world and the Deaf world.

It is still quite common for some professionals involved with deafness (doctors, speech-language pathologists, teachers, etc.) as well as for some parents to believe that the knowledge of sign language will hinder the development of the oral language in deaf children. This is unfortunate as it is now well accepted that a first language that has been acquired normally, be it spoken or signed, will greatly enhance the acquisition and use of a second language.

In the case of deaf children, whether they have a cochlear implant or not, sign language can be used early on to communicate while the oral language is being acquired; it can be used to express emotions, to explain things as well as to communicate about the other language; and linguistic skills acquired in sign such as discourse rules and even general writing skills, acquired through sign writing, can be transferred to the oral language. It has been shown that the better the children's skills are in sign language, the better they will know the oral language.

As I state in my "The right of the deaf child to grow up bilingual," a short text that has been translated into some thirty-five languages in a collaborative project with Gallaudet University, one never regrets knowing several languages but one can certainly regret not knowing enough, especially if one's own development is at stake.

References

Grosjean, F. (2010). Bilingualism, biculturalism, and deafness. *International Journal of Bilingual Education and Bilingualism,* 13(2), 133–145.
Grosjean, F. (2000). The right of the deaf child to grow up bilingual. *WFD NEWS,* 13(1), 14–15.
Plaza-Pus, C. and Morales-López, E. (2008). *Sign Bilingualism: Language Development, Interaction, and Maintenance in Sign Language Contact Situations.* Philadelphia and Amsterdam: John Benjamins.

7.4 DYSLEXIA IN BILINGUALS AND SECOND-LANGUAGE LEARNERS[3]

(Interview with Fred Genesee)

Dyslexia is the most common learning disability and yet we know very little about it when two or more languages are involved. An expert on the topic answers our questions.

---

[3] The original title of this post was, "Dyslexia, bilingualism and second language learning."

The National Institute of Neurological Disorders and Stroke (NINDS) defines dyslexia as a brain-based type of learning disability that specifically impairs a person's ability to read.[4] The British National Health Service (NHS) gives a fuller definition: it is a common learning difficulty that can cause problems with reading, writing, and spelling. The NHS also lists a number of problems that people with dyslexia have: they read and write very slowly, confuse the letters of words, put letters the wrong way round, have poor or inconsistent spelling, have difficulty with information that is written down, and so on.[5]

Dyslexia is the most common learning disability and has been the object of much research published in books, chapters, and articles. Unfortunately, we know much less about it in bilinguals, in second-language learners, or in students schooled in a second language. The latter can be in immersion or bilingual school programs, or can come from minority language groups being educated in the majority language. Dr. Fred Genesee, Professor Emeritus at McGill University, is one of the leading experts on this topic and he has very kindly agreed to answer a few of our questions. We thank him wholeheartedly.

Are there more dyslexics among bilinguals than among monolinguals?
There is no evidence that dyslexia is more common among bilinguals than among monolinguals.

Does being bilingual cause dyslexia or increase the probability of becoming dyslexic?
Again, there is no evidence that bilingualism causes dyslexia. Dyslexia is linked to neuro-cognitive factors that are inherited. It is thought that children with dyslexia have an inherited impairment processing the sounds of language. This means that children born with the genetic profile that is linked to dyslexia will have difficulty learning to read whether they are bilingual or monolingual.

When talking about dyslexia in children, shouldn't one insist on something that you have put forward in your writings – the distinction between *reading impairment* and *difficulty learning to read?*

---

[4] www.ninds.nih.gov/disorders/all-disorders/dyslexia-information-page
[5] www.nhs.uk/conditions/dyslexia/

Yes, this crucial. Reading impairment is due to underlying neurocognitive factors mentioned in my previous answer whereas difficulty learning to read is linked to other factors, such as the child's learning environment, motivation, quality of instruction, or general health. For example, some children have difficulty learning to read in school because the quality of instruction they receive is not always optimal; because they have undetected visual impairment which makes it difficult to see and process written language; or because they are uninterested in learning to read because they find the reading materials in school boring. These children's difficulties are not genetic in nature and are not true dyslexia.

Concerning children who are in the process of learning a second language, can they be at greater risk for *difficulty learning to read* than children learning through their first language?
Yes, this may be the case because they are still learning the language which is being used to teach reading in school and some teachers may not have modified instruction to take this into account. Second-language learners might also have greater difficulty than monolingual students learning to read because the cultural content of the reading material is unfamiliar, or because the teacher's cultural expectations of how they should behave in class is foreign or even difficult for them.

Unfortunately, tests that assess progress in learning to read can make it appear that bilingual children have an impairment because they do not consider the linguistic level of the children. But, none of these factors are symptomatic of reading impairment or dyslexia per se.

Going back to actual dyslexia, what are the difficulties faced by second-language learners who are dyslexic?
The core difficulties faced by second-language learners who are dyslexic are the same as those of monolingual children with dyslexia. The core problem for these children is difficulty learning to decode written words accurately and fluently so that they can make sense of them and understand written text. If children's word reading skills are impaired, then their comprehension of written text will also be impaired because they cannot read the individual words accurately and fluently enough to create meaningful text.

In addition, second-language learners with dyslexia face the challenges encountered by all second-language learners – limited vocabulary and grammatical competence and lack of familiarity with the cultural or social context of the text. In this respect, their challenges are different from monolingual children.

Can the effects of dyslexia in bilinguals be stronger in one language than in the other?
Dyslexia in bilinguals is evident in both languages. This is the case because the impairment that underlies dyslexia is part of the learner's genetic profile and, thus, its effects will influence the child's ability to learn to read in any language. Of course, since many bilinguals are more proficient in one language than the other, the magnitude of their impairment will be more evident in their weaker language.

A bilingual child who has a reading problem in only one of his/her languages does not have dyslexia. This child has difficulty learning to read in one of his/her languages that is due to other factors, as we discussed earlier.

It is often recommended that the parents of children who are thought to be dyslexic stop using the home language on the assumption that this will make it easier for their child to overcome their dyslexia. What is your opinion on this?
There is no evidence to support this assumption. If the child is from a minority language community where the language is important for communication with parents, extended family members, or others in the community, parents should continue to use the home language. There are many reasons for this. First, proficiency in the home language is important if the child is to become an engaged and well-adjusted member of his family and community. In addition, parents of minority language children are often more proficient in the home language and, thus, they are better able to assume their full parental responsibilities if they interact with their child in that language.

What are the other reasons?
Encouraging parents who speak a minority language to use it in the home also allows them to enrich their child's home language experiences and competence. We know that strong skills in the home language prepares children to learn a second language and to do well in school because there are significant positive effects of the home language on second-language learning.

This means that parents who continue to use the minority/home language can facilitate their child's chances of becoming proficient second-language learners. This is particularly true if they use the home language in literacy-related activities where the cross-linguistic correlations are strongest.

What about parents who wish to put their dyslexic child in a bilingual program? Should they avoid doing so?
There is no evidence that children with reading impairment or even difficulty learning to read cannot benefit from participation in a bilingual program. This is true for both children from minority language homes and children from majority language homes. To the contrary, there is considerable research now that shows that educating minority language children in school programs that use both the home language and the majority language results in higher levels of achievement than programs that use only the majority language.

If parents are concerned that their child has a reading or other learning disability, they should pay special attention to whether the school has the know-how and resources to provide their child with the additional support they need in both languages.

When children being schooled in a second language start showing reading difficulties, should one have a wait-and-see attitude whilst they are making progress in their new language, or should one intervene immediately?
If children who are being educated entirely or partially through a second language appear to have difficulty learning to read, then it is best to start giving them additional support as soon as possible. This is recommended whether the child simply has difficulty learning to read or has clinically-identified dyslexia. Research shows that additional support that is early and individualized to meet each student's needs is the most effective way to alleviating long term problems.

More generally, how does one know if a child's problems are due to dyslexia or simply to the fact that she is in the process of learning a second language?
It is not always easy to tell if a second-language learner who is struggling learning to read has an underlying reading impairment or simply needs more time to learn to read like other students of the same age. To make a more definitive decision that a child is struggling to read because he/she has a reading impairment, it is necessary to rule out other possible

contributing factors that are not indicative of dyslexia. For example, does the student have health-related problems; has he/she experienced recent trauma or emotional upset related to family or immigration issues; does he/she have normal intellectual and sensory motor abilities; and so on. If an individual child's difficulties can be linked to these other kinds of factors, then his/her difficulties are probably not due to reading impairment.

What kind of help and support can be given to dyslexic children being schooled in a second language?
Students being educated in a second language who are struggling readers can benefit from the same kinds of support that are used to help struggling monolingual students. At the same time, it is important to provide support that incorporates adaptations that are suitable for students who are still learning the language and who may be from a different cultural group; for example, provide lots of scaffolding, support vocabulary development, and use culturally familiar and appropriate materials at an appropriate linguistic level.

Should the intervention take place in both languages or just in one? What should professionals be aware of?
Support should be provided in whichever language is the primary language of instruction or in both languages if instruction is bilingual. Professionals providing support for struggling readers should understand the nature of bilingual development and they should consider similarities and differences in the written and oral conventions of the two languages when they provide support.

Knowledge of these aspects of second-language learning can ensure that they will make appropriate adjustments when they provide additional support. Professionals also need to know their student's individual capabilities and challenges so you can individualize support and build on each child's strengths.

Do you have any final words?
Scientific studies have shown that the fears about raising or educating children are largely unfounded. To the contrary, we now know that children have the capacity to learn two languages as naturally and as easily as one in the home or in school. Meeting the learning challenges of struggling second-language learners calls for educators, professionals, and parents who can create learning environments that allow them to achieve their full capacity.

References

Genesee, F. (2015). Myths about early childhood bilingualism. *Canadian Psychology*, 56(1), 6–15.

Paradis, J., Genesee, F., and Crago, M. (2011). *Dual Language Development and Disorders: A Handbook on Bilingualism and Second Language Learning*, 2nd ed. Baltimore, MD: Brookes.

7.5 STUTTERING IN BILINGUALS: WHAT WE KNOW TODAY

(Interview with Valerie Lim)

Many aspects of stuttering in bilinguals are still being researched. A recognized stuttering specialist helps us uncover the major issues.

Even though stuttering in bilinguals has a relatively long research history, there are still many questions that cause debate: Do bilinguals stutter in just one language or in all of their languages? Is stuttering severity affected by language proficiency? Does one stutter differently in structurally different languages? Does language dominance have an impact on stuttering? and so on. Dr. Valerie Lim, a speech-language therapist in Singapore, has kindly agreed to answer some of these questions for us. She is a recognized stuttering specialist who has successfully treated bilinguals who stutter. What better person to tell us about a topic that is still being researched actively. We thank her wholeheartedly.

Do we know if there are proportionally more bilinguals who stutter than monolinguals?
There are currently no studies that provide information about whether there are proportionally more bilinguals who stutter than monolinguals. The impression some of us have that this might be the case, although unfounded as of today, is related to the fact that the number of bilinguals has grown worldwide.

Do bilinguals usually stutter in just one of their languages or in all of them?
Stuttering is considered to be a motor speech disorder. So it is not surprising that there is more evidence to show that bilinguals stutter in both, or all of their, languages. If stuttering only occurs in one language (i.e. language specific stuttering), it is probably an exception and related to a significant imbalance in proficiency in each language.

For the majority who stutter in all their languages, is the type of stuttering and its severity dependent upon the language acquired first?
There is still a debate as to whether stuttering manifests itself similarly or differently in both languages. However, there is more evidence to substantiate that stuttering occurs "differently" across languages. In John Van Borsel's review of the literature, bilinguals who stutter in both languages have been reported to exhibit several kinds of profiles. For example, some have shown a difference in stuttering frequency (number of stutters) across languages, but not the location of the stutters (e.g. within the sentence). Others have shown a difference in stuttering frequency, type and location across the two languages.

What about the role of language proficiency?
The different manifestations of stuttering across languages have been attributed to language proficiency. While some studies have reported that adults show a greater degree of stuttering in the more proficient language, it is more common to find increased stuttering in the less proficient language. But this has to be confirmed with additional data.

The manifestation of stuttering in bilingual children may be different and will be dependent on factors such as the age of the child and his/her stage of language development.

In a study you published in 2008, you showed clearly that language dominance influences the severity of the stuttering. Can you tell us about it?
In our study, we investigated the influence of language dominance on the severity and type of stuttering in English–Mandarin bilinguals who stutter. Our thirty English–Mandarin stutterers were put into one of three groups: English-dominant, Mandarin-dominant, and balanced bilinguals.

We found that both the English-dominant and Mandarin-dominant bilinguals exhibited higher stuttering frequency in their less dominant language. On the other hand, the frequency scores for the balanced bilinguals were similar across languages.

Did these bilinguals stutter in the same way in their languages even though the languages are very different?
Interestingly, we found no difference in the types of stutters between English and Mandarin for any bilingual group.

Based on our results, we concluded that language dominance seemed to affect the frequency of stuttering but not the type of stuttering behavior. This means that speech-language pathologists should assess all the bilingual's languages, if possible, in order to obtain a clear diagnostic.

When young monolingual stutterers start learning and using a second language, does their stuttering increase in frequency and/or severity?
It is common for stuttering to increase when children (monolingual or bilingual) start putting words together, or when they start producing longer or more complex sentences.

For monolingual children who stutter and who are also learning a second language, the appearance of stuttering in the second language will depend on their level of proficiency in that language, and/or how often they use it. For example, if a child is only able to speak a few words of the second language, it is typical for parents to report no stuttering in that language. However, when the child gains proficiency in the second language, or when he/she starts joining more words together, or uses the language more often, parents do notice an increase in stuttering.

For parents of young bilingual stutterers, are there any strategies they can adopt to help their children learn and maintain their languages?
Based on what we know from the literature, there is no evidence to support the notion that bilingual families should only focus on using one language to avoid stuttering. We encourage parents to continue to use both languages in their daily life.

We often show parents how to provide language modelling (i.e. how to produce appropriate sentence structure and vocabulary in each language), and how to support the child when he/she is trying to join words or say a sentence. We start stuttering treatment as soon as we deem it clinically necessary for the child and the family.

Concerning speech therapy, should it take place early?
There is strong evidence that early intervention for monolingual childhood stuttering is highly effective if the treatment is done before six to seven years of age (see Professor Mark Onslow's work presented in the references below). This is no different for bilingual children who stutter. Treatment for older bilingual children and adults who stutter can also help to reduce the stuttering.

Should therapy be done in all of the bilingual's languages or in only one of them?
Research has shown that the treatment for bilinguals who stutter is effective whether or not it is conducted in one language or in both languages. When the treatment is delivered in one language only, we know from the literature that treatment effects can generalize from the treated to the non-treated language.

Similarly, when the treatment is conducted in two languages, stuttering can be reduced in both languages whether or not the treatment is delivered simultaneously (both languages are treated at the same time) or consecutively (one language is treated first and the other language is treated later).

The decision regarding the delivery of treatment for bilinguals who stutter will be made by the clinician who will take into consideration the evidence as well as the individual needs of the child and family. Important factors will be the frequency and type of stuttering, the child's language background, the impact of stuttering on the child and family, the age of the child, and so on.

References

Lim, V. P. C., Lincoln, M., Chan, Y. H., and Onslow, M. (2008). Stuttering in English-Mandarin bilingual speakers: The influence of language dominance on stuttering severity. *Journal of Speech, Language, and Hearing Research, 51,* 1522–1537.

Onslow, M. (2018). Stuttering and its treatment: Eleven Lectures. Australian Stuttering Research Centre, The University of Sydney.

Van Borsel, J. (2011). Review of research on the relationship between bilingualism and stuttering. In P. Howell and J. Van Borsel, eds., *Multilingual Aspects of Fluency Disorders.* Bristol: MPG Books Group, pp. 247–270.

8

Second Language Learning

INTRODUCTION

In this chapter, we start with second language learning in school and then progressively move to older learners of foreign languages. Post 8.1 presents a quick review of the way second languages are acquired in the school setting. From a subject taught in a rather formal way, the second language is increasingly becoming a medium of instruction through immersion and dual-language teaching.

Post 8.2 is an interview with Dr. Fabrice Jaumont who has played a leadership role in establishing dual-language programs in the public school system in the New York area. The movement is led from the bottom-up by families who want their children to acquire a second language in a more natural way.

In Post 8.3, Dr. Aneta Pavlenko, an applied linguist, offers the first of five posts in this chapter. It is a discussion of the key differences between learning a second language in the classroom and learning it in a naturalistic setting, "in the wild" as she writes.

Post 8.4 stays in the classroom and evokes the practice of translanguaging in bilingual children, that is the use in the classroom of the speaker's entire linguistic repertoire. Dr. Ofelia García, one of its most visible proponents, answers our questions.

The final five posts are proposed by Aneta Pavlenko. In Post 8.5, she explains how learning a foreign language is a bit like dating: it spurs anxiety. Her message is that one needs to strike a balance between foreign language anxiety and the positive emotions that are intrinsic in language learning.

In Post 8.6, Aneta Pavlenko asks whether a second language can help you learn a third language. The answer is complex as there are indeed many advantages to already knowing a second language, but the latter may team up with the first language to make things more difficult.

In Post 8.7, she asks whether musicians make better language learners. Or is it the other way around: is it our experience with several languages that makes us better musicians?

In Post 8.8, Aneta Pavlenko interviews William Fierman, a highly successful learner of many languages. He explains what his learning strategies are, and how they depend on his goals for the language in question as well as the availability of teachers and of learning material.

Finally, in Post 8.9, Aneta Pavlenko stays with multilingualism and discusses whether it makes any sense that the media differentiate between "regular" multilinguals and polyglots.

8.1 FROM SECOND LANGUAGE LEARNING TO BILINGUALISM IN SCHOOLS

Learning a second (or foreign) language has been possible in schools since the beginning of education. For a long time, however, it was just a subject matter learned in a rather formal way. Now interesting new approaches are being used to develop bilingualism and biliteracy in schools.

We are many who feel that education should help children and adolescents acquire a second or third language while retaining their first language. Education should also encourage the active use of those languages, if at all possible.

Currently, many educational systems throughout the world follow one of UNESCO's objectives in its 2002 Universal Declaration on Cultural Diversity which encourages, among things, "the learning of several languages from the earliest age." But there are many different ways of doing so, as we will see below.

First, there is the traditional way of teaching a second or foreign language that many of us have experienced as children in whatever country we have grown up in. The language is a subject that is taught in a rather formal way at specific times during the week. It rarely becomes a means of communication and it is not a medium used to teach other subjects. Despite this, second language (or foreign language) teachers (see Post 14.1 that is dedicated to them) usually make every effort to transform language learning into an enjoyable and lively activity. For example, they now use Web-based and other audiovisual methods including singing and music, as well as diverse communicative strategies, to teach the language in question.

At the end of their schooling, students come away with formal knowledge of the second language and its accompanying culture(s) and, often, its literature. But if the classes were rather large, and they only met a few times a week, students may not have made all the progress wanted and will not have used the language orally that much. And with time, unless they visit a country or region where the language is used, or take additional courses, their knowledge of the language may well wither away.

In order to remedy this, educators and psychologists from McGill University (Wallace Lambert, Richard Tucker, and others), set up "immersion programs" in the second half of the last century, first in the small town of St. Lambert in Quebec, Canada, and then elsewhere in the country and abroad. What is interesting with this approach is that students acquire a language by learning subject matters in that language – it is the medium of instruction – instead of acquiring it through formal instruction. Thus, in the St. Lambert project, English-speaking children were taught in French, by French-speaking teachers, starting in kindergarten.

From first grade on, the teachers never spoke English to the students or with one another, so as to create, as far as possible, a totally French-speaking environment. The children were taught to read and write in French starting in grade one. In grade two, they started having English-language classes for about an hour a day, but the rest of the program was in French. Little by little, more English was brought in, so that by grade six, more than half the teaching was in English.

The approach proved to be highly successful as the children were in no way behind control groups who had been taught in English only. Their intelligence level was equivalent to that of the controls, and their knowledge of French was far better than that of other English-speaking children their age. The one thing missing was the active use of French outside the school which was left to the families to work on.

The immersion approach is now used widely in many countries of the world as well as in language-revival programs. There are numerous versions of it such as late-immersion or language-switch programs which start the instruction in the second language in later grades. There are also partial-immersion programs that use the second language for half of the day and for certain subjects only. Whatever the version, though, children become much more fluent in the second language than do children in more traditional programs. In addition, children in immersion programs benefit from many of the advantages of bilingualism.

Another type of program – the dual-language or two-way immersion program – promotes bilingualism and biliteracy, as well as a very real understanding of the people and cultures involved. Here two languages are used throughout schooling and, what is new, the students come from both language backgrounds. An example of such a program is the Amigos School in Cambridge, Massachusetts. It is open to students of families in which Spanish is the dominant language as well as to students for whom English is the main language. Every student group, or class, has a balance of native-English and native-Spanish speakers. Groups rotate between their English classroom and their Spanish classroom.

What is special about these programs (there are still very few available nation-wide) is that students become literate in two languages, discover the culture of the other language group, interact with speakers of that language and culture, and help one another out. Thus, students who are dominant in one language work with, and help, students dominant in the other language. This allows them to have a better understanding of what it means to be able to help someone who does not understand what is being said and to be helped by someone when you are in the same situation.

Both immersion and dual-language programs are extremely promising approaches as they aim for bilingualism, and in the case of dual-language programs, for biculturalism also. They clearly benefit all those concerned, whatever the culture they come from.

References

Grosjean, F. (2010). Education and bilingualism. Chapter 19 of *Bilingual: Life and Reality*. Cambridge, MA: Harvard University Press.

Baker, C. (2017). *Foundations of Bilingual Education and Bilingualism*. Clevedon, England: Multilingual Matters.

Juan-Garau, M. and Lyster, R. (2019). Becoming bilingual through additive immersive programs. In Annick De Houwer and Lourdes Ortega, eds., *The Cambridge Handbook of Bilingualism.* Cambridge: Cambridge University Press, pp. 213–232.

8.2 PARENTS WHO FIGHT FOR BILINGUAL EDUCATION

(Interview with Fabrice Jaumont)

Groups of parents working with teachers and school officials have helped found dual-language programs in New York public schools. Dr. Fabrice Jaumont tells us about it.

Many of those interested in bilingual education in the United States have been observing the New York area. There, groups of parents working with teachers and school officials have helped found dual-language programs in the public school system. How did they go about it? What were the challenges they had to face? How did they obtain the support they needed? What were the problems they had to solve? Dr. Fabrice Jaumont played a leadership role in this grassroots movement and his book, *The Bilingual Revolution,* describes what happened and gives the necessary ingredients for those who plan to start such a program. He has kindly accepted to answer a few of our questions and we thank him wholeheartedly.

Bilingual education has existed for a long time in the United States, both in private schools and in public schools. In what way is the dual-language educational movement you describe in your book "revolutionary"?

The bilingual revolution that I have directly contributed to over the last twelve years, and that I describe in the book, is led from the bottom up by families who appreciate the value of bilingualism because it is part of their American identity. Although the roots of bilingual education in the United States can be traced back to the seventeenth century, the book shows how this new movement is driven by parents and educators who have founded dual-language programs in public schools.

Like these parents, I am convinced that bilingual education is a universal good that should be offered to all students. These pioneers illustrate how these programs can positively transform a child, a family, a school, a community, and even a country.

In an earlier post, we describe immersion programs as well as dual-language programs.[1] Why is it that you have favored the latter?
I actually like them both! My first encounter with immersion schools was in Massachusetts in the late 1990s. As a native of France, these programs immediately caught my attention because they offered immersive curricula in French, from kindergarten to high school, to children in the United States who did not necessarily have a particular connection to the French language or a French-speaking country.

More importantly, these programs were in public schools, free of charge, and therefore accessible to every student and family. This made a strong impression on me as I witnessed children mastering my own native language, eventually becoming bilingual and biliterate themselves. Now, as the father of two bilingual and bicultural girls who attend a dual-language program in a public school in Brooklyn, I am deeply attached to the concept of dual-language education as a way to both sustain a cultural heritage and acquire a second language.

There are a growing number of dual-language programs created not only to serve English language learners, but also students for whom English is a native language. This can be explained by the overwhelming evidence that educating children in multiple languages offers a competitive advantage in the global economy, boosting not only their foreign language skills but also improving their English reading and comprehension, and even their math skills. These programs concentrate on the advantages of bilingualism for all students involved, regardless of the language skills they come in with.

When did the New York grassroots movement start and what triggered it?
New York City provides the backdrop for my book, where parents have fought for access to various bilingual public school programs from pre-school to high school over decades. Of course, similar programs have developed in hundreds of cities in the United States and around the world. New York has been particularly active on this front since the 1960s. Throughout the Civil Rights era, the Latino community played a pioneering role in calling for bilingual education, not only as a way of educating their children, but also as a means to realize the promise of equal citizenship.

[1] See Post 8.1.

The grassroots movement that I describe in my book is more recent. It started fifteen years ago and is triggered by parents and communities, and their desire to educate their children bilingually. This, in part, can be explained by the fact that more and more people understand and value the unique characteristics of the bilingual brain and person, and will explain how being bilingual can help improve a child's ability to learn, focus, communicate, and understand the world.

How can parents, most of whom are not educators or teachers, become adequate proponents of dual-language programs, all the way from the initial conception to the maintenance of the program once it has started? I wanted the book to be directed toward families, with the goal of providing accessible knowledge, guidance, and encouragement as they consider implementing a dual-language program in their community or school. In that spirit, the book provides a roadmap for parents willing to embark on such an initiative, along with suggested steps to follow, examples, and testimonies from parents and educators who have chosen a similar path.

As such, my book doubles as a "how to" manual for setting up your own dual-language program and, in so doing, launching your own revolution. This is a role I have held for the last ten years, providing tips and resources to many program founders and schools. I felt it was time for me to share this knowledge in a book.

The Bilingual Revolution **describes many real successes but also some failures. Why did some programs fail and what can one learn from them?** Some of these stories illustrate many of the challenges and accomplishments new initiatives can face. Sometimes these group leaders face obstacles in finding a school and maintaining the interest of the parents involved. Sometimes it is a lack of commitment on behalf of the public schools. In many cases, these stories highlight the importance of perseverance for communities and parents invested in their children's education. In my book, I have compiled these trials and errors, and the lessons learned from them in a way that can be both useful and interesting to read.

Your book has been translated into several languages. Is it to get parents in other school systems, in other countries, interested in what you have done? *La Révolution bilingue* is already available in English and French, and there are eight additional translations in Arabic, Chinese, German, Italian,

Japanese, Polish, Russian, and Spanish. The Portuguese version will be added soon. In offering all these, I wanted to reflect the various dual-language programs and linguistic communities that are featured in the book, and to help other communities in the United States and elsewhere to follow in their lead.

Also, for some of these translations, I do hope my book will help raise awareness about the advantages of dual-language education and inspire a few people in other countries to create their own programs.

References

Jaumont, F. (2017). *The Bilingual Revolution: The Future of Education is in Two Languages.* New York, NY: TBR Books.

Juan-Garau, M. and Lyster, R. (2019). Becoming bilingual through additive immersive programs. In Annick De Houwer and Lourdes Ortega, eds., *The Cambridge Handbook of Bilingualism.* Cambridge: Cambridge University Press, pp. 213–232.

8.3 HOW DO WE LEARN LANGUAGES IN THE CLASSROOM AND "IN THE WILD"?

Key differences between second language learning in the classroom and naturalistic learning lie in the memory systems involved, and in the depth and nature of language processing.

Post written by Aneta Pavlenko.

Today, we take it for granted that language immersion, that is, acquiring a language in the context where it is spoken, is beneficial. Yet we rarely ask the more interesting question: What is it about immersion that facilitates second language acquisition?

Psycholinguistic findings suggest that the key differences between second language learning in the classroom and "in the wild" lie in the memory systems involved and in the depth and nature of language processing. Memory is a set of dynamic integrated systems, commonly divided into *implicit* memory that requires little to no conscious awareness and *explicit* memory that encodes our knowledge about the world and is subject to conscious recall.

Foreign language learning in the classroom engages explicit memory, both for memorization of new words and rules and for their conscious recall during classroom activities, quizzes, and tests. The reliance on explicit memory is also supported by patient foreign language teachers who are willing to wait and smile encouragingly, while we hunt for the right word.

Yet even the most superior conscious recall is too slow for everyday interaction – in "the real world," transactions and interactions rely on automatic processes and few people are willing to wait while we fumble to retrieve our new words and order them just so. This pressure, however, gives learning "in the wild" an edge – to fit in, and keep up, naturalistic learners have no choice but to engage the same automatic processes and the same implicit memory that subserve native language use. Such engagement does not guarantee either accuracy or native-likeness, but it does ensure that both learning and retrieval of information rely on the same memory system.

A second advantage of naturalistic learning is in the depth of language processing. Classroom tasks vary widely in the degree to which they engage the learners: some can be accomplished mechanically, while others require only a modicum of attention because they focus on form and not on meaning. Even activities that try to imitate real-life situations are often experienced by students as boring because they do not have any immediate relevance to their lives. Studies in cognitive psychology show that such tasks engage what is known as "shallow" or minimal processing, which results in weak memory traces and substandard retention of the information.

In contrast, outside the classroom, every interaction has meaning and personal relevance, be it banter at a holiday party, an argument over rental property, or even something as simple as getting a falafel sandwich (why am I being asked to repeat my order? was I not clear?). In the absence of predetermined answers, second language conversations force us to pay attention and engage "deep" processing that results in stronger memory traces and superior retention and recall of new information. This standard can be reached only by the best of the classroom tasks, designed with learners' immediate needs and interests in mind.

A third advantage of immersion involves the nature of language processing. Recent discoveries in cognitive science, wonderfully described by Benjamin Bergen in his book *Louder than words*, suggest that we understand language by simulating in our minds what it would be like to experience the things described. This process, called embodied simulation, relies on our mental images and previous experiences and makes use of the same parts of the brain that are dedicated to interacting with the world, with simulation of action, for instance, activating the same part of the brain as direct physical action.

Classroom learning, however, offers few if any opportunities to encode new mental images and experiences that would accompany new words and structures. Instead, learners link new words to their translation equivalents in the native language. Such linking is supported by foreign language textbooks where words are translated and at times illustrated by single pictures of a typical "jacket," "house," or "glass." This approach works well if the words are indeed translation equivalents but it fails when they are not, which is very often the case.

As a result, speakers of English and Russian learning each other's languages in the classroom may misuse everyday words for years, because coats and jackets do not easily map onto the categories *pal'to* (long overcoat), *plashch* (raincoat), *kurtka* (jacket as outerwear), *pidzhak* (men's sportcoat), and *zhaket* (women's suit jacket), while paper and plastic containers we call *stakan* (glass) in Russian are actually *cups* in English.

Naturalistic learning allows you to notice such differences, to generalize the key features across multiple exemplars, and to integrate information from multiple modalities with emotions and autobiographical memories (my teal winter jacket, my black Spanish coat), consolidating memory traces and forming mental images that are more closely aligned with those native speakers rely on.

The differences between the two contexts do not imply, however, that immersion guarantees successful learning by osmosis – it does not. Nor are classroom and naturalistic contexts mutually exclusive – the best results are often achieved by learners who had the advantage of both. Nor would I ever say that one cannot learn a language outside of the context where it is spoken – just look at classicists happily debating the nuances of Ancient Aramaic, and chattering in Latin.

The key lesson to retain is that language requires context – this context can be natural but it can also be created, in part, through books, social media, and especially movies and soap operas that offer plentiful opportunities for embodied simulation.

References

Bergen, B. (2012). *Louder than Words: The New Science of How the Mind Makes Meaning.* New York: Basic Books.
Paradis, M. (2009). *Declarative and Procedural Determinants of Second Languages.* Amsterdam/Philadelphia: John Benjamins.

8.4 WHAT IS TRANSLANGUAGING?

(Interview with Ofelia García)
Many teachers of bilingual children practice translanguaging in the classroom. But what is it exactly and what are its linguistic and cognitive underpinnings?

In the last ten years or so, a new term has appeared in the field of bilingualism, most notably in the area of bilingual education – translanguaging. One of its most visible proponents is Professor Ofelia García of the Graduate Center of the City University of New York. In a 2015 publication with Ricardo Otheguy and Wallis Reid, she defines translanguaging as, "... the deployment of a speaker's full linguistic repertoire without regard for watchful adherence to the socially and politically defined boundaries of named (and usually national and state) languages." Ofelia García has very kindly accepted to answer a few of our questions and we wish to thank her wholeheartedly.

You are a strong defender of allowing bilingual students in school to use their entire language repertoire through translanguaging. You write, "... forbidding bilinguals to translanguage, or assessing it negatively, produces an inaccurate measure of their language proficiency." Can you expand on this a bit?
If we are truly interested in knowing what bilingual students know and what they can do with language, we must separate their ability to use certain forms of one language or another from their ability to use language. For example, in schools, students are asked to find the main idea of a text, to support an argument with text-based evidence, to infer, to make a convincing oral presentation, to work out a math problem. Especially emergent bilingual students may not be able to show that they can do these things if only allowed to use the language legitimized in school. Only by drawing from their entire language repertoire will bilingual students be able to demonstrate what they know, and especially what they can do with language. Being able to perform with language-specific

features legitimized in schools is not the same as having general language ability or being knowledgeable of content.

Translanguaging in the classroom functions well when the children and the teacher share the same minority language. But in many other classrooms, students come from many different language backgrounds. How can translanguaging take place then?
Translanguaging pedagogy requires a different type of teacher, a co-learner. Classrooms are increasingly multilingual in the world. It is impossible for teachers to know all the languages of students. But it is possible for teachers to build a classroom ecology where there are books and signage in multiple languages; where collaborative groupings are constructed according to home language so that students can deeply discuss a text in the dominant school language with all their language resources; where students are allowed to write and speak with whatever resources they have and not wait until they have the "legitimate" ones to develop a voice; where all students' language practices are included so as to work against the linguistic hierarchies that exist in schools; where families with different language practices are included. Any teacher, including a monolingual one, can take up translanguaging to enable their bilingual students to make deeper meaning and legitimize their home language practices.

Given that bilingual students, as they grow older, will increasingly find themselves interacting with monolinguals, especially in their future workplace, should schools also encourage them to "keep to one language" and measure their proficiency at doing so?
Translanguaging leverages the fluid language practices of all bilingual students and communities to learn deeply, while also equipping students to recognize when to use what features for what purposes. Of course schools must develop bilingual students' critical metalinguistic awareness, and their ability to suppress some language features from their repertoire at appropriate times. And schools must give students affordances to perform with only some of their features at times. And teachers must assess what students can do using their entire repertoire of language features, as well as selected ones. Yet, teachers should not evaluate bilingual children's performances using only certain of their language features as being valid performances, and should not compare those performances to those of monolingual children in that language.

Turning to the more linguistic and cognitive aspects of translanguaging, how does the notion that a bilingual is not two monolinguals in one person – something I stressed as early as 1985 – tie in to translanguaging?
Your notion is essential to the concept of translanguaging. Translanguaging is based on Grosjean's idea that bilinguals are not two monolinguals in one. That is why their performances in one or another language cannot be compared to that of monolinguals, since they would then be expected to draw only from less than half of their entire repertoire. This puts bilinguals in an unfair position.

In what way is translanguaging different from interacting with other bilinguals, changing base language freely, translating whenever needed, and intermingling one's languages in the form of codeswitching and borrowing?
There is an epistemological difference between the theoretical position on language contact that has led to the constructs of borrowing, code-switching, calques, language interference, etc., and the concept of translanguaging. Language contact studies start with named languages as categories, and then look across these named categories. Linguists often refer to the behavior of bilinguals when they go across these named language categories as code-switching. It is an external view of language. But translanguaging takes the internal perspective of speakers whose own mental grammar has been developed in social interaction with others. For these bilingual speakers, their language features are simply their own. Translanguaging is more than going across languages; it is going **beyond** named languages and taking the internal view of the speaker's language use.

The linguistic phenomena mentioned in the previous question have been studied by researchers for more than sixty years. What are the benefits of replacing them with "translanguaging" when the behavior is clearly the same?
The behavior may look to be the same from the external social perspective, from a perspective that doesn't question why named languages and language hierarchies exist or the relationship between language and power. But seen from the internal perspective of the bilingual speaker, translanguaging behavior is clearly different. Translanguaging legitimizes the fluid language practices with which bilinguals operate. It posits that bilinguals have a much more complex and expanded repertoire than monolinguals. Bilingual speakers then appropriate all their linguistic features, no matter their social standing, instead of categorizing

them as belonging to one national group or another to which they may
not belong.

**In your 2015 paper with Ricardo Otheguy and Wallis Reid, you state that we
all have our own idiolect – a collection of individual lexical and structural
features – and that there are large areas of overlap among idiolects so that
we can communicate with one another. People call this sharing a language
(e.g. English), something that is psychologically real for them, and yet you
state that language is only a social and political construct, not a lexical or
structural one. Can you explain?**
Linguists can only describe linguistic features, but they cannot say as linguists which features constitute one language or another. The naming of
a language is always a social, political, and economic decision, not
a linguistic one. Thus, it is not true that separate named languages have
linguistic reality. However, it is true that languages are social constructs that
have had very important real and material consequences in the lives of
people, some bad, and some good. This social construction of language also
has an important identity function for groups and individuals that cannot
be denied. But named languages have often been constructed by a process
of standardization that leaves out the practices of minoritized populations.

**Bilinguals, according to you, only have one idiolect made up of more
lexical and structural features than monolinguals and a more complex
socio-cultural marking of which features to use and when. What evidence
do you have, cognitive or neurolinguistic, that bilinguals do not have
separate idiolects, one for each of their languages?**
I am a sociolinguist who has specialized in the education of bilinguals. My
evidence comes from the classrooms and from listening to bilingual
children. From the bilingual eleven-year-old who once told me:
"Spanish runs through my heart, but English rules my veins," concretely
expressing that for him there is one language system that cannot be
separated because otherwise it would lead to his death. From the five-
year-old Spanish speaker who was learning English by repeating after the
teacher, "That tree is grander." From the teacher who tells me that her
young first graders are always talking to themselves in Spanish, even when
working through English. The work of neurolinguists is also beginning to
show that when bilingual speakers perform linguistically, all the features
of their repertoire are activated and available, even though speakers
selectively suppress some features depending on the communicative
situation in which they find themselves.

References

García, O. (2009). *Bilingual Education in the 21st Century: A Global Perspective.* Malden, MA and Oxford: Blackwell/Wiley.

Otheguy, R., García, O., and Reid, W. (2015). Clarifying translanguaging and deconstructing named languages: A perspective from linguistics. *Applied Linguistics Review,* 6(3), 281–307.

8.5 FOREIGN LANGUAGE LEARNING IS LIKE DATING: IT SPURS ANXIETY

Anxiety and embarrassment are often seen as a detriment to success in foreign language learning but recent studies hint that small doses of anxiety don't hurt. Post written by Aneta Pavlenko.

Learning a foreign language is a bit like dating: your tongue is tied in knots, as you tiptoe anxiously around the object of your desire, afraid that the smallest transgression could incur enormous costs. In affairs of the heart, this anxiety may be helpful, making you bite your tongue just as you are about to mention the previous love of your life. But what about speaking a foreign language, where habits of the tongue are not as easy to control? In her book, *Lost in Translation,* Polish–English bilingual Eva Hoffman (see Post 14.10) offers a compelling description of frustrations and loss of face that accompany such communication:

> . . . it takes all my will to impose any control on the words that emerge from me. I have to form entire sentences before uttering them; otherwise, I too easily get lost in the middle. My speech, I sense, sounds monotonous, deliberate, heavy – an aural mask that doesn't become or express me at all. . . . I don't try to tell jokes too often, I don't know the slang, I have no cool repartee. I love language too much to maul its beats, and my pride is too quick to risk the incomprehension that greets such forays. I become a very serious young person . . . I am enraged at the false persona I'm being stuffed into, as into some clumsy and overblown astronaut suit. (pp. 118–119).

Psychologists studying language learning and use distinguish between two main types of anxiety – trait and state. Trait anxiety is a personality attribute exhibited in persistent and sometimes unrealistic worry about mundane things. This pervasive worry also underpins many excuses we come up with to avoid foreign language learning and use: "I am not good at languages," "I am too old to learn a new language," "My memory is poor," "I do not have a good ear for languages," "I have forgotten everything I learned," and so on.

The other type, state anxiety, is experienced by all of us, triggered by a job interview, a visit to the dentist, a conference presentation, or a particularly hard test. Communication in a foreign language – especially one in which we have limited competence – is one such situation. Foreign language anxiety, in this view, involves fears and apprehensions of goofy slips, silly errors, and mortifying stumbling and mumbling that trigger sweating, shaking, and palpitations, and permanently tie our tongues: "I will sound dim-witted," "Everyone will laugh at me," "I am really ashamed of how poorly I know the language I ought to know much better by now," etc.

To understand the effects of anxiety on language learning and use, University of London professor Jean-Marc Dewaele and his colleagues analyzed responses to foreign language anxiety questionnaires. Their results revealed several groups particularly affected by foreign language fright, including girls, perfectionists, and introverts. Girls experience – or at least report experiencing – foreign language anxiety more intensely than boys. Perfectionists may set impossibly high performance standards and then feel debilitating anxieties that lead them to procrastinate and put off angst-inducing tasks. As for quiet and reserved introverts, they may outperform everyone else on pen-and-pencil tasks but become tongue-tied when required to speak.

At the other end of the anxiety spectrum are a few lucky extroverts who fearlessly ask for directions, order meals, and make jokes using a vocabulary of a dozen words. Their exploits show that anxiety also colors our perceptions of how good we are: highly anxious speakers tend to underestimate their language competence, and speakers with low levels of anxiety tend to overestimate it. Research findings also show that some types of foreign language communication are more anxiety-provoking than others. Talking on the phone or speaking with strangers stirs more worries than communication in the same language with friends.

The angst is not limited to the second language (L2). In a study with Turkish immigrants in the Netherlands, Yeşim Sevinç and Jean-Marc

Dewaele found that some immigrants may experience anxiety in the slowly deteriorating or incompletely acquired first language (L1) and the non-native L2. These findings suggest that at the heart of anxiety is not the situation itself but our perception of it: if we think that we should have a better mastery of a particular language, we may become tongue tied out of shame and guilt. Future studies in highly multilingual contexts may add an additional twist: foreign language anxiety may turn out to be a uniquely Western construct, triggered by the unrealistic monolingual or native-like standard.

Yet not all is doom and gloom. When they expanded the scope of their studies, Dewaele and his team found that many learners experience both anxiety and enjoyment, and that, in small doses, anxiety doesn't hurt language learning, as it focuses our attention on the task at hand. The key is to articulate realistic expectations and to strike a constructive balance between foreign language anxiety and positive emotions intrinsic in language learning, including pride in one's achievements, excitement about new challenges, and confidence that comes with practice.

References

Dewaele, J.-M., MacIntyre, P., Boudreau, C., and Dewaele L. (2016). Do girls have all the fun? Anxiety and enjoyment in the foreign language classroom. *Theory and Practice of Second Language Acquisition*, 2(1), 41–63.

Hoffman, E. (1989) *Lost in Translation: A Life in a New Language*. London/New York: Penguin Books.

Sevinç, Y. and Dewaele, J.-M. (2016). Heritage language anxiety and majority language anxiety among Turkish immigrants in the Netherlands. *The International Journal of Bilingualism*, DOI: 10.1177/1367006916661635.

8.6 CAN A SECOND LANGUAGE HELP YOU LEARN A THIRD?

What role does your second language play in the process of third-language learning? Is it an asset that facilitates and speeds up the process or is it an obstacle that interferes and slows it down?

Post written by Aneta Pavlenko.

As bilinguals, one of our greatest hopes is that the efforts we have invested in learning a second language (L2) will also pay off when we learn the third one (L3). The more languages we know, the easier it should be to learn them, right? A positive answer to this question can have tremendous implications for language education. And yet researchers limit themselves instead to the non-committal "it depends." Why is that? And what does our success in L3 learning depend on?

The first undeniable advantage involves strategy. If you learned your L2 as a teenager or an adult, you have managed to figure out what strategies work best for you. The more extroverted among us enjoy talking to target language speakers, while the introverts prefer to pore over textbooks and grammar books. I, for one, am an avid reader and foreign movie watcher, always hoping that new words will find their way into my memory effortlessly, in the process known as incidental learning. Research also shows that learners who are literate in both of their languages, and those who have metalinguistic knowledge, are in a particularly advantageous position because, among other things, metalinguistic awareness allows them to make comparisons and generate creative hypotheses.

Another area of potential advantage involves cross-linguistic similarities: learning a language typologically similar to the language or languages we already know allows us to utilize our prior knowledge through the process known as positive transfer or reliance on already familiar sounds, words, and grammatical categories. Unfortunately, not all of the similarities we perceive are real. Sometimes, our interlingual connections are erroneous, leading to what is known as negative transfer, which includes, for example, our reliance on false cognates, or *faux amis* (see Posts 3.7 and 3.8). It was such superficial similarity between the Spanish word *embarazada* (pregnant) and the English embarrassed that led the marketing people at Parker Pen to enter the Mexican market with a bold slogan: "*No te embarazará chorreándose en tu bolsillo*" (It won't impregnate you by leaking in your pocket).

And here is where it becomes interesting when a third language is concerned. We know that our first language (L1) affects the process of learning other languages, but we do not always expect that our L2 also wants to play an active role in the learning of L3. Yet this is precisely what happens and it is the influence from L2 Spanish that leads English-speakers learning L3 Italian to produce forms like *aiudarono* (helped, a blend of L2 Spanish *ayudaron* and L3 Italian *aiutarono*) or *uccido* (killed, a blend of L3 Italian *ucciso* and an L2 Spanish past participle *–ido*).

But then again it shouldn't really come as a surprise that there is an interaction between typologically related languages. My own Spanish mercilessly interferes with my Italian, while Polish and Russian emerge, uninvited, every time I try to speak Ukrainian. While inconvenient, this is hardly surprising. What is utterly counterintuitive is to see a typologically distant L2 (e.g., French) actively interfere with the L3 (e.g., German), as in the case of an English speaker who asked his German colleague in L3 German: ***Tu as** mein Fax bekommen?* (Did you [Fr] get my fax [G]?). The replacement of the L3 German *Du hast* with the similarly sounding French *Tu as* caught them both by surprise yet this is exactly what happens time and again – the previously learned foreign language suddenly pops out. Such interference, dubbed a foreign language effect, is so frequent that it may lead us to suspect that our brain has a separate section for all languages learned later in life.

Studies using neuroimaging techniques suggest that this is not the case. Rather, it appears that language processing is not restricted to single sites in the brain but spread across various parts. In addition, the same areas subserve different languages of multilingual speakers. The only difference is that the use of the native or the dominant language is optimized and thus more automatic, and the use of other languages requires more cognitive resources. The shared representation, in turn, means that all languages are connected in the multilingual mind. Like our second language, our native language does not remain an independent observer in the process of L3 learning. Instead, it influences it, through both positive and negative transfer, in ways that are sometimes subtle and at other times pretty visible, as we have just seen. Our L1 may even team up with the L2 in messing with our L3. And our first language is not immune from influences either, as experienced by the English speaker who upon returning from a short, two-week, trip to Germany joyfully informed his friends that He had *drinken* many beers (although, in this case, we may also be seeing a beer effect).

All in all, we should probably expect that the effects of the previous languages on L3 learning will be diverse. On the one hand, we come to the learning process as more experienced and better-equipped learners but, on the other, our languages are not immune to playing tricks on us. The best we can do is to relax and enjoy the learning process, as well as appreciate the insights we invariably gain about our languages and ourselves.

References

De Angelis, G. (2007). *Third or Additional Language Acquisition.* Clevedon, UK: Multilingual Matters.
De Bot, K. and Jaensch, C. (2015). What is special about L3 processing? *Bilingualism: Language and Cognition,* 18(2), 130–144.

8.7 DO MUSICIANS MAKE BETTER LANGUAGE LEARNERS?

Do people with musical training have an easier time learning foreign languages? Or is it the other way around and it is our language experience that makes us better musicians?

Post written by Aneta Pavlenko.

YouTube videos and Wikipedia's lists of famous multilinguals usually include singers who perform in several languages, like the Russian soprano Anna Netrebko (Russian, Italian, French, German, English, Czech), Italian tenor Andrea Bocelli (Italian, Spanish, English, Latin, German), and Colombian phenomenon Shakira (Spanish, English, Portuguese, Arabic, French, German). Their communicative abilities in these languages vary greatly, from native and native-like to just a few words, but when they sing these words they sound quite impressive to their fans.

These singers, as well as musicians like the cellist Yo-Yo Ma (Chinese, French, English), provide grist for the mill for those who believe that people with musical talent – or at least musical training – have an easier time learning foreign languages. Common sense suggests that years of paying close attention to pitch and rhythm give musicians a leg up. Their fine-tuned ears must be better at picking out sound patterns of the second language (L2) and the advantage in perception should trans-late into superior pronunciation. But before we start separating music majors into special sections of foreign language classes, let's see what research has to say about brain connections between music and language.

Neuropsychological studies show that music and language are represented in distinct areas of the brain, indicating thereby that the link between musical ability and second language learning is not as direct as one would think. Additional evidence of separation comes from cases of selective impairments, that is, people with language impairments, such as aphasia, who retain their musical skills, and individuals with intact linguistic skills who lose their musical abilities. These differences in cortical representation do not tell the whole story, however, because music and language do rely on common – or at least similar – processes: detection of differences in pitch, meter, rhythm, phrasing and interpretation, tonal memory, memory for long sequences, and the ability to imitate and improvise based on familiar sequences. These similarities led researchers to ask two questions: Are abilities in one domain easily transferred to another? And are musicians better L2 learners than the rest of us?

To answer these questions, researchers turned to languages that differ in the uses of pitch or perceived frequency of vibration. Pitch is central in music, where one greatly envied and admired gift is absolute pitch, that is, the ability to identify and recreate musical notes without the use of a reference tone. Pitch is also central in language, revealing the meaning of utterances (question or statement? angry or ironic?). Tone languages also rely on pitch to differentiate between meanings of similar-sounding words. In Mandarin Chinese, for instance, "ma" could mean "mother," "hemp," "horse," or "scold" depending on the accompanying tone. The tone system is extremely challenging for speakers of English who habitually pay attention to pitch height and never to pitch contours of individual words (a change of pitch in English can transform the word "book" from a statement into a question but it cannot make it mean "horse").

To see how musical ability affects the learning of L2 Mandarin by L1 English speakers, Anita Bowles and her colleagues asked 160 native speakers of English to learn a small lexicon of Mandarin pseudo-words by listening to recordings. The challenging aspect of the task was the fact that the words were similar in sound but different in tone and therefore in meanings, and participants had to acquire not just sound-meaning but sound-tone-meaning correspondences. The participants also completed a questionnaire about their musical experiences and undertook a battery of cognitive tests that measured pitch perception, auditory memory, musical aptitude, general cognitive ability, and general L2 aptitude. The results revealed that months of private music lessons were a better predictor of the accuracy of tonal word learning than general cognitive ability and L2 aptitude measures.

These findings were corroborated by other studies where English-, French-, and Italian-speaking musicians outperformed non-musicians in identifying Mandarin tones, yet the findings by Bowles and colleagues also had a twist – on the whole, musical variables were not a powerful predictor. The key predictor – not surprisingly – was success on linguistic tasks involving tone discrimination (same or different). The correlation between these tasks and musical training could arise, in the researchers' opinion, because musical training enhances pitch ability and/or because people with high levels of pitch ability gravitate toward musical training. Other than a minor advantage in discriminating tones, however, there does not appear to be any conclusive evidence that musicians are better at L2 learning or have superior pronunciation skills.

Diana Deutsch and her colleagues suggested that the question should perhaps be turned around, asking whether speakers of tonal languages have superior sensitivity to pitch. To test their hypothesis, Deutsch and her colleagues asked speakers of two tonal languages, Vietnamese and Mandarin, and speakers of English to read aloud lists of words in their native languages on two different days. The analysis of pitch revealed that native speakers of Vietnamese and Mandarin maintained precise and stable pitch in enunciating words, while English speakers were significantly less consistent on different days. Follow-up studies found that speakers of tonal languages were better at identifying musical pitches than speakers of English or French and more likely to have absolute pitch.

So where do we stand on the relationship between music and language? We certainly should not jump to the conclusion that speakers of tonal languages make better musicians. There is more to musical talent than sensitivity to pitch – not every speaker of Chinese becomes a Yo-Yo Ma. By the same token, not every musician is a polyglot – there is much more to L2 learning than tonal discrimination and when it comes to syntax, vocabulary, or pragmatics, musicians have no advantage over the rest of us. Yo-Yo Ma is trilingual because he was born to a Chinese family in Paris and grew up in New York, while opera singers put years of hard work into learning foreign language diction.

This is not to say that music is not useful in learning a language. The most widely accessible tool – songs – help L2 learners acquire new patterns of stress and rhythm, strengthen pronunciation skills, and make an emotional connection to the language of choice. Many learners owe their success to listening or even singing along with popular songs. This strategy can be used by everyone – including those with a deaf ear for music.

References

Bowles, A., Chang, C., and Karuzis, V. (2016). Pitch ability as an aptitude for tone learning. *Language Learning*, 66(4), 774–808.

Deutsch, D., Henthorn, T., and Dolson M. (2004). Absolute pitch, speech, and tone language: Some experiments and a proposed framework. *Music Perception: An Interdisciplinary Journal*, 21(3), 339–356.

Zeromskaite, I. (2014). The potential role of music in second language learning: A review article. *Journal of European Psychology Students*, 5(3), 78–88. DOI: http://dx.doi.org/10.5334/jeps.ci

8.8 THE SECRETS OF A SUCCESSFUL LANGUAGE LEARNER

(Interview with William Fierman)

What are the secrets of successful language learners? What strategies do they use? Professor William Fierman answers questions about his unusual multilingualism.

Interview conducted by Aneta Pavlenko.

Our guest today is William Fierman, an Emeritus Professor of Central Eurasian Studies at the University of Indiana in Bloomington and an expert on language policies in Central Asia. Bill, could you please tell us a little about your language-learning history?

I grew up in a St. Louis suburb where I had the good fortune to study Russian in junior high and Chinese in high school. While in high school I spent two months on an exchange in Brazil, living in a family with no English speakers, and learned some Portuguese. Later, I improved my knowledge of Portuguese by studying in a school for foreign students in Lisbon. I got a Bachelor's degree in Russian and Chinese. Then, I began to study Uzbek on my own in preparation for a dissertation on Soviet language policy. I have since studied Kazakh and can read several other Turkic languages. I learned a lot of Czech while living with a family a couple of months in Prague. Fairly recently I tried learning Hungarian and reached a point where I could communicate about everyday matters. But I was vanquished by that language and gave up.

I am absolutely amazed by the variety of your languages and the levels of proficiency you manage to achieve. You are one of the few non-Russians with whom I correspond in Russian and your mastery of colloquial Russian is such that I often forget that my interlocutor is not a native speaker, in linguistic terms. What brought you to Russian and how did you get to be so native-like?
When in junior high school I had to choose one of five languages to study; my parents told me to select any language *except* Russian. Russia fascinated me though because it seemed so remote. I was a highly motivated student and I had absolutely fabulous language instructors both in the United States and Leningrad (now St. Petersburg), where I studied for one semester. In the mid-1970s, I also lived for a year in Tashkent. Some of my closest friends have been native Russian speakers.

Our colleagues in Kazakhstan tell me that your Kazakh is equally impressive and you are famous there as the American who lectures in Kazakh. Why Kazakh?
As noted above, I started with Uzbek as a graduate student. However, after the USSR's demise, I began to focus more on language policy in Kazakhstan. It is a more important political issue there than in Uzbekistan and it is relatively easy for an American scholar to work in Kazakhstan. Even Russian-dominant Kazakhs are thrilled to meet an American who can speak "their language." So there has always been great positive reinforcement.

What do you see as the key differences in ways in which multilingualism is treated in Kazakhstan and the United States?
There are many differences. Most important, though: the dominant and unofficial state language of the United States is a world language, whereas Kazakhstan has a state language that is quite weak. So there is widespread knowledge of another language, Russian. Most of the population of Kazakhstan knows at least two languages, whereas most US citizens are monolingual.

What are your favorite language learning strategies and do they differ across languages?
They do differ. It depends on my goals for the language, as well as availability of teachers/informants, and of instructional and other

materials. Much of my learning has been without a teacher, sometimes even without an easily accessible informant. I like to immerse myself in speech or texts for a language I am learning, even if I do not understand everything. Then I like to go back (especially with texts) to figure out everything I can with a dictionary and, if possible, a native speaker. I force myself (I can't say I enjoy it) to read or listen to "deciphered" texts over and over, thinking in the language. Eventually I begin to use some of those words and constructions in speech or writing. I use flashcards for vocabulary but do not find translation exercises helpful. I read every foreign language public sign and listen to public announcements, trying to figure them out. I love working with a native informant in learning a new language, discovering I can make myself understood.

I use languages I know better to learn new ones, especially in acquiring reading and listening skills. I have used this approach with Turkic languages (building on Uzbek), Portuguese (for Spanish), Czech (for Polish), and now I am learning to read Ukrainian by using online translators to see Russian equivalents. The problem with this approach is that if I try to speak or write in the "new" language acquired this way (which for me is the case most often with Turkic languages), I am plagued by interference.

What are your future plans in terms of language learning?
I want to learn to read Ukrainian, maybe Belorussian, too. I'm always trying to improve my Turkic language (especially reading) skills. I am working on Azerbaijani and then plan to make the short jump to Turkish. Then I want to return to Tajik – a non-Turkic language, form of Farsi, but sharing much common vocabulary with Uzbek and Azerbaijani.

Thank you, Bill, for sharing your experiences and good luck with your new language-learning adventures!

8.9 THE DARK SIDE OF THE RECENT POLYGLOT HYPE

The recent media surge of interest in polyglots is a positive development but it has a darker side: by differentiating between "regular" multilinguals and polyglots, journalists trivialize the complexity of the language-learning process. To see if there is a difference between the two, we turn to Cleopatra, the celebrated polyglot of antiquity.

Post written by Aneta Pavlenko.

In his book *The World until Yesterday,* Jared Diamond recalls an evening in Papua New Guinea when he went around the campfire circle asking members of different tribes how many languages they speak. The smallest number of languages anyone spoke was five, several people spoke eight to twelve languages, and the champion spoke fifteen. And these were mutually unintelligible languages, belonging to different families! Now, does this mean that all New Guineans – or at least the ones around the campfire – have unique language abilities? Are they polyglots? Or is there a fine line, separating multilinguals from polyglots?

And if there is such a line, where should we place that celebrated polyglot of antiquity, Cleopatra VII, who, according to Plutarch, easily passed from one language to another in her melodic voice, and rarely needed an interpreter to speak to the representatives of barbarian nations: "to most of them she spoke herself, as to the Aethiopians, Troglodytes, Hebrews, Arabians, Syrians, Medes, Parthians, and many others, whose language she had learnt" (Plutarch, *Antony*, p. 497). And what about the famous explorer of antiquity, Heinrich Schliemann, who boasted of more than twenty languages, including ancient Greek?

Lately, the media has shown a heightened interest in polyglots, with numerous articles, blog posts, and even a book, *Babel No More,* dedicated to people who speak multiple languages. Diamond and Plutarch allow us to reevaluate this trend, with an eye on who writes these reports, for whom, and to what effect. One thread that links many reports involves authorship: they are usually written by journalists who, by their own admission, are monolingual English speakers or have English and a modicum of Spanish or French. As a result, they are more likely to be impressed by the rapid barrage of foreign words, to mistake speed for fluency, and to buy into the speaker's own descriptions of their abilities, without picking up on the limitations and inconsistencies.

Now, far be it from me to say that monolinguals should not write about multilingualism. My concern is about reports that describe people who can learn dozens of languages "rapidly" and speak them "fluently," without a solid basis for such descriptions, not unlike Plutarch's second-hand portrayal of Cleopatra. This is all the more pertinent because, at closer inspection, some self-reports turn out to be greatly exaggerated, including Schliemann's – classics experts who examined his ancient Greek writing found it to be truly appalling.

The second thread that unites many reports is selective portrayal. The polyglots featured by the media are usually Westerners. Missing from the picture are Cameroonians, New Guineans, and many others, for whom everyday interaction in multiple languages is the norm, or even classicists who work in, but do not necessarily "speak," their "dead" languages and who are among the most impressively multilingual people I have ever met.[2]

On the face of it, there are good reasons to focus on "exceptional" learners – their stories of learning languages for pure love and "against all odds" are more dramatic and exciting. They also allow journalists to speculate on the elusive and mysterious language talent – aka language aptitude or the secret of the multilingual brain – that could explain why some people have an easier time learning languages. But what is the secret? Is it prodigious memory or the skills of immediate pattern recognition? Or maybe it is a uniquely tuned ear or a nimble tongue that easily mimics foreign sounds? Or, perhaps, it is a chameleon-like ability to dispense with all inhibitions and become someone else, if only for a moment?

Alas, the reports come short on substance, because different polyglots have different abilities and go about language learning in different ways, using strategies that match the unique circumstances and preferences of each learner: some pour over books and grammars, others favor listening to songs and movies, and yet others prefer to learn by speaking and making new friends. But then again, this is what multilinguals do as well, isn't it? (See the preceding post on this.)

Perhaps, the only difference between multilinguals and polyglots is that the latter spend their time studying languages they do not need for everyday practical purposes. In this they may be akin to amateur

---

[2] See Aneta Pavlenko's blog post on a multilingual archeologist, Rachel Mairs: www
.psychologytoday.com/intl/blog/life-bilingual/201812/what-does-it-mean-be-
multilingual-archeologist

musicians who learn to play dozens of musical instruments. Interestingly, we do not see reports on such musicians – even though they undoubtedly exist and have valuable knowledge and expertise – because we know that the end result still lands them quite far from Yo-Yo Ma.

I have no doubt that the journalists writing about polyglots mean well: they want to inspire and maybe even shame us a little into learning the language we always wanted to speak. But by differentiating between "regular" multilinguals and polyglots – extraordinary learners with unique abilities – the polyglot hype trivializes the complexity of the language learning process, obscures the amount of time and effort necessary to master a language, detracts from the normativity of multilingualism in many places around the world, and reinforces the very monolingual norms it purports to challenge. At the end, it gives the readers a sense that without an aptitude for languages they should not even try.

And as to Cleopatra, Plutarch's description gives us a good sense of where she falls in the multilingual–polyglot dichotomy and why he found her achievements worthy of reporting: they were "all the more surprising because most of the kings, her predecessors, scarcely gave themselves the trouble to acquire the Egyptian tongue" (p. 497). In other words, Cleopatra was not a collector of languages but a multilingual ruler who used her knowledge – whatever it was – strategically, to differentiate herself from the other Ptolemies and to enhance her royal prestige.

References

Diamond, J. (2012). *The World until Yesterday: What we Can Learn from Traditional Societies.* New York: Penguin Random House.

Erard, M. (2012). *Babel no More: The Search for the World's Most Extraordinary Language Learners.* New York: Free Press.

Laes, C. (2013). Polyglots in Roman Antiquity: Writing Socio-cultural History Based on Anecdotes. *Literatūra,* 55(3), 7–26.

Plutarch's Lives, volume II. (1992). The Dryden Translation, edited by Arthur Hugh Clough. New York: the Modern Library.

9

Biculturalism and Personality

INTRODUCTION

Many bilinguals are also bicultural, but we know much less about biculturalism than we do about bilingualism. This chapter attempts to make up for this in part.

Post 9.1 gives an overview of what it means to be bicultural, evokes cultural dominance, and explains how bicultural people navigate a situational continuum that requires different types of behavior.

Posts 9.2 and 9.3 concern the identity quest of bicultural bilinguals. In Post 9.2, the process by which biculturals come to terms with their own identity is explained. This may require them to identify with only one culture, with none or, preferably, with all. And in Post 9.3, an author, Dr. Julie Choi, talks about the ambiguity and vulnerability of a multilingual and multicultural existence, and the pros that outweigh the cons.

Post 9.4 concerns a dimension of becoming bicultural, that of discovering hidden aspects of the host culture that you have to be introduced to. In it, I relate how my family and I discovered Thanksgiving by first being invited to the celebration by an American family. Then, over the years, we made it into a family event.

Post 9.5 is a personal reflection on how I have become a mosaic of the four cultures I have lived in, and how I keep them alive within me. It is easier to do so in this day and age than it used to be before.

Post 9.6 concerns the many advantages of being bicultural and describes a study that shows that biculturals appear to have greater creativity and professional success. This is accounted for by a psychological mechanism known as integrative complexity.

The last three posts concern the longstanding belief that bicultural bilinguals change their personality when they change language. In Post 9.7, this is developed and it is argued that there is, in fact, no direct causal relationship between language and personality. In Post 9.8, some of the comments to the first post received are discussed, and then a study is described that seems to show that we are not all aware to the same extent that we may be different when we change language.

Finally, in Post 9.9, which was written several years after the first two, the change of language, change of personality myth is put to rest by showing that within just one language, people also modulate their personality to fit the social situations they are in. Thus, it is the environment, the culture, and the interlocutors that cause bilinguals to adapt their attitudes, feelings, and behaviors (along with language) – and not their languages as such.

9.1 HOW CULTURES COMBINE AND BLEND IN A PERSON

Many people are both bilingual and bicultural and yet we know much more about bilingualism than about biculturalism. This is unfortunate as biculturalism permeates every aspect of one's being and one's behavior.

Bicultural people are characterized by at least three traits. First, they take part, to varying degrees, in the life of two or more cultures. Second, they adapt, at least in part, their attitudes, behaviors, values, etc., to these cultures. And third, they combine and blend aspects of the cultures involved. Certain characteristics come from one or the other culture whereas others are blends based on these cultures.

Thus, contrary to bilingualism where it is possible to deactivate a language and only use the other in particular situations (at least to a very great extent; see Post 3.7), biculturals cannot always deactivate certain traits of their other culture(s) when in a monocultural environment. A Colombian–American bicultural, for example, blends aspects of both the Colombian and the American culture, and this often comes through in both a Colombian and an American environment, however hard the person tries to adapt fully to the one or the other situation.

Contrary to general belief, bilingualism and biculturalism do not always go hand in hand. People can be bilingual without being bicultural (think of Europeans who use two or more languages in their everyday lives but who live in only one country and within one culture), and people can be bicultural without being bilingual (such as British expatriates who have lived in the United States for many years). But of course, many bilinguals are also bicultural; they use two or more languages in their everyday lives and they navigate within and between their different cultures.

People can become bicultural at different points in time. Children can be born within bicultural families or come into contact with a second culture outside their home or in school; adolescents may pursue their studies in another culture; and many adults emigrate to other regions or countries and slowly acculturate into their new culture.

Cultures rarely have exactly the same importance for bicultural people; one culture often plays a larger role leading to cultural dominance (similar to language dominance in bilinguals). In addition, cultures can wax and wane in one's lifetime, become dominant for a while before taking a secondary role later on, and vice versa.

Bicultural people navigate along a situational continuum that requires different types of behavior: at one end they are in a monocultural mode since they are primarily with monoculturals. Here they usually deactivate as best they can their other culture(s). If their knowledge of the culture in question is adequate, and the deactivation is sufficient, then they can behave in a monocultural way (e.g. hold a meeting according to the rules of that culture, deal with monocultural business partners, welcome acquaintances, etc.).

However, because of the blending component in biculturalism, certain attitudes, behaviors, feelings, etc., may not be totally monocultural. For example, biculturals often produce blends in their greeting behaviors such as when shaking hands with someone (how firm the handshake? at the beginning and at the end of the encounter?), greeting a woman friend with a kiss (who exactly? how many kisses?), and so on. Cultural blends can also be observed in hand gestures, the amount of space to leave between yourself and others, what one talks about, etc.

At the other end of the situational continuum, bicultural people are in a bicultural mode since they are with other biculturals who share their cultures. They use a base culture to interact in and bring in the other culture, in the form of cultural switches and borrowings, when they choose to.

Bilingualism expert, Aneta Pavlenko, gave me an example of Russian–American teenagers in Philadelphia who may spend Friday evening with their families laughing over a popular Soviet-era comedy and then go out on Sunday night together to see a new Hollywood blockbuster. They'll chat about the movie in English but slip in a few Russian adjectives or a reference to a popular character from a Russian movie.

Biculturals often say that life is easier when they are with other people with the same bicultural background as them. They can relax and do not have to worry about getting things right all the time. They often state that their good friends (or dream partners) are people like them, with whom they can be totally at ease about their languages and their cultures.

References

Grosjean, F. (2008). The bicultural person: A short introduction. Chapter 12 of *Studying Bilinguals*. Oxford: Oxford University Press.
Nguyen, A-M. and Benet-Martinez, V. (2007). Biculturalism unpacked: Components, measurement, individual differences, and outcomes. *Social and Personality Psychology Compass*, 1, 101–114.

9.2 WHO AM I? THE IDENTITY QUEST OF BICULTURAL BILINGUALS

Those people who are both bilingual and bicultural have to come to terms with their own identity. Reaching the point of accepting fully one's biculturalism can be for some a long and challenging process.

In addition to navigating within and between their cultures (see the post above), biculturals have to come to terms with their own identity. To be able to reach the point of saying, "I am bicultural, a member of *both* culture A *and* culture B," biculturals may have to go through a long and challenging process[1].

First, biculturals have to take into account how they are perceived by members of each of their cultures. The latter base themselves on such

---

[1] Note that in what follows we will limit our discussion to two major cultures but what is said also applies to people who belong to three or more cultures. See also the next post.

factors as kinship, language, physical appearance, nationality, education, attitudes, and so on. The outcome may be similar (X is judged to be a member of culture A by all concerned) or contradictory (X is seen as belonging to culture A by members of culture B and vice versa). Rarely do biculturals receive the message that they are *both* A *and* B.

Faced with this double categorization, biculturals have to reach a decision as to their own cultural identity. They take into account how they are perceived and they bring in other factors such as their personal history, their identity needs, their knowledge of the languages and cultures involved, the country they live in, and so on. The possible outcomes are to identify solely with culture A, solely with culture B, with neither culture A nor culture B, or with both culture A and culture B.

Although sometimes necessary, the first three solutions may not be satisfactory in the long run as they do not reflect the fact that biculturals have roots in two or more cultures. They may regret at some point having turned away from one of their cultures or, if they have rejected both cultures, they may feel ambivalent about who they are.

Paul Preston interviewed a number of hearing adults whose parents are Deaf and who grew up in the hearing and in the deaf worlds. Many expressed the feeling that they did not belong to either world. Here is how one of them expressed this: "I always felt like I didn't belong either place. I didn't belong with the deaf 100 per cent and I didn't belong with the hearing. I didn't feel comfortable with (the) hearing. I felt more comfortable with (the) deaf but I knew I wasn't deaf."

The fourth outcome, identifying with both cultures A and B, is the optimal solution since bicultural people live their lives in two or more cultures even if one culture is dominant. Those who have the chance of belonging to established bicultural groups such as Mexican Americans, Italian Americans, and so on, find support among their members. The writer Veronica Chambers relates how she progressively discovered her dual identity group in Panama among the Afro-Antillanos: "I was thrilled to learn there was actually a society for people like me."

For isolated biculturals, the process of identifying with both cultures and admitting that one is indeed bicultural may take time. The Franco-British journalist and writer, Olivier Todd, spent most of his life searching for his dual identity after philosopher and writer Jean-Paul Sartre told him that his problem was that he was divided between England and France. I had the pleasure of meeting him a few years ago and I asked him about his biculturalism. I stressed the fact that one could be both A and B even if one culture is dominant. After a long silence he admitted that I was right and that he was indeed bicultural, although he was reluctant to adopt the word "bicultural."

Bicultural people are invaluable in today's world since they are bridges between the cultures they belong to. They act as intermediaries between the two and they can explain one culture to members of the other. As Phil, one of Paul Preston's interviewees said, "We can see both sides because we're on both sides."

References

Preston, P. (1995). *Mother Father Deaf.* Cambridge, MA: Harvard University Press.
LaFromboise, T., Coleman, H., and Gerton, J. (1993). Psychological impact of biculturalism: Evidence and theory. *Psychological Bulletin,* 114, 395–412.

9.3 A MULTIVOCAL SELF: A MULTICULTURAL MULTILINGUAL SPEAKS[2]

(Interview with Julie Choi)

Dr. Julie Choi of the University of Melbourne, author of "Creating a multivocal self," talks about the ambiguity and vulnerability of multilingual existence and the pros that outweigh the cons.

Interview conducted by Aneta Pavlenko.

Would you please introduce yourself to our readers and say a few words about yourself and your languages?

I am a lecturer in Education specializing in English language teacher education at the Melbourne Graduate School of Education in Australia. I was born and raised in New York, living largely within a Korean–American community and speaking Korean (with my family), English (in school), and

[2] The original post was entitled, "A multivocal self."

Konglish, that is, Korean filled with English loanwords, with other Korean–American friends. I left New York some time ago and I don't quite see myself as American nor do I necessarily think of myself as Korean even though this is my ancestral background and I have strong familial ties to Korean.

I have spent equal numbers of years in Beijing and Tokyo being completely immersed in the languages and local and expat cultures but I never felt that I developed a meaningful identity in Chinese as I did in Japanese. My Korean acquaintances gasp in horror when I say this but my Japanese is much more fluent and "grown-up" than my Korean in all of the macro skill areas because I learned it formally in school and through work. I have a history in all of these labels, languages, and places, but I don't have any strong attachments to any of them.

What prompted you to write a book about your own multilingualism?
I've been keeping a diary since I was a little girl. When I started working on my Master's thesis, I found research related to growing up in multiple languages. What researchers could see and say about their participants' multilingual identities was fascinating, rich, and valuable for me to read as a grad student but I felt there was a gap – I wanted to hear how multilinguals themselves make sense of their lives through research practices. I wondered how one would do that kind of work in academia.

So I started to piece entries together in my Master's thesis using narrative methods. At the end of that journey I was left with many more questions about diaries, materials that kept falling out of the diaries (e.g. letters, pictures, cards, teachers' notes, etc.), and how we come to make sense of our linguistic and cultural identities and realities. I wanted to rewrite my thesis (my life) with more critical insights so I decided to continue pursuing this area further in a PhD using autoethnography. The product of this ten-year journey is this book.

You begin your book with a fascinating story of the many names you had in English, Korean, Chinese, and Japanese. Do all of these names refer to the same person?
I think they do, although the people using these names may have a very particular view of me. For instance, my name Juri when used by my family embodies me with my position and history as the youngest sister, daughter, cousin, etc. For my Japanese friends, my name is associated with being their Korean–American friend who speaks Japanese and teaches English. My Chinese name Zhu Li is used by my school teachers who see

me as a Korean–American student and by my Chinese students who see me as their Korean–American teacher who speaks Chinese.

In English, I only respond to the name Julie. My birth name, Juria, is so foreign to me. I get annoyed when people try to call me by this (when I have told them I don't respond to it!). I could get rid of all the ambiguity by just changing my name to Julie legally but I can't quite bring myself to that (yet) either. I quite like living in the ambiguity of it all. It makes me stop and think about the "cracks" in multilingual lives.

One of the dominant themes in your book is your sense of vulnerability, foreignness, and displacement. Do you regret being multilingual or do the pros outweigh the cons?
I think I've worked hard to get to where I am today but none of the things I value today would have been possible without my multilingual foundations. My interests, work, and the connections I have made with particular friends and colleagues have all been made possible to me through this inherent multilingual and transnational configuration.

The process of writing my autoethnography and unpacking all of those histories helped me to see what can emerge *from within* those feelings of vulnerability if one channels them in healthy directions. So I now understand the kinds of vulnerabilities I went through and am going through as being necessary conditions for who I have, and can continue to, become.

What have you learned about yourself in the process of writing this book?
At some point in the research-writing process, I came to see myself as no longer concerned (or constrained?) by the label "multilingual." I became more interested in the historical, political, ideological, social, and cultural embodiment of the languages in my repertoire, the care and ethics I wanted to convey in my writing and how to package this all together into a scholarly voice that I was comfortable with. So in a sense I started sensing a shift from a "multilingual" to a "multivocal self." It sounds corny but I felt liberated in so many respects. This was a radical shift for me.

What does your multilingual life look like these days?
My whole world revolves around teaching and learning these days so even though I don't do anything special to maintain my other languages, I engage with the languages of my students, and future teachers. Together, we produce classroom activities that bring other languages to the fore in the English language classrooms.

I like being away from the pressure of having to "speak" or perform in any one language for extended periods of time. I like listening to others about their multilingualism and exchanging bits and pieces of different languages in conversations. Australia is a really great environment for this kind of playfulness and relaxed attitude toward multiple language usage.

Reference

Choi, J. (2017). *Creating a Multivocal Self: Autoethnography as Method.* New York/ London: Routledge.

9.4 BECOMING BICULTURAL: DISCOVERING HIDDEN ASPECTS OF THE OTHER CULTURE

When you come to live in a new country and begin the process of becoming bicultural, differences in the way people live, work, and socialize are often quite visible. But other aspects, engrained in the host culture, are hidden, and you have to be introduced to them. Thanksgiving is a case in point.

When my wife, our two-year-old son, and I first came to live in the United States, we were struck by the many differences that existed between our original culture and our new culture. Many of the things that related to how people lived and worked, what they ate, how they socialized, and so on, were quite apparent, but some were not. They were hidden and we had to be introduced to them.

As we acculturated to our new life in the United States, and slowly became bicultural, we initially passed by very traditional American events, most notably Thanksgiving. When our first Thanksgiving weekend arrived, we had been in the United States for some four months only and we thought it was like any other extended weekend. In our original culture, there were many such weekends, and so we didn't pay much attention to this one. On the Thursday itself (we didn't yet know it was called Thanksgiving Day), we simply went on a hike in the nearby hills!

As we were coming back in the afternoon, we found everything terribly quiet in our neighborhood; never did we realize what was going on in millions of homes all over the country!

In the fall of our second year, quite by chance, we met an American friend whom we had known a few years before in our home university. We started chatting with her and at some point she asked us if we would like to celebrate Thanksgiving with her family. We gratefully accepted, not quite realizing what that meant.

We were asked to arrive at 2 p.m. which we thought was a bit late for lunch (we had little knowledge of how the day was organized) and we were greeted warmly by her parents, siblings, cousins, friends, and many children. Then, as we went from the kitchen to the children's room, and then to the living room where a football game was showing on TV, we realized that we wouldn't be eating for some time yet. That afternoon and then evening, we discovered a totally new celebration with its well-established traditions, both culinary and social.

A year later, our first Thanksgiving Day initiation was long over, and we weren't really thinking about doing anything special. But our son enrolled in a preschool program started talking about Thanksgiving as well as the size of the turkey we would have and all the trimmings that would go with it. So we decided to give the meal a try. In addition, since the playground we took him to was next to a football field, we watched with interest the local game that morning without really understanding the rules.

Little by little, Thanksgiving became part of our family tradition, just like Halloween. Our son, through his contacts at school and his neighborhood friends, knew more about these holidays than we did and was instrumental in helping us get things straight. (It is a well-known phenomenon that parents acculturate to a new culture in part through their children.)

With time we felt sufficiently comfortable with the Thanksgiving menu that we invited a Belgian couple who had just arrived to join us on that day. It was fun telling them about the tradition (we had done our homework beforehand) and to talk about the events that take place. I had started enjoying football and had learned from friendly colleagues what to look at, and not look at, when watching a game, so we switched on the TV.

With time, our Belgian friends took over organizing the Thanksgiving dinner and, over the years, the number of faces around the table increased as our children were born (their four and our additional one). We continued this tradition of going to their house on that day until we returned to Europe.

During our first years back, we continued celebrating Thanksgiving on Thanksgiving Day, just as if we were in the States. Our boys would invite a few friends over and we would give them a crash course on the tradition, without the football games though, much to my regret. But with time, things changed a little. We found it more convenient to have the meal on a Saturday since there is no school the next day. Also, we replaced the turkey with a smaller bird (more easily available in our local stores) and we added a European dessert in place of the customary pumpkin pie.

We do phone or email with our Belgian–American friends each year on Thanksgiving Day, however, to get their latest news and give them ours. We keep promising that we will come to their home for the next Thanksgiving, like in the old times, but we still haven't made it over. This said, it is definitely time to do so as our Thanksgiving ritual is becoming much too European . . . and is slowing waning!

Reference

Grosjean, F. (2010). Bilinguals who are also bicultural. Chapter 10 of *Bilingual: Life and Reality*. Cambridge, MA: Harvard University Press.

9.5 KEEPING MY FOUR CULTURES ALIVE

Over the course of my life, I have become a mosaic of four cultures. I now have the challenge of keeping them alive within me.

In my book, *A Journey in Languages and Cultures: The Life of a Bicultural Bilingual*, I explain how I came into contact with four different cultures during my life and how I lived within each of them for a number of years, becoming bicultural – more precisely, quadricultural – as a consequence.

My early years were spent in a small village just outside Paris, and until the age of seven and a half, I was a normal French boy, both linguistically and culturally. But then I moved to an English-speaking boarding school in Switzerland, acquired English, and acculturated into both English and American cultures. My English side was consolidated with four years of boarding school in England.

I moved back to France for my university studies and stayed there for ten years, before immigrating to the United States where my family and

I stayed for some twelve years. Our boys became totally American, and at the end of our stay, we were basically an English-speaking family, acculturated into life in America. But then we came back to Europe and settled down in Switzerland where we have been for some thirty years. The four cultures I came into contact with, and lived in, have found their place in a mosaic of cultures that characterize me.

Now that I am retired, and concentrate on writing books, chapters, and articles, an interesting challenge has been to keep alive my four cultures. I would regret losing my French, English, American, and Swiss sides, since they are definitely part of who I am. Fortunately, there are ways of keeping all of them alive, as people like me have discovered.

First, it is important to maintain ties with family members and close friends in your cultures. We visit ours whenever we can and they come over to see us. We also communicate via email and messaging services, something that was simply not possible thirty years ago. In addition, my wife and I go up to Paris several times a year. It is the city where we studied, where we met fifty years ago, and where we have many friends. We are always amazed by how these short trips revive our French cultural side!

Internet is a great way to stay in touch with every aspect of one's cultures. I'm an avid online newspaper reader and I start my day with the latest news from America and Great Britain before shifting over to the French and Swiss media. And throughout the day, I check on headlines on my favorite sites, navigating between countries and languages.

I also listen to radio programs, and sometimes watch TV, in my four countries whilst I am doing various activities at home. For example, as I am preparing lunch, I listen to WBUR, Boston's NPR news station. I am physically in Switzerland but my mind is in Boston where I "wake up" with New Englanders who are listening to Morning Edition. I learn about the weather they have there, whether the inbound commute is fluid or not, and whether my favorite Bostonian teams have won or lost the day before. I can visualize all that I hear having lived there so many years. I repeat this in the evening as I work out and do various house chores.

Choosing one's radio programs carefully is a wonderful way of keeping abreast of events that are happening "back home" and assessing how people are reacting to them. Of course, having lived for extended periods of time in all my countries, I am attuned to their differences. So I'm not too surprised by the slow-paced BBC4 news discussions and the more heated, and sometimes less organized, debates on French radio.

The web also allows me to interact with all those involved in my writing projects, across my different cultures. These can be coauthors or invited authors, publication editors, as well as production managers. I have written books and articles, and given interviews, in all the countries I identify with, and in both my working languages.

Finally, the content of my writing – bilingualism and biculturalism – encourages me to keep studying the linguistic and cultural diversity of my four cultures. When I wrote a recent book in French on bilingualism, *Parler plusieurs langues: le monde des bilingues*, I did a lot of background work to show how linguistically diverse France is, contrary to general belief. I have been doing the same thing for the United States for my books in English and for this very blog which is in its tenth year.

I am proud to have roots in all these cultures and am doing my best to keep them alive!

Reference

Grosjean, F. (2019). *A Journey in Languages and Cultures: The Life of a Bicultural Bilingual.* Oxford/New York: Oxford University Press.

9.6 THE ADVANTAGES OF BEING BICULTURAL

There are many advantages to being bicultural, two of which are greater creativity and professional success, as shown in some interesting research. The underlying psychological mechanism that accounts for this is enhanced integrative complexity.

It has long been known that there are many advantages to being bicultural such as having a greater number of social networks, being aware of cultural differences, taking part in the life of two or more cultures, being an intermediary between cultures, and so on. Recent research shows that biculturals are also characterized by greater creativity and professional success.

In a paper, comprising three studies, researchers Carmit Tadmor, Adam Galinsky, and William Maddux compared the results of bicultural participants to those who were not bicultural. In the first study, MBA students at a large business school in Europe, who had lived abroad for an average of four years, were given a creative uses task. They were shown the picture of a brick and were given 2 minutes to write down as many creative uses of it as they could think of. When three components of creativity were examined, the biculturals exhibited more fluency (they generated more ideas), more flexibility (their ideas fell into more categories), and more novelty (they were more creative in their suggestions).

In a second study, the researchers examined how biculturalism affects real-world innovations in a group of MBA students at a business school in the United States. Here again the participants had lived abroad and came from different countries of origin. The study examined how many new businesses the participants had started, how many novel products or services they had invented, and how many breakthrough process innovations they had created. Biculturals once again did better than the other participants.

Finally, in a third study, the question asked was whether being bicultural leads to professional success (as measured by the rate of managerial advancement), and to an increase in managerial reputation (as judged by peers). This time, the participants were Israeli professionals in the United States who had worked on the West Coast, primarily in Silicon Valley, for slightly more than eight years on average. What was found is that biculturals achieved higher promotion rate and had more positive reputations than those who were not bicultural.

The authors of the study explained this enhanced creativity and professional success in biculturals by means of a psychological mechanism, integrative complexity, which is the capacity and willingness to acknowledge the legitimacy of competing perspectives on the same issue, on the one hand, and the ability to forge conceptual links among these perspectives, on the other. It is a capacity that involves considering and combining multiple perspectives.

According to the authors, biculturals have an enhanced ability to carefully weigh the merits of alternative perspectives. They view things from these different perspectives and integrate them into a coherent whole. They also recombine different existing ideas to make novel connections between concepts.

The enhanced integrative complexity that biculturals show has implications for a number of tasks such as effective information search, greater tolerance for ambiguous information, less susceptibility to information overload, and so on.

As a bicultural myself, and always interested in pursuing alternative perspectives, I wrote to the senior author of the paper, Dr. Carmit Tadmor of Tel Aviv University, to enquire whether one can't develop integrative complexity by remaining monocultural. I felt I had experienced one way of doing so in my English school during my youth by taking part in the debates that took place once a week. We were given the task of defending or opposing a particular position without being able to choose the side we were on. Thus we often spoke in favor of a point of view that was not ours and hence we were forced to see both sides of an issue.

Carmit Tadmor replied that you can indeed achieve higher levels of integrative complexity in a number of ways such as the one I had mentioned to her, among many others. Biculturalism is one such way but not the only way. I came away from our exchange, feeling relieved for monoculturals and happy for biculturals – an optimal best-of-both-worlds situation!

Reference

Tadmor, C. T., Galinsky, A. D., and Maddux, W. W. (2012). Getting the most out of living abroad: Biculturalism and integrative complexity as key drivers of creative and professional success. *Journal of Personality and Social Psychology*, 103(3), 520–542.

9.7 CHANGE OF LANGUAGE, CHANGE OF PERSONALITY? I

There is a Czech proverb that says, "Learn a new language and get a new soul," and it is true that many bilinguals do indeed report being different in each of their languages. How can one explain this?

Bilingual 1:   *"When I'm around Anglo-Americans, I find myself awkward and unable to choose my words quickly enough . . . . When I'm amongst Latinos/Spanish-speakers, I don't feel shy at all. I'm witty, friendly, and . . . . I become very out-going."*

Bilingual 2: *"In English, my speech is very polite, with a relaxed tone, always saying "please" and "excuse me." When I speak Greek, I start talking more rapidly, with a tone of anxiety and in a kind of rude way. . . ."*

Bilingual 3: *"I find when I'm speaking Russian I feel like a much more gentle, "softer" person. In English, I feel more "harsh," "businesslike."*

Could it be that bilinguals who speak two (or more) languages change their personality when they change language? After all, the Czech proverb does say, "Learn a new language and get a new soul."

Despite the fact that many bilinguals report being different in each of their languages, only a few researchers have attempted to get to the bottom of this question. Early in her career, Berkeley Professor Susan Ervin-Tripp conducted a study in which she asked Japanese–American women to complete sentences she gave them in both Japanese and English. She found that they proposed very different endings depending on the language used. Thus, for the sentence beginning, "When my wishes conflict with my family. . . ." one participant's Japanese ending was, ". . . it is a time of great unhappiness," whereas the English ending was, ". . . I do what I want."

More than forty years later, Baruch College Professor David Luna and his colleagues asked Hispanic American bilingual women students to interpret target advertisements picturing women, first in one language and, six months later, in the other. They found that in the Spanish sessions, the bilinguals perceived women in the ads as more self-sufficient as well as extrovert. In the English sessions, however, they expressed more traditional, other-dependent, and family-oriented views of the women.

The spontaneous reports by individual bilinguals, and the results of studies such as those mentioned here, have intrigued me over the years. I noted first of all that monocultural bilinguals who make up the majority of bilinguals in the world are not really concerned by this phenomenon. Although bi- or multilingual, they are in fact members of just one culture. But what about bicultural bilinguals? I proposed in my first book on bilingualism, *Life with Two Languages*, that what is seen as a change in personality is most probably simply a shift in attitudes and behaviors that correspond to a shift in situation or context, independent of language. Basically, the bicultural bilinguals in these studies were behaving biculturally, that is, adapting to the context they were in (see Post 9.1).

As we saw in Post 1.5, bilinguals use their languages for different purposes, in different domains of life, with different people. Different contexts and domains trigger different impressions, attitudes, and behaviors. What is taken as a personality shift due to a change of language may have little, if anything, to do with language itself.

Imagine the way we speak to a best friend and the behavior that we adopt. Then, think of how all this changes when we are speaking the same language to a superior (e.g. a school head, religious authority, or employer). We behave differently and sometimes change attitudes and feelings even though the language is the same.

The same is true for bilinguals except that here the language may be different. It is the environment, the culture, and the interlocutors that cause bicultural bilinguals to change attitudes, feelings, and behaviors (along with language) – and not their language as such. In essence, there does not seem to be a direct causal relationship between language and personality.

A Swiss German–French–English trilingual gives us a concluding statement that is fitting: *"When talking English, French or German to my sister, my personality does not change. However, depending on where we are, both our behaviors may adapt to certain situations we find ourselves in."*

References

Ervin, S. (1964). An analysis of the interaction of language, topic, and listener. In J. Gumperz and D. Hymes, eds., The Ethnography of Communication, special issue of *American Anthropologist*, 66, Part 2, 86–102.

Luna, D., Ringberg, T., and Peracchio, L. (2008). One individual, two identities: Frame switching among biculturals. *Journal of Consumer Research*, 35(2), 279–293.

Grosjean, F. (2010). Personality, thinking and dreaming, and emotions in bilinguals. Chapter 11 of *Bilingual: Life and Reality*. Cambridge, MA: Harvard University Press.

9.8 CHANGE OF LANGUAGE, CHANGE OF PERSONALITY? II

Many bilinguals report feeling different in each of their languages and some even state that a change of language leads to a change in personality. As more research is conducted on this topic, new issues are raised and new explanations are provided.

My first post on the topic (see above) received many comments which I went through carefully. On the question of personality change, my respondents, probably all bilingual, were undecided. About a third thought there was no change in personality, a second third thought there was, and the remaining third didn't actually mention this aspect. This mixed reaction is not a surprise as even among researchers it is difficult to find a consensus as to how to define personality.

One respondent who believed in a personality change addressed the issue of whether there may sometimes be a direct causal relationship between change of language and change of personality (and not always an indirect relationship as I proposed). He raised the intriguing possibility that an "initially indirect causal relationship can develop into a direct one" and he cited Pavlov's well-known study involving his dogs' reaction to the ringing of a bell. This might explain, in part, another respondent's remark. She found that a teacher was quite strict and a bit intimidating when speaking one language and more friendly in the other. She continued as follows: "If you were in a room with her and she was giving you a hard time, it was a good idea to manipulate the conversation over into the other language!"

Although divided on the personality issue, most respondents agreed with the fact that different contexts, domains of life, and interlocutors – which in turn induce different languages – trigger different impressions, attitudes, and behaviors. Thus, as bicultural bilinguals we adapt to the situation or the person we are talking to, and change our language when we need to, without actually changing our personality. One respondent put it very nicely: "... it is not a personality change but simply the expression of another part of our personality that is not shown as strongly in our other language(s)."

Future research will hopefully use both explicit and implicit tests of attitudes and self-concept as suggested by yet another respondent. This is all the more important as it could be that not everyone is equally apt at judging that they "feel different" when they change language. In a study, researcher Katarzyna Ożańska-Ponikwia examined why some people report feeling different while others do not. She asked some 100 bilinguals made up of people who had grown up speaking two languages, immigrants who acquired their second language later on in life, as well as students who had stayed in a foreign country for an extended period of time, to give answers to two personality questionnaires and to give scale values to statements such as, "I feel I'm someone else while speaking English," or "Friends say that I'm a different person when I speak English."

What she found was that only people who are emotionally and socially skilled are able to notice feeling different. According to her, some people do not report changes in their behavior as well as in their perception or expression of emotions when changing language, not because they do not exist, but because they are unable to notice them. She speculates that it is people with an above-average level of social and emotional skill who can notice that they adapt aspects of their personality and behavior when using another language.

I personally look forward to reading more studies on this topic in the years to come. Not only will they allow me to update my own thinking on the subject but they may also help me understand my bilingual conduct in case I belong to the category of those who do not notice changes in their attitudes, feelings, and behavior when changing language!

Reference

Ożańska-Ponikwia, K. (2012). What has personality and emotional intelligence to do with "feeling different" while using a foreign language? *International Journal of Bilingual Education and Bilingualism*, 15(2), 217–234.

9.9 CHANGE OF LANGUAGE, CHANGE OF PERSONALITY? UNCOVERED DATA

A look at how monolinguals change their personality ratings depending on the context helps to demystify the change of personality issue in bilinguals.

In Posts 9.7 and 9.8, I asked whether bilinguals who speak two or more languages change their personality when they change language. In the former, I concluded that there is no direct causal relationship between language and personality. And in the latter, I stated that many of my readers agreed with the fact that different contexts, domains of life, and interlocutors – which in turn can induce different languages – trigger different impressions, attitudes, and behaviors, whether one is monolingual or bilingual.

These two posts, out of a total of 152 posts, have received the most views on my blog, showing thereby the interest readers have for this issue. I have noted over the years how Professor Jean-Marc Dewaele of Birkbeck College (University of London), among others, has attempted to explain why bi- and multilinguals feel different when switching languages. I have also noticed that many researchers are now preferring to couch the issue in terms of cultural frame switching or cultural accommodation along the lines of what I have proposed.

In the personality literature, I have looked for studies *within just one language* that show that personality ratings can be modulated depending on the situation/context the participant is put into. If that is the case, and if the modification is greater than that found when there is a change of language, then the question would be largely resolved, at the personality level at least.

It is only recently, and quite by accident, that I have come across two studies that show experimentally that we do indeed modulate our personality traits depending on where we are and who we are with. Let me describe one of them. Oliver Robinson from the University of Greenwich in England used an adapted version of the Ten-Item Personality Inventory (TIPI) which is a measure of the five-factor model of personality also known as the Big Five Inventory. These concern the following dimensions: Extraversion, Agreeableness, Openness, Emotional Stability/Neuroticism, and Conscientiousness.

His participants were given pairs of items such as "extraverted, enthusiastic," "dependable, self-disciplined," and "sympathetic, warm," and they had to judge how strongly they felt these applied to them in three different situations: with their parents, with their friends, and with their work colleagues. To do so, they had to write a number down from a scale of 1 (disagree strongly) to 7 (agree strongly).

Oliver Robinson regrouped the results under the five personality dimensions tested, and showed that the ratings were strongly influenced by context. Thus, the mean rating for Extraversion was 4.72 with work colleagues, 5.18 with parents, all the way up to 5.78 with friends. For Agreeableness, the corresponding mean ratings were 4.88, 4.54, and 5.17, respectively. The other three traits showed similar variation. The author concluded that the majority of people adapt or modulate their personality to "fit in" to social situations they are put into.

It is now worth comparing Oliver Robinson's results with those obtained in personality studies that asked bilinguals to give ratings in their different languages. For example, Sylvia Chen and Michael Bond of the Hong Kong Polytechnic University used the Big Five Inventory to measure the perceived personality of their participants. The rating scales they used ranged from 1 (strongly disagree) to 5 (strongly agree). In their first study, they asked half of their Chinese–English bilinguals to assess their own personality traits in English only, and the other half of the bilinguals to do so in Chinese.

If a change in language induces a real change in personality, then the results due to language should be very different. In fact, the ratings in Chinese and in English were very similar. Over the five personality traits, the mean of the absolute differences between the ratings in Chinese and those in English was a mere 0.124! In Robinson's monolingual study, on the other hand, once the 1 to 7 scale had been adjusted to a 1 to 5 scale, the mean difference was practically four times larger (0.45)!

What happens if the *same bilinguals* give ratings in one language and then, some time later, in another? This is exactly what Nairán Ramírez-Esparza and her coauthors looked at in a study using English–Spanish bilinguals. The absolute differences between the ratings in the one and in the other language were again extremely low (mean of 0.116), and very similar to those in the Sylvia Chen and Michael Bond study.

Thus, as I stated in the very first post on the topic, it is the environment, the culture, and the interlocutors that cause bilinguals to adapt their attitudes, feelings, and behaviors (along with language) – and not their languages as such.

References

Chen, S. X. and Bond, M. H. (2010). Two languages, two personalities? Examining language effects on the expression of personality in a bilingual context. *Personality and Social Psychology Bulletin*, 36(11), 1514–1528.

Dewaele, J.-M. (2016). Why do so many bi- and multilinguals feel different when switching languages? *International Journal of Multilingualism*, 13(1), 92–105.

Robinson, O. C. (2009). On the social malleability of traits: Variability and consistency in Big 5 trait expression across three interpersonal contexts. *Journal of Individual Differences*, 30(4), 201–208.

Ramírez-Esparza, N., Gosling, S. D., Benet-Martínez, V., Potter, J. P., and Pennebaker, J. W. (2006). Do bilinguals have two personalities? A special case of cultural frame switching. *Journal of Research in Personality*, 40, 99–120.

10

When the Heart Speaks

INTRODUCTION

In this chapter, several facets of emotions in bilinguals are addressed, such as how they are expressed and processed, but also how they can be brought about by different languages and cultures, as well as by other bilinguals. In Post 10.1, the myth that bilinguals always express their emotions in their first language is discussed and it is shown that, in fact, there are no set rules. In Post 10.2, Aneta Pavlenko, an expert on the question, asks whether we process emotions differently in our respective languages. Even when the levels of proficiency are comparable, she writes, languages learned earlier and later in life offer different processing advantages.

Post 10.3 is an interview with the author, Lauren Collins, on her book, *When in French: Love in a second language.* A longtime monoglot, she claims, she became a late-life bilingual when she met her French husband and moved to Europe. In Post 10.4, how partners in bilingual couples learn to appreciate each other's humor, as well as partake in it, is discussed, even when it can be so very different from their own.

The next two posts examine how one can fall in love with a culture and a language. In Post 10.5, Julia Child, the iconic cooking expert, is followed as she discovers the French culture and language, as well as its cuisine, and becomes enamored of all three. And in Post 10.6, the American songwriter and composer, Jimmy Davis, is evoked. His *coup de foudre* for France was for very different reasons, and he was one of the rare expatriates in the world of jazz who stayed in France all his life.

The final two posts are personal expressions of emotion. In Post 10.7, I pay a tribute to a bilingual couple who inspired me when I was a young man. They made me more confident in my work and more serene as a bilingual and bicultural person. And in Post 10.8, in a letter to my newborn grandchild, I celebrate the bilingual and bicultural person whom he will grow up to be.

10.1 EMOTIONS IN MORE THAN ONE LANGUAGE

The language bilinguals express their emotions in is both a complex and a fascinating topic. There is a myth that they do so in their first language but there are many instances of this not being so. In the end, there seems to be no set rule.

It is often believed that bilinguals express their emotions in their first language (when they haven't acquired both languages simultaneously), usually the language of their parents. Like all myths, there are instances when it is true. Thus, a Portuguese–English bilingual who acquired English at age fourteen wrote to me that if something makes him angry and he allows his anger to come out, there is no doubt that he will use Portuguese to express himself. And it makes sense that bilinguals who have lived in the same place all their lives, who use their first language with family and friends and their other language(s) mainly at work, will express affect in their first language.

However, as Temple University researcher Aneta Pavlenko, herself multilingual, writes, things are much more complex than that. In her book on the topic, she dismantles this myth and shows that the relationship between emotions and bilingualism plays out differently for different individuals and distinct language areas. Basically, it is too simplistic to suggest that late bilinguals have emotional ties only with their first language and no ties with their other languages.

When a childhood in one language lacked affection or was marked by distressing events, then bilinguals may prefer to express emotion in their second language. For example, an adult English–French bilingual who moved to France in early adulthood once wrote to me that she found it easier to speak of anything connected with emotions in French, her second language, whereas in English she was rather tongue-tied. She then explained that it was in French that she had discovered what love meant. She ended by stating, "Perhaps one day I'll even manage to say, 'I love you' in English."

The Canadian and French novelist, Nancy Huston, gives a similar testimony. Nine years after having moved to Paris from North America, her daughter Léa was born. She had married a Bulgarian–French bilingual with whom she spoke French. Huston tried to use English baby talk with her daughter but couldn't continue. She explains that the memories and feelings stirred up were simply too strong (her English-speaking mother had abandoned the family home when she was six).

On a less poignant level, many late bilinguals state that they can swear more easily in their second language. Both the English–French bilingual above and Nancy Huston have said the same thing. The former stated that she has a wider range of vulgar vocabulary in French and Nancy Huston wrote her master's thesis on linguistic taboo and swearwords in French. As she wrote, "The French language in general . . . was to me less emotion-fraught, and therefore less dangerous, than my mother tongue. It was cold, and I approached it coldly." (p. 49)

When bilinguals are angry, excited, tired, or stressed, their accent in a language can reappear or increase in strength. In addition, they often revert to the language(s) in which they express their emotions, be it their first or their second language, or both. I was once bitten by a stingray in California and recall clearly switching back and forth between English and French. I used English to ask the English-speaking friends I was with to take me to see a doctor and I cursed in French to help me ease the pain.

The language used in therapy is also quite informative. Paul Preston, who has written a book on the sign language/spoken language bilingualism of the hearing children of deaf parents, interviewed several of them who said they felt blocked when in a therapy session. They wanted to use sign language but couldn't do so (the session was taking place in English). And Nancy Huston claims that she could not finish her own psychoanalysis because it was conducted in French, the language in which her neuroses were under control.

In sum, emotions in two or more languages have no set rules; some bilinguals prefer to use one language, some the other, and some both. It is fitting to finish with an extract from Aneta Pavlenko's book about her own habits: *"'I love you,' I whisper to my English-speaking partner. 'Babulechka, ia tak skuchaiu po tebe [Grandma, I miss you so much],' I tenderly say on the phone to my Russian-speaking grandmother."*

As the author states prior to this: "I have no choice but to use both English and Russian when talking about emotions" (pp. 22–23).[1]

---

[1] See Post 10.2, which is written by Aneta Pavlenko.

References

Pavlenko, A. (2005). *Emotions and Multilingualism.* Cambridge: Cambridge University Press.

Huston, N. (2002). *Losing North: Musings on Land, Tongue and Self.* Toronto: McArthur.

Grosjean, F. (2010). Personality, thinking and dreaming, and emotions in bilinguals. Chapter 11 of *Bilingual: Life and Reality.* Cambridge, MA: Harvard University Press.

10.2 AFFECTIVE PROCESSING IN BILINGUAL SPEAKERS[2]

Do we process emotions differently in our respective languages? An answer can be found in the language chosen by bilingual poets, in swearwords used by bilinguals, and in experimental studies of affective processing.

Post written by Aneta Pavlenko.

Vladimir Nabokov, a native speaker of Russian, best known as an English-language writer, was a superb stylist, brilliant lecturer, and sparkling conversationalist. He did not feel the same emotional connection to his English as he did to Russian and complained once in a letter to a friend: "I envy so bitterly your intimacy with English words." This lack of intimacy did not affect the sophistication and richness of his English-language prose, where he displayed a superior ability to depict and express emotions, but it did influence his language choice for poetry. While Nabokov did try his hand at poetry in English and French, his unambiguous preference was for Russian, and upon finishing a book in English, he usually rewarded himself with a "tryst" with his "ruddy robust Russian muse."

Nabokov's choice highlights an interesting dissociation in the relationship between our languages and emotions: we can express emotions in all of our languages (see the post earlier), but we do not experience language emotionality in the same way in all of them. The difference is particularly noticeable in our use of taboo and swearwords: research by Jean-Marc Dewaele at the University of London shows that swearwords in the mother tongue affect us more strongly than those in the languages learned later in life. Such intimate connection between language and

---

[2] The original title of this post was, "Poetry and the language of the heart."

emotions is a must for modern poetry where everything is designed to act directly upon you: a poet's word choices aim to trigger your memories, associations, and images, their tone, meter, and rhythm reach for your body, while their rhymes, repetition, and alliteration land on your tongue to be tasted and savored. To get this unmediated access to the readers' senses, the poet has to be physically connected to the language and this connection appears to be tighter in languages learned early in life. But what does an intimate or "tight" connection between a language and emotions actually mean?

For an answer, we turn to studies of language emotionality, examined by psychologists under the umbrella of affective processing. In lay terms, affective processing is what happens when you walk into a crowded room and realize that the object of your dreams and desires is right there by the window: you see this person before you see anyone else, your heart starts beating faster, you have butterflies in your stomach, you may even start sweating and become tongue-tied. The strength and range of responses undoubtedly depend on the stimuli (I, for one, dislike mice but am indifferent to spiders) and on our contexts and trajectories (the person who triggered an array of feelings in us just a year ago may elicit nothing but indifference today). Yet one thing remains constant: some stimuli are detected faster and earlier than others (a phenomenon termed *perceptual prioritization*) and elicit stronger physical reactions (termed *increased arousal*).

The key question in research with bilinguals is whether we process emotional words similarly or differently in our respective languages. To answer this question, Catherine Caldwell-Harris and her coauthors at Boston University presented Turkish–English bilinguals with an array of words and examined electrical conductivity of the skin. Our skin is particularly sensitive to threatening and relevant stimuli – these stimuli increase the level of adrenaline in the blood and lead to sweating, which increases electrical conductivity of the skin, measured via fingertip electrodes. The analysis of conductivity revealed that these bilinguals displayed stronger physical responses to Turkish words and especially to taboo words and childhood reprimands. Some mentioned that they could hear, in their mind, Turkish family members addressing reprimands to them. These findings, corroborated by other studies, suggest that affective processing in the first language may be deeper than in the languages learned later in life.

The implications of this difference were examined at the University of Chicago, where Boaz Keysar and associates offered bilinguals an array of decision-making tasks in their respective languages. In one task, for instance, participants were given the same choices in a gain frame (if you choose medicine A, X people will be saved) and in a loss frame (if you choose medicine A, X people will die). The findings demonstrated that in their native language participants were more prone to display a bias toward positive framing, while in their second language they were less affected by negative framing and loss aversion. These findings were linked to the greater emotional distance provided by the second language.

Now, what do these findings mean for our everyday lives? To begin with, they remind us that language is situated not only in the mind but also in the body, and languages learned at different points in our lives may inhabit our body in different ways. The findings also suggest that even when the levels of proficiency are comparable, languages learned earlier and later in life offer different processing advantages. The increased emotionality and sensitivity to threat in the first language make it perfect for poetry and arguments, while languages learned later in life make it easier to lie, to recall traumatic events, and to resist framing effects and advertising pressures.

This difference seems almost intuitive until we try to determine the precise point of transition to "later in life" or start thinking about the fact that Nabokov, who had an English nanny, was actually exposed to English from early childhood, while Marc Chagall, who wrote poetry in Russian, started learning it at age thirteen.

References

Harris, C., Ayçiçegi, A., and Gleason J. (2003). Taboo words and reprimands elicit greater autonomic reactivity in a first language than in a second language. *Applied Psycholinguistics*, 24(4), 561–571.

Keysar, B., Hayakawa, S., and An, S. G. (2012). The foreign-language effect: Thinking in a foreign tongue reduces decision biases. *Psychological Science*, 23, 661–668.

10.3 LOVE IN A SECOND LANGUAGE

(Interview with Lauren Collins)
Lauren Collins is the author of "When in French: Love in a second language"
about life, love, and language.
Interview conducted by Aneta Pavlenko.

Our guest today is Lauren Collins, author of *When in French: Love in a second language,* **an unputdownable story of an American who fell in love with a Frenchman – and with French. Lauren, would you please tell us a few words about your life as a bilingual today?**
I am a longtime monoglot who became an improbable late-life bilingual upon meeting my husband, Olivier; moving to Switzerland with him; and, eventually, settling in France with our nearly two-year-old daughter, whose language abilities will very soon be giving mine a run for their money. Learning a language in what I'm forced to admit is midlife has been a transformative experience for me, a sort of intellectual lottery win that's given me greater resources than I'd ever have dreamed of.

You talk about the isolating nature of language classes, yet you also challenge the myth of learning by osmosis, by simply living in the foreign-language environment or watching TV. What motivation and strategies worked best for you?
For me, all the positive motivation in the world is useless; I think "wouldn't it be nice if" is a far weaker incentive than "what if I don't?" Especially for adult learners, life can be so busy that there has to be a sense that something unpleasant is going to happen if you fail! I got to a point where I no longer wanted to be the silent idiot at the dinner table; I didn't want to be isolated in the community I was living in. I especially didn't want to not be able to partake in my daughter's life and upbringing in France. The stakes started to feel high, and that's when I got serious.

Taking an immersion class – 5 hours a day for a month – seemed like a necessary first step, as I'm the kind of person who prefers as methodical an approach as possible. I now see that such an approach to language learning is impossible, but it at least helped to have a basic grounding in French grammar before throwing myself into the messy process of second-language acquisition.

I was fascinated by your comment that, in English, you try to speak in a distinct voice and avoid clichés, while in French you just want to fit in

and master the clichés. Do you still feel this way and, if so, have you gathered enough French clichés to argue with your husband?
I think that goes back to the old idea, "You can only break the rules when you know them." As I'm still in the rule-internalizing stage, nothing gives me a greater sense of accomplishment than deploying some shopworn but situationally apt saying like, "*Revenons à nos moutons*" (literally, "Let's get back to our sheep"; figuratively, "Let's get back to the matter at hand"). OK, I still haven't actually used that one, but just figuring out the call-and-response of daily life, the banal response, the proper filler, seems to me like a big part of mastering a language beyond the textbook sense. I can argue with anyone in French! All you have to say is "*C'est une provocation*" or "*C'est insupportable*," ideally with the word "*polémique*" thrown in somewhere. Every language has its formulas, and I enjoy trying to get the tincture just right.

You describe yourself as an All-American girl who found languages faintly irrelevant until she stumbled into French, but the sheer delight you take in words betrays you as a language aficionado. How did being a writer affect your learning of French?
Being a writer has surely affected my learning of French positively in that I'm already in the longstanding habit of being intrigued by words, or turns of phrase, that aren't familiar to me, and making the effort to seek out their meanings and to retain them. But there's a negative side, too, in that, as a person who uses words professionally, I'm perhaps not always as willing or able to make a fool of myself, in the way that one needs to in order to learn a language. When you feel like you have a decent command of your native language, sometimes it's just so much easier to revert to it, and the pressure you put upon yourself to be articulate can be inhibiting.

Interestingly, it's not just that being a writer has affected my learning of French, but also that my learning of French has affected my being a writer. I was surprised to find out that bilingualism is a two-way street, the second language influencing the first as much as the first influences the second. I've come to see French as a source of inspiration (and even outright theft) for the way I express myself in English.

Your book ends with the birth of your daughter. What are the joys and challenges of raising a bilingual child?
Ask me in a few years. I'm so early in the process that it's hard to tell. Right now, it's a lot of joy, but I already fear for the day our daughter begins *maternelle* and surpasses my French approximately three weeks later. For

the moment, English is her stronger language. My husband had the funny but marginally unnerving experience just this week of hearing her say a word – "scoot in" – that he didn't know.

Your memoir is all the more interesting for the engaging links it makes to academic research. What insights did you gain from this work?
As a journalist, my first instinct was to try to gird my own observations with fact, and the work that I encountered in my research was invaluable in helping me to understand these strange transformations of mind, body, and spirit that I sensed I was undergoing. Whether in learning that researchers at the University of Michigan proved that small amounts of alcohol improve people's language skills (haven't we all guessed as much?), or in coming across your own proposal that perhaps the denial of Whorfian effects was a big whopping Whorfian effect itself, I found it enlightening to connect my personal experiences, through science, with those of bilinguals across time and space.

How did your family receive your book and when can we expect a French edition?
So far, so good. A French edition *"Lost in French: les aventures d'une américaine qui voulait aimer en français"* sort le 11 janvier, 2017, chez Flammarion.

Reference

Collins, L. (2016). *When in French: Love in a Second Language.* New York: Penguin Press.

10.4 HUMOR IN BILINGUAL COUPLES

Humorous talk is a bonding agent in relationships; it creates intimacy and helps deal with stress. How do partners in bilingual couples learn to appreciate each other's humor, and even partake in it, when it can be so very different from their own, both linguistically and culturally?

British novelist George Eliot once wrote, "A difference of taste in jokes is a great strain on the affections." This is all the more so when the people involved, in our case bilingual couples, have different language and cultural backgrounds. And yet, humor and, more precisely, jokes, puns, banter, understatement, and forms of irony, to name but a few, are an integral part of a relationship within couples. It is well known that humorous talk of this kind is a bonding agent; it creates intimacy and helps deal with stress.

In an interesting chapter, Professor Delia Chiaro of the University of Bologna, a British and Italian bilingual and bicultural, reports on a survey she undertook of some fifty-nine bilingual and bicultural couples and their use of humorous talk together. Each member of the couple had been born and raised in a country different from his/her partner's. And on average, the couple had been together for an average of ten years.

For most domains of life, they reported using the one or the other language, which confirms once again that languages in bilinguals are often used for different purposes, in different domains of life, and with different people (see Post 1.5). However, for humorous interaction all possibilities were found – language A, language B, or both languages. It is interesting to note that talking about food was done in all three ways as well, as was intimate communication.

Among the examples of humorous talk the author gives, we find word jokes. For example, a Dutch–Swedish couple reports using a Swedish word that resembles a Dutch word which is funny normally but which is especially funny with other people around who do not understand it. Translating names is also mentioned, among other forms of humor. Thus, an Italian–British couple might talk of "Cassio Argilla" when talking about "Cassius Clay" or of "Joe Green" when referring to "Giusseppe Verdi."

This said, learning to appreciate the humor of one's partner, which can be so different from one's own, and actually starting to use it takes time and effort. The first step is to acknowledge that it is indeed humor! As British English speaker Sandra states (she has an Italian husband): "British humor is particularly hard for Italians to get, especially the difference between sarcasm and irony and as for understatement . . . they are just totally unknown concepts here."

Amália, who is Hungarian, comments as follows: "I must say that it really took me a while to get used to my English partner's sense of humor. . . . I must admit . . . that occasionally I still look at him in disbelief at some of his jokes."

Of course, translating a joke or another form of humorous talk is particularly difficult, as any bilingual can report. Colm, one of the author's respondents, declares that "sometimes you lose the complete meaning if you don't translate well" and Claudia, another respondent, actually feels that translating a joke is "always a disaster."

Humorous talk in one's non-native language can be a problem though as it can be misinterpreted by outsiders. Sandra states: "I don't often do puns in Italian with other Italians as they tend to leap in to correct your Italian if they are not linguists!"

But with time and effort, many respondents in the survey indicate that they have learned the humor of their partner, they are starting to enjoy it and even partake in it. As Anne, who is British with a German partner, says: "After 15 years in Germany I can now watch some modern German comedy shows and even find them almost as funny as British ones!"

Delia Chiaro concludes her chapter with this remark: ". . . humorous interaction in cross-cultural, bilingual couples may well be an important bonding agent to help overcome the myriad of intercultural difficulties such relationships inevitably face." I'm sure she would agree with Frank A. Clark who once wrote: "I think the next best thing to solving a problem is finding some humor in it."

Reference

Chiaro, D. (2009). Cultural divide or unifying factor? Humorous talk in the interaction of bilingual, cross-cultural couples. In N. Norrick and D. Chiaro, eds., *Humor in Interaction*. Amsterdam/Philadelphia: John Benjamins, pp. 211–231.

10.5 FALLING IN LOVE WITH A CULTURE AND A LANGUAGE I

Some people fall in love with a new culture and language. The way Julia Child discovered the French culture and language, and French cuisine – and became enamored with all three – is very moving.

Over the holidays, I happened to see the ending of the movie *Julie & Julia*, with Meryl Streep portraying Julia Child. I was instantly captivated by Julia Child's story and so I plunged into her book, with Alex Prud'homme, *My Life in France*. It is a love story between Julia and Paul, her husband, between Julia and French cuisine, but also between Julia and a new country and its language.

As I was reading it, my mind wandered back to other people I had known who had fallen in love with a new culture and language. I thought of that French au pair in the United States who was totally captivated by America, Americans, and their language; the American professor visiting a French university for a year who then stayed on for several more years and who has gone back almost every year since; the student so enamored with the new language she was learning, Chinese, that she would get all her friends to learn the Mandarin tone system along with her; or even my own mesmerizing encounter with American Sign Language and the culture of the Deaf many years ago.

The reasons behind such *coups de foudre* are many, and different from person to person. It is worth following Julia Child's own story to uncover a few of them.

Julia arrived in France with her husband in 1948. Paul had been asked to fill a position at the US Information Agency in Paris, a city he had lived in as an artist and poet in the 1920s. For Julia, on the other hand, France was "a misty abstraction ..., a land I had long imagined but had no real sense of." Paul spoke good French but Julia could neither speak nor understand the language.

They drove from Le Havre to Rouen and Julia was immediately impressed by the many differences with America (recall this was in 1948): the horse and buggies, the boys in wooden shoes, the women dressed in black, the absence of billboards. ... "Oh, la belle France," she writes, "without knowing it, I was already falling in love!"

To add to her first impressions, Paul, a connoisseur of fine cuisine, took her to La Couronne in Rouen for lunch. They had oysters, sole meunière in butter sauce, salade verte and cheese accompanied by a Pouilly-Fumé. Julia writes that it was absolute perfection and that it was the most exciting meal of her life.

They arrived in Paris and found an apartment in a beautiful area of the city. Even though life in Paris was enthralling, there were some difficult moments also, especially with the language. Like many people who are making progress speaking and understanding a new language, there comes a time when you feel you are no longer making any headway. Julia writes that she hated her American accent, her impoverished syntax, and her inability to communicate correctly.

But with Paul's help, with language lessons and, especially, with the conversations she had with people at the cooking school she attended, and the vendors at the market place, her language skills improved rapidly. After one year in Paris, she spoke French quite well and concluded, with a smile, that she was probably French but that no one had ever told her! "I loved the people, the food, the lay of the land, the civilized atmosphere, and the generous pace of life."

By the time the couple left for Marseille in 1952, Julia had started her own cooking school with her friends, Simone Beck and Louisette Bertholle, her future coauthors of the bestseller, *Mastering the Art of French Cooking*. Two years later, the Childs finally left France for Germany, much to their regret. A few years later, on their return to the United States, Julia Child published her book and became a household name for all those who enjoy fine French cuisine.

The Childs came back almost every year to the small house they had in Provence. On arrival in Nice, they invariably had a leisurely meal at the airport. It was a reminder that they should slow down and open their senses: "You are here in *la belle France!*," they would say to one another.

When Julia finally closed down their house in 1992, and said goodbye to her second country, she couldn't help but reflect that France had become a part of her, and she a part of it – ". . . and so it has remained ever since," she observed.

Reference

Child, J. with Prud'homme, A. (2006). *My Life in France*. New York: Alfred A. Knopf.

10.6 FALLING IN LOVE WITH A CULTURE AND A LANGUAGE II

People who fall in love with a new culture and language are always of interest. Here we follow Jimmy Davis, an American songwriter and composer, best known for his song "Lover Man," who first went to France during World War II as a soldier and who finally settled there for good.

In the preceding post, I told the story of how Julia Child, the well-known chef and author, discovered the French culture and language, and French cuisine, and fell in love with all three. Not all people who have a *coup de foudre* for a new culture and language are as famous as Julia Child though. Jimmy Davis, the subject of our story, is one such person. He grew up in Englewood, New Jersey, and probably never thought in his younger years that he would spend the major part of his life across the ocean, in France. After attending the local high school where he was a regular student, preferring music and the debating club to sports, he was accepted to the Juilliard School of Music where he studied piano and composition.

Jimmy Davis quickly started making a name for himself as a songwriter and composed his famous, "Lover Man," with Roger (Ram) Ramirez and Jimmy Sherman, in the early 1940s. It became a worldwide hit when Billie Holiday recorded it in 1944. Since then, it has been sung by many artists, most notably Sarah Vaughan, Ella Fitzgerald, Whitney Houston, Norah Jones, and scores of others.

When the United States entered World War II, Jimmy Davis was called up but asked to be deferred or be given an exempt status since he was opposed to "serving in military forces that segregate and discriminate because of race, creed or color ...," as he wrote in his letter of appeal in 1942. Army units were segregated at the time – hence the expression "Jim Crow army" – and African American soldiers repeatedly suffered from discrimination and mistreatment. After a spell in prison, Jimmy Davis finally accepted to be inducted and served his country for three and a half years.

Even though he became a Warrant Officer and was a bandleader, these were difficult times for him as he was in daily contact with practices he had fought against. In one letter to his great friend, the poet, novelist, and playwright, Langston Hughes, he wrote: "Whenever I encounter Jim Crow of any sort now, I can't seem to control my emotions; I have no desire, no will power to do anything; I care about nothing."

In March 1945, two months before the end of the war, Jimmy Davis was sent to France and fell under the spell of the country and its people who accepted him as he was. He wrote to his friend Langston that, after so many years of misery, "Paris is just what the doctor ordered." Professor Michel Fabre reports in his book on Black American writers in France that Jimmy Davis was at Soissons, Northern France, when the war ended. He continues, "... along with a couple of other black

American officers, (Jimmy Davis) was invited to the home of a French family. While they were feasting, white American officers attempted to teach their host how to treat (them) – by excluding them – and were thrown out of the house."

Even though he only spent six months in France before coming back home with his army unit, he had time to follow a two-month course in French language and civilization offered at the Sorbonne for some 600 GIs. In addition, he met several people in the jazz world who were interested in his work. Starting in the 1920s, jazz had become very popular in France and many American artists had come over for stays of varying length.

Jimmy Davis spent two years back in the States where he studied dramatic art at the Actors' Lab in Hollywood. But even though he was talented, he was offered no roles of any importance and again suffered from discrimination. And so, in 1947, he came back to France where he settled down for good and was known as Jimmy "Lover Man" Davis. He continued his study of French and over the years, became extremely fluent in it. In all, he authored more than 130 copyrighted songs in English, French, and Spanish. He also started a career as a singer and a pianist and in one of his records, released in 1954, he can be heard singing in each of his three languages.

Life in his country of adoption was not always easy as he never became as famous as some of his fellow musicians and singers, many of whom would come over from the States for short stays. In his letters to Langston Hughes, which range over twenty-five years, he talks of his hopes to have a song or two take off and also of his money problems. Things picked up a bit in the seventies with small roles in movies and plays, and Valerie Wilmer, the renowned jazz expert and a personal friend of his, was able to write in 1975: "Today, Jimmy Davis is alive and well and living in Paris where he divides his time between acting on stage and on screen and continuing to write songs."

Jimmy Davis was liked by all who met him. Professor Fabre talks of a friendly, soft-spoken person, who managed to live happily on little, occasionally hosting American friends on their visits to Paris. In my recent quest to discover Jimmy Davis – for reasons I reveal in my 2019 autobiography – I have interviewed several of his friends, some quite elderly now, and what comes through is that he was a very fine human being, a true gentleman, with a very attaching personality and an innate elegance.

Jimmy Davis was one of the rare expatriates in the world of jazz who stayed in France all his life. He died in 1997 in Paris and his funeral ceremony was an improvisational performance, in English and in French, of life and of grief and of hope, according to Pastor David J. Wood, who officiated. Jimmy Davis' ashes rest in a small cemetery in the center of France, the country which welcomed him and which he adopted. There, a small plaque states, in both French and English, "To you, Jimmy Davis, who will remain forever our "Lover Man", because it was so."

References

Fabre, M. (1991). *From Harlem to Paris: Black American Writers in France, 1840–1980.* Chicago: University of Illinois Press.

Wilmer, V. (1975). Blues for a Lady. *Melody Maker*, 50, May 3, p. 40.

Grosjean, F. (2019). *A Journey in Languages and Cultures: The Life of a Bicultural Bilingual.* Oxford, England: Oxford University Press.

10.7 THE ROSE: REMEMBERING TWO INSPIRATIONAL BILINGUALS

We all have one or two key people who have inspired us in our careers. We might not have chosen our particular domain, and been who we are, had we not met them. A bilingual couple played that role in my career and in my life.

The end of a year[3] is always a time of reflection, on the events that are to come but also on the years that have gone by, as well as on important moments in one's life. My own life as a bilingual, and researcher on bilingualism, would not have been the same had I not met, and become friends with, Einar and Eva Haugen.

When I was preparing my master's thesis at the University of Paris, I came across a book with a specialized title, *The Norwegian Language in America* but an appealing subtitle, *A Study in Bilingual Behavior.* I quickly became enthralled by its scientific content but also by its very human touch. Clearly, the author, Einar Haugen, a Harvard professor and

[3] This post was published on December 29, 2010.

a bilingual himself, had analyzed bilingualism in both its academic and its human perspectives. His book was later to become a classic.

Never did I dream that I would meet Einar Haugen some years later and become friends with him. Having moved to the United States, and while I was preparing my first book on bilingualism, in the early eighties, I phoned him (we happened to live close by in Massachusetts), and asked if I could come and see him. I expected him to give me an appointment in his university office but he very kindly asked me over to his home.

I was greeted by a rather tall, very genteel, elderly man who showed me into his living room. As he was getting me a drink, Eva Haugen came in and introduced herself. She looked like a dream grandmother with very fine features, her grey hair in a bun, a soft voice, and a wonderful smile.

The first part of our meeting was more academic – I told Einar Haugen about my manuscript, and we talked about topics in bilingualism such as language planning, language choice, and code-switching. After about an hour, Eva joined us. Little by little, I realized that she too had had an impressive career as an author, editor, and translator of several books related to Norwegian–American subjects.

The Haugens were clearly comfortable in their lives as bilinguals and biculturals, and in their love of both America and Norway. They were ideal examples of bilingualism and biculturalism as it can be lived, as well as very fine scholars in their respective fields.

My first visit was followed by many others and, each time, I came away feeling more confident in the work I was doing and more serene as a bilingual and bicultural person myself. These visits had a very real impact on my career and on my life.

When I returned to Europe after some twelve years in the United States, I stayed in touch with the Haugens and visited them every time I came back. Then, in 1994, I heard that Einar Haugen had passed away. I wrote to Eva and promised that I would come and see her and, indeed, the following summer, when I was back, I gave her a call. There was no answer. So I drove to her home but found no one there. I went to the neighbor's and asked if they had seen her. They replied that she had had an accident and had broken her hip. She was now recuperating in a nursing home nearby.

I visited her the next day and, despite her health problems, I found her as lovely and as warm as usual. We talked about many things and she mentioned her move to the Midwest a few days later where she would live with one of her daughters. I suddenly had an idea: "Do you want to go and see your house before leaving?" She hesitated and then declined, "It wouldn't be wise," she said. This may have been because the house had been rented for the summer. But then, several minutes later, she changed her mind and said with a smile, "Oh, I would love to see my home again." So she got prepared and I drove the car up to the nursing home entrance as she could walk only with great difficulty.

When we reached her home, she looked at it for a long while and then said that she would like to see the yard. We walked around it slowly, Eva holding on to my arm, and she commented on her favorite trees and plants. We only stayed a short while and when I had helped her back into the car, I asked her to wait just a bit. I went to the side garden and carefully cut off a rose that had been climbing up the wall of her house. I brought it back to her and said: "To accompany you on your trip, Eva." She thanked me with one of her wonderful smiles. I then drove her back to her nursing home and spent a bit more time with her before giving her a goodbye hug.

Eva left for her daughter's home a few days later and I flew back to Europe. She passed away just three months later.

Reference

Haugen, E. (1969). *The Norwegian Language in America: A Study in Bilingual Behavior.* Bloomington: Indiana University Press.

10.8 BORN TO BE BILINGUAL: A LETTER TO MY NEWBORN GRANDCHILD

Bilinguals and biculturals of all ages need to be celebrated from time to time. This is a letter to my newborn grandchild who will grow up bilingual and bicultural.

My dearest little one,

One day you may read this letter written a few days after your birth. Your parents, your extended family, as well as many friends, have been celebrating your arrival among us. We have been marveling at how beautiful and how delicate you are, and we have wondered at your every move, awake or asleep.

While I was admiring you during my last visit, I could not help but think that your life will be surrounded by languages and cultures. Since your mother speaks primarily two rhythmically different languages, you came to the world already attuned to those languages. And in your first year, you will start acquiring those two languages simultaneously. Your father, and his family, will speak one language to you, and your mother, and her family, the other. Being bilingual and bicultural will be a normal part of your life.

You will reach the main milestones of language acquisition – babbling, first words, first phrases – at a rate similar to that of monolingual children. Some sounds or sound groups that are easier to produce will appear sooner than those that are more difficult, some words will have their meaning overextended, and simpler grammatical constructions will be used before more complex ones. The main difference, of course, will be that you will be doing all of this in two languages – like millions of other bilingual children – and not just one.

Of course, if one language receives more input than the other in your first years, it may become your dominant language – sounds will be isolated more quickly, more words will be acquired, and more grammatical rules will be inferred. And your dominant language may well influence your other language. But this can be corrected quickly if you change environment and your weaker language starts being used more often. It may even take over as your dominant language if the change lasts long enough.

Very quickly you will know which language to use with whom and for what. At first, you will create a strong bond between a person and his or her language. You will address that person in the appropriate language and you may be at a loss – to the point of being upset – when the wrong language is used by your interlocutor. You may even offer to interpret for that person in order to maintain the person–language bond.

You will also intermingle your languages at times as a communicative strategy or to fill a linguistic need. In the latter case, you may suddenly find yourself having to say something in a language that you do not normally use for that particular domain, object, or situation. But very quickly you will learn that with people who only know one of your languages, you have to speak just their language.

As the years go by, you will sometimes play with your languages. You will violate the person–language bond and will jokingly speak to someone in the wrong language. Or you may mix your languages on purpose to raise some eyebrows. A bit later, you will translate idiomatic expressions literally into the other language and produce them with a straight face. You may even imitate family members who speak one of your languages with an accent when you could say the same utterance without one.

Since your parents and grandparents have roots in different cultures, you will be introduced to them and will become bicultural. You will learn to adapt to each culture as you navigate between them, and you will combine and blend aspects of these cultures. Hopefully, each of your cultures will accept you as a bicultural person and will not force you to choose one over the other. As you grow up, you will be a bridge between the cultures you belong to, and you will sometimes act as an intermediary between the two.

There may be times when you are frustrated because of your bilingualism or biculturalism. Someone may remark on your way of saying or doing something, or may not know how to situate you. You may also struggle with a written language that you do not (yet) master well. But your parents and your extended family will be there to ease you through the difficulty and make things better.

Be proud of your linguistic and cultural roots and enjoy going back and forth between your languages and cultures. I will personally marvel at how you do so, and will help you, as best I can, to meet the challenges that you will sometimes have to face.

Welcome, my dearest little one. May you have a wonderful life![4]

Reference

Grosjean, F. (2010). *Bilingual: Life and Reality*. Cambridge, MA: Harvard University Press.

---

[4] At the time of going to press, my grandchild is already eight years old! He is indeed an active bilingual and on his way to becoming bicultural.

11

Language Processing

INTRODUCTION

The first two posts ask a fundamental question: Does the state of activation of the bilingual's languages change – both are active or only one is active – depending on factors such as the proximity of words in the two languages, the interlocutor's language knowledge, and the situation? Post 11.1 describes a production study that shows that the bilingual processing system can indeed operate in different activation states.

Post 11.2 shows that this is also true in language perception. Eye-tracking experiments have demonstrated that the system can be selective at times (only one language is involved), or nonselective at other times (both languages are involved).

Post 11.3 describes two studies – one on language production, the other on language perception – that examine how bilinguals react when they are confronted with a language they do not expect. These studies show how one can bring into the laboratory what bilinguals sometimes experience in "real life."

A study that received a lot of press when it came out is evoked in Post 11.4. It was taken to show that bilinguals are more efficient at phonological competition than monolinguals during spoken word recognition. I contacted the main author and found out what the main conclusion was really meant to be.

Post 11.5 relates the long life of a research result first obtained in the 1970s. It showed that a slight delay can occur in the perception of code-switches. Many researchers questioned the original experiment but further studies showed the result to be quite robust. The factors that modulate the delay, or that may even cancel it, are then discussed.

Post 11.6 reveals how certain processing mechanisms in a second language learned after childhood will never be acquired, or only partly acquired, after a specific point in time. In this case, it concerns the use of gender-marking cues when listening to speech.

Post 11.7 examines why it is that many people listening to a second language feel that the speech rate is faster than that in their first language. Research has investigated whether there is evidence for this and, if so, how it can be accounted for.

Finally, Post 11.8 is an interview with the late Dr. Lu-Feng Shi, a well-known speech-language-hearing researcher on the clinical assessment of speech perception and comprehension in bilinguals. A number of issues are discussed, such as which languages to use to test patients and which to employ during rehabilitation.

11.1 WHEN BILINGUALS SPEAK

Psycholinguists have developed very refined experimental procedures to show that bilingual language production is a dynamic process that can operate in different language activation states. A study illustrates this.

Anyone observing bilinguals speaking to different people during any one day will notice quite readily that they keep to one language when they are communicating with people who do not know their other language(s). However, they may well code-switch into, or borrow from, their other language(s) when their interlocutors know the same languages and the situation is conducive to language intermingling (see Post 3.4).

Bilinguals navigate along a continuum with two endpoints – a monolingual language mode where only one language is fully active and a bilingual language mode where several languages can be active (see Post 3.1). The consequence of this is that the state of activation of bilinguals' languages will vary from moment to moment. Numerous factors, both internal and external, control the level of activation at any given time.

Psycholinguists have developed very refined experimental procedures to show that bilingual language production is a dynamic process that can operate in different language activation states. Here is an illustration. Dutch researchers Daan Hermans, Ellen Ormel, Ria Besselaar, and Janet van Hell undertook a study that shows that even the lexical similarity between the two languages known by the bilingual, under certain circumstances, can play a role in changing the level of activation of the bilingual's languages. They did this by manipulating the presence of cognates, that is, translation equivalents that have similar orthographic and phonological forms in two languages, such as "apple" in English and "appel" in Dutch.

The researchers asked Dutch–English bilinguals to look at pictures on a computer screen followed by a letter representing a phoneme (e.g., the letter "b" represents the phoneme /b/). The bilinguals had to decide whether the phoneme was part of the English name of the picture being presented; they did so by pushing on a "yes" or a "no" button. There were three conditions in this phoneme monitoring study:

(a) In the affirmative condition, the phoneme was indeed part of the English name of the picture. For example, the picture was that of a bottle and it was followed by a "b" or a "t"; the answer was "yes" therefore.

(b) In the cross-language condition, the phoneme was not part of the English name but rather of the Dutch name of the picture. For example, "f" was presented and it is part of "fles," the Dutch translation equivalent of "bottle." Here the answer was "no" therefore (recall that participants had to base themselves on the English name of the picture).

(c) Finally, in the unrelated condition, the phoneme was neither part of the English nor of the Dutch name. For example, "p" is not part of "bottle" nor of "fles."

Now came the subtlety permitted by a good experimental design. The pictures shown to the bilinguals were divided up into two categories: half the pictures were used in the experimental condition where there was an English name that had a noncognate translation equivalent in Dutch. Examples were English "bottle" and Dutch "fles," English "pillow" and Dutch "kussen," etc. The other half of the pictures were used in the filler condition. It is here that the experiments that were run by the researchers differed from one another (we will look at two of them). In the first, all the filler pictures also had noncognate names in Dutch and English. Hence, if one adds the two halves of the experiment, no picture was followed by a letter that corresponded to a sound in the Dutch name of the picture. In sum, the experiment was monolingual, both overtly and covertly.

The results they obtained in this first experiment showed that there was no difference between the cross-language condition and the unrelated condition (the two conditions of interest), be it in reaction times or in accuracy scores. Basically, the Dutch translation equivalents of the English names of the pictures were not active. In other words, the participants were in a monolingual English mode.

In their second experiment, all the authors did was to change the pictures in the filler condition. They now had cognate names in English and Dutch, such as "moon" and Dutch "maan," "mouse" and Dutch "muis." (Note that they did not change the pictures in the experimental condition.) This time the two critical conditions (cross-language and unrelated) did produce different response latencies and accuracy scores. It took the participants more time to do the task in the cross-language condition than in the unrelated condition, and they were less accurate in the former condition. What was happening there was that the phonological representations of the Dutch picture names were activated, and they slowed down the response regarding the presence of a phoneme in the English name.

Based on these findings, the authors concluded that the bilingual language production system is indeed dynamic and that it can operate in different activation states depending on a number of factors. The level of activation of the bilingual's languages will be due to linguistic factors, such as mentioned above, but also psycholinguistic and sociolinguistic factors such as who you are talking to, whether you are using the "right language" to talk about the subject in question, how well you know the language you are speaking, how recently you have spoken the other language, and the presence of speakers of the other language(s). The bilingual production process is wonderfully sensitive to all these factors, and this promises many intriguing research findings in the years to come.

References

Hermans, D., Ormel, E., Besselaar, R., and van Hell, J. (2011). Lexical activation in bilinguals' speech production is dynamic: How language ambiguous words can affect cross-language activation. *Language and Cognitive Processes*, 26(10), 1687–1709.

Grosjean, F. (2013). Speech production. In F. Grosjean and P. Li, eds., *The Psycholinguistics of Bilingualism*. Malden, MA and Oxford: Wiley-Blackwell, pp. 50–69.

11.2 WHEN BILINGUALS LISTEN

When bilinguals are listening to, or reading, just one language, are their other languages involved? For many years, researchers answered positively but positions are evolving as new studies are being done and more factors are controlled.

In Post 11.1, we saw that bilingual language production is a dynamic process that can operate in different language activation states depending on a number of factors. These can be linguistic but also psycholinguistic and sociolinguistic. Is this also true of language perception? Researchers have spent considerable time examining the way bilinguals listen to, or read, their languages, and for many years they came to the conclusion that perceptual processing is nonselective, that is, that all the bilingual's languages are involved in the processes that take place during the acts of listening to, or reading, just one language.

Although many different experimental tasks have been used to study this question, I will concentrate on one used quite extensively in bilingual speech processing research. It is the eye-tracking technique that allows the experimenter to see where the participant is looking while listening to speech. In a first study, researchers Michael Spivey and Viorica Marian asked their Russian–English participants to look at a board situated in front of them, which contained a number of objects. For example, there was a target object, a stamp, which had to be moved; there were also, along with the stamp, a competitor object (a marker), or a control object (a ruler), as well as filler objects.

In the Russian-language session, the participants heard sentences such as "Poloji marku nije krestika" (Put the stamp below the cross), and researchers examined whether they looked at interlingual competitor objects (in this case, the marker) whose English name ("marker") shared the same onset as the target object ("marku"). This was compared to what happened in a control condition where the name of the control object (e.g., "ruler") had no phonetic similarity with "marku."

The researchers found significantly more eye movements to the interlingual competitor objects than to the control objects, which seemed to show that the word onset of the target object (e.g., "marku") not only activated Russian words but also activated English words. Based on this, they concluded that processing is nonselective, that is, both Russian and English were involved in the processing.

This first study led to many other studies by other researchers with different pairs of languages. Viorica Marian and Michael Spivey came back to this question four years later because they realized that the contextual factors in their first study had probably pushed their participants toward a bilingual mode of processing, thereby activating both languages, and hence encouraging nonselective processing. Among the factors they mentioned was the fact that the participants knew they were taking part in an experiment on bilingualism, they were tested by bilingual experimenters who were fluent in both languages, and the two languages (Russian and English) were tested in adjacent experimental sessions.

Thus, this time they attempted to put their participants in as close to a monolingual mode as possible, the kind of situation many bilinguals find themselves in on a daily basis (e.g., at work where no one else speaks their other language(s)). They used different experimenters for the Russian and English sessions, the experimenters spoke only one language, and the participants only took part in one or the other session.

The result they found this time (in the Russian session again) was that the competitor objects were not looked at more than the control objects. Hence, in this case, the other language had been totally put aside (deactivated) and processing only took place in Russian.

So, how does listening take place in bilinguals? What seems clear is that the incoming speech wave is processed by the language(s) that contain(s) elements of that input. This can indeed lead to nonselective processing when words from different languages have similar word beginnings, or when homophones and cognates are involved. If the input, however, contains elements of just one language, then only one language will process it ordinarily.

Other factors that play a role are "top-down" factors such as who is speaking and the accompanying context, both linguistic and situational. Sometimes these factors contradict the "bottom-up" information (the speech signal) as when a listener is shocked to hear the speaker use a language that is not expected. (Imagine coming out with a sentence in Spanish to your bilingual Spanish–English friend who has never ever heard you speak one word of Spanish.) When this happens, the listener may even have to ask the speaker to repeat what was said.

Another important factor is the listener's proficiency in the language being spoken. If it is the stronger language that is being processed, then the weaker language may not intervene as much or at all. However, if it is the other way around, that is, the weaker language is being processed, then there is a fair chance that the stronger language may be active, and may be influencing processing.

In sum, the bilingual's language perception system, much like its production counterpart, is dynamic and can operate in different activation states depending on a number of linguistic, psycholinguistic, and sociolinguistic factors.

References

Spivey, M. and Marian, V. (1999). Cross talk between native and second languages: Partial activation of an irrelevant lexicon. *Psychological Science*, 10, 281–284.

Marian, V. and Spivey, M. (2003). Competing activation in bilingual language processing: Within- and between-language competition. *Bilingualism: Language and Cognition*, 6, 97–115.

Grosjean, F. (2013). Speech perception and comprehension. In F. Grosjean and P. Li, eds., *The Psycholinguistics of Bilingualism*. Malden, MA and Oxford: Wiley-Blackwell, pp. 29–49.

11.3 HOW DO BILINGUALS REACT TO AN UNEXPECTED LANGUAGE?[1]

Bilinguals often associate a particular language with a specific speaker. How do they react when they are confronted with a language they do not expect?

Many bilinguals have a story or two of being surprised, if not shocked, when a person suddenly uses a language they did not expect, even though they know it. Some report not understanding what is said at first. There are even threads on the web that refer to this topic. Thus,

[1] This post was originally entitled, "Why aren't you speaking the right language? Part 2."

an American in Japan writes that he gets many shocked looks from Japanese people when he speaks Japanese in front of them for the first time. A Serbian notes that she is very surprised when foreigners in her country speak Serbian. And a teacher in India reports that her eyes nearly popped out when she heard a French student utter something in Hindi.

Language choice by bilinguals – basically which language you use with whom and for what – is governed by a number of factors several of which pertain to the participants in the exchange (see Post 3.1). For example, when you do not know the speaker, visual cues can prime a particular language as has been shown in an interesting study.

Shu Zhang and her colleagues at the Columbia Business School in New York wanted to know if facial characteristics could lead to language expectation. They asked a number of Chinese students who had been in the United States for about a year to take part in a computer-mediated communication task. The participants viewed the photo of either a Chinese or a Caucasian face of a certain Michael Lee and listened to him on a recording talk with a standard American accent about campus-life topics. The very same recording was played irrespective of the photo. The students then spoke about these same topics in English and were recorded.

When the researchers assessed their verbal fluency and measured their speech rate when speaking to Michael Lee, they found fascinating results. The students' fluency ratings were lower, as was their objective speech rate, in the Chinese face condition than the Caucasian face condition. Basically, they had expected the Chinese face to speak Chinese and hence their English language output was disrupted when interacting with Michael Lee in English.

Of course, only static pictures were used in this study, and they were clearly associated with visual cues representing different cultural groups. But what about situations where you associate a specific language to a given speaker you have actually seen speaking that language? And what impact does this have, not so much on your production of speech, as in the previous study, but on its perception? If, as some researchers still believe, both languages are always active when bilinguals process speech, then it shouldn't have an impact on your perception (nor should bilinguals be shocked by an unexpected language). If, on the other hand, one language is activated and the other deactivated, or even inhibited, when faced with a particular interlocutor who is known for speaking a particular language, then this should show up in the results obtained.

Monika Molnar and her colleagues at the Basque Center on Cognition, Brain and Language in Spain examined this very issue. They first asked proficient Basque–Spanish bilinguals, who had acquired both languages before the age of three, to familiarize themselves with three types of interlocutors via video recordings: Basque speakers, Spanish speakers, and bilingual Basque–Spanish speakers. The interlocutors introduced themselves and talked about various topics such as their family background, hobbies, and work. The Basque and Spanish speakers only spoke their respective language whereas the bilingual speakers used both Basque and Spanish and code-switched from time to time.

In the second part of the study, the bilingual participants saw each interlocutor on video produce a word or a made-up word, and they simply had to decide whether the item was a real word or not by pressing one of two keys. Seventy-five percent of the time, the Basque and Spanish interlocutors presented words in the language they had spoken during the familiarization phase (the experimenters called this the congruent trials since they corresponded to the language they had used before) and the remainder of the time, they produced words in the other language (the incongruent trials). Thus, the monolingual speakers surprised the participants at various points by uttering words in the wrong language. Until this happened, the participants did not know that the interlocutors also spoke the other language. As for the bilingual interlocutors, they presented words in one or the other language equally.

The results showed the importance of interlocutor identity when bilinguals process speech. The participants responded faster to words produced in the language previously associated with the monolingual interlocutors (e.g., Spanish words produced by Spanish interlocutors) than to words produced by them in the other language (e.g., Basque words produced by these same Spanish interlocutors). As for the words produced by the bilingual interlocutors, in the one or the other language, they were responded to the slowest.

With these two studies, researchers have been able to bring into the laboratory a phenomenon that bilinguals experience from time to time in "real life" – being confronted with a person using the wrong language. They have also confirmed that a language can be deactivated in certain situations. Future studies of this type, in which sociolinguistic factors are taken into account, will be fascinating to follow as they will certainly extend our knowledge of how bilinguals process their languages – individually, or together in a bilingual mode (see Post 3.4).

References

Zhang, S., Morris, M. W., Cheng, C.-Y., and Yap, A. J. (2013). Heritage-culture images disrupt immigrants' second-language processing through triggering first-language interference. *Proceedings of the National Academy of Sciences*, 110 (28), 11272–11277.

Molnar, M., Ibáñez-Molina, A., and Carreiras, M. (2015). Interlocutor identity affects language activation in bilinguals. *Journal of Memory and Language*, 81, 91–104.

11.4 DOES PROCESSING LANGUAGE DIFFERENTLY MEAN MORE EFFICIENTLY?

Current research is helping us understand in what way bilinguals are different from monolinguals when they process language and in what way they are similar. But where does efficiency come in? An example is taken from a study that received worldwide attention when it came out.

I have defended over the years a view that proposes that bilinguals are not the sum of two complete or incomplete monolinguals (see Post 1.2). The coexistence and constant interaction of the two or more languages in bilinguals have produced specific processing characteristics that cohabit with general characteristics common to all users of language.

In the domain of speech perception and comprehension, for example, bilinguals go through the same major stages as monolinguals when processing an utterance: they identify the speech sounds and recognize the words that are uttered; they do syntactic and semantic processing; and they undertake pragmatic processing, which takes into account the context in which the utterance is said, the listener's knowledge of the world, and the rules of communication to produce a final enriched meaning of the utterance.

However, because bilinguals speak two or more languages, they differ from monolinguals in a number of ways when they process language. We know, for example, that the perception system of bilinguals is dynamic and will operate in different activation states – monolingual or bilingual – depending on a number of linguistic, psycholinguistic, and sociolinguistic factors (see Post 11.2). We know also that certain mechanisms in the bilinguals' second language will never be acquired, or only partly acquired, in particular when they started learning it late (see Post 11.6).

With the increased use of brain imaging, along with more traditional behavioral experimentation, great strides are being made in our understanding of how bilinguals process language. One study, which was talked about extensively in the media, was conducted by Professor Viorica Marian along with colleagues from Northwestern University and the University of Houston. They wanted to study phonological competition during spoken language processing in both monolinguals and bilinguals, and they obtained both behavioral data – accuracy and response time – and brain imaging data.

English monolinguals and Spanish–English bilinguals were placed individually in a scanner and were asked to search for a picture of an object (the target) that corresponded to a spoken word presented to them in English. They saw an array of four pictures and used a button box to indicate the position of the target picture. At various points during the experiment, the word representing one of the other objects had the same beginning as the word representing the target. So, for example, if the target object represented a candy, the other object represented a candle. The presence of this other object created a momentary competition that ended when "candy" was fully heard and the participants pressed on the "candy" button. This type of phonological competition is common in spoken word recognition, even when we are not looking at something since many other words in our minds have the same beginning as the one being uttered, and we have to deactivate them (some say, inhibit them) as we are listening.

The results obtained showed that both monolinguals and bilinguals were very accurate in their responses, but they did respond more slowly when the competitor picture was present than when it was absent, as was expected. There were no differences between monolinguals and bilinguals at this level. However, when the imaging results were compared, the researchers found that bilinguals displayed substantially less cortical activation compared to monolinguals who showed greater activation in frontal regions (executive control areas) as well as the primary visual cortex. The conclusion the study arrived at makes sense: both monolinguals and bilinguals experienced competition, as indexed by slower response times in competition conditions, whereas the two groups recruited different neural resources to manage this competition.

The interpretation the authors had of these results will be debated for some time though. They proposed that bilinguals may be more efficient at managing phonological competition. General media accounts amplified this interpretation and took it out of context to produce titles such as "Study shows that people who speak two languages have more efficient brains" (*Washington Post*), "Bilingual people are like brain 'bodybuilders'" (*Discovery News*), and "Bilingual brains may be better at processing language and cognitive information" (*The Hearing Review*).

I wrote to Viorica Marian to ask her a few questions and two of her answers reassured me. First, she clearly stated that monolinguals and bilinguals are both competent language processors and are able to process language in real time. She also stated that monolinguals are just as efficient as they need to be to process the types of linguistic demands that they typically face. As concerns bilinguals, Viorica Marian thinks that their experiences involve between-language competition in addition to within-language competition, and that this may change the way they process language.

In the long run, both monolinguals and bilinguals have to do extensive processing of language (think of the number of hours a day we listen to people speaking), and have to do it efficiently. They'll do it in similar ways at some levels and differently at others – and this is what bilingualism processing research will continue to examine in the years to come.

Reference

Viorica, M., Chabal, S., Bartolotti, J., Bradley, K., and Hernandez, A. E. (2014). Differential recruitment of executive control regions during phonological competition in monolinguals and bilinguals. *Brain and Language*, 139, 108–117.

11.5 THE RESEARCH FINDING SOME OF US DIDN'T WANT
TO BELIEVE

A very old research finding related to the slight delay that can occur in the perception of spoken code-switches by bilinguals has had a long and interesting life.

There is a very old study that was done with bilinguals in Canada and whose results I couldn't quite believe at first. McGill researchers John Macnamara and Seymour Kushnir, back in 1971, asked French–English bilinguals to listen to short sentences containing code-switches. These are complete shifts to the other language for a word, a phrase, or a sentence, before coming back to the base language, that is, the language of the interaction (see Post 3.4). The researchers presented statements such as "A monkey can drink *eau* (water)" and recorded the time it took the participants to say whether they were true or false. They compared the results obtained with those found for statements that contained no code-switches and found that those containing switches took about a quarter of a second longer to process. If there were two switches, the delay approached half a second.

Macnamara and Kushnir's methodology was questioned by a number of researchers and I was one of them. Their code-switches did not follow the precise grammatical constraints of natural code-switching; there were grammatical problems with the French segments (e.g., one would say, "de l'eau" in the example above); it was unclear whether the participants were regular code-switchers themselves, and so on. So a few years later, my colleague Carlos Soares and I, both active code-switchers in our everyday bilingual lives, undertook a study where we did away with these potential problems. We also made sure our bilingual participants were as fluent in the one as in the other language, and that they were indeed code-switchers when the situation and the interlocutor permitted it. We also told them that they would be hearing sentences with and without code-switches, thereby removing, we thought, the surprise component of code-switching.

Much to our amazement, given all the precautions we had taken, we again found that the processing of code-switches took more time than that of base-language words. This time the difference was 152 milliseconds. Since then, other studies examining reaction time but also electrical activity of the brain (EEG) have replicated this finding. If one calculates the mean delay time for the published speech perception code-switching studies over the last forty-five years, it is 133 ms. This is not a particularly long time and does not deserve the label "switching cost" that some researchers have used since, but it is nevertheless present.

Macnamara and Kushnir proposed an interesting explanation for the phenomenon. They hypothesized that as listeners we have certain expectations and that one of them is that all the words in a sentence should be in a single language. We now talk about a "base-language effect," that is, the fact that in normal bilingual speech, elements belonging to the language being spoken – the base language – are favored over guest-language elements. This is because the base language is being processed primarily and is the most active.

A number of studies have gone beyond just finding a switching delay and have examined the factors that modulate it, or remove it. Here are a few that have emerged over time. First, the amount of code-switching that takes place before the point at which code-switching processing is measured seems to play a role. The greater the amount of code-switching, the more the guest language is activated, and hence the more readily a code-switch is processed. A second factor concerns the situational context bilinguals are in. Yu-Lin Cheng and David Howard showed quite convincingly that bilinguals can process mixed-language utterance with no significant processing delay when they are in a situation where both languages are used interchangeably and frequently. Other factors concern one-word switches – their frequency, their syllabic configuration, the way they are pronounced, the presence of a near homophone in the other language, etc.

Since many studies have shown that the perception of code-switches does take extra time, although various factors can affect the delay and may even make it disappear, researchers have asked how long the delay lasts after the code-switch. If it is carried over to the next word(s), then the bilingual listener may start falling behind the speaker – especially if the latter is code-switching a lot – something that seems quite counterintuitive to all those who practice code-switching on a daily basis. In my laboratory, two master's degree students, Corinna Domenighetti and Dolorès Caldognetto, showed that the switching delay appears to be short-lived. By the time the next words arrive, any delay that might have occurred has been made up. Other speech studies have shown that the persistence of the delay depends on the switching direction – is it a switch into the first or into the second language? – as well as on the proficiency one has in the switch language.

When Macnamara and Kushnir undertook that first speech delay study many years ago, they could not have imagined that the line of research they inaugurated would still be alive and well almost fifty years later. As researchers, we should salute their seminal work even though many of us didn't want to believe their results at first. But then, didn't French medieval scholar, Pierre Abélard, write, "It is by doubting that we come to investigate, and by investigating that we recognize the truth?".

References

Grosjean, F. (2018). Processing bilingual speech. In F. Grosjean and K. Byers-Heinlein. *The Listening Bilingual: Speech Perception, Comprehension, and Bilingualism.* Hoboken, NJ: Wiley, pp. 109–128.

Macnamara, J. and Kushnir, S. L. (1971). Linguistic independence of bilinguals: The input switch. *Journal of Verbal Learning and Verbal Behavior,* 10, 480–487.

Cheng, Y-L. and Howard, D. (2008). The time cost of mixed-language processing: An investigation. *International Journal of Bilingualism,* 12(3), 209–222.

11.6 PERCEPTUAL INSENSIBILITY IN A SECOND LANGUAGE

It is a well-known fact that producing the correct gender of nouns is sometimes difficult for speakers of a second language. But can they nevertheless make use of this cue when they are listening to speech? A study examined this and found some fascinating results.

Winston Churchill once said on French radio, with his characteristic English accent when he spoke French, "Despite working so hard and coming so far with the French to help them win their freedom, I have never mastered the gender of French nouns!" His problem was a classic one for those who learn French late: Is it "le bateau" or "la bateau" (the boat)? It's "le bateau." Is it "le montagne" or "la montagne" (the mountain)? It's "la montagne" and so on.

Not only is gender difficult for late learners of French (as it can be for late learners of Spanish and Italian, among other languages), but gender agreement marking on other words that accompany the noun, such as an article, an adjective, or a pronoun, can also be difficult. This explains why you may hear a non-native speaker of French say, "le petit montagne" (the small mountain) instead of "la petite montagne."

We have known for some time that native listeners of languages with gender make use of gender-marking cues (such as the pronunciation of the "t" in "petite" but not in "petit") to speed up the recognition of the following noun (e.g., "montagne"). The question my colleague, Delphine Guillelmon, and I asked was whether bilinguals would show the same effect. And does it depend on when they acquired their gender-marking language?

Even though late learners of a gender language make more gender errors than early learners when speaking, we expected that in perception both early and late bilinguals would be sensitive to gender marking to the same extent. After all, we reasoned, if a language offers you a gender cue to speed up your recognition of the following noun, why not use it?

We asked early and late English–French bilinguals to do a very simple task: they were to listen to short phrases such as "le joli bateau" (the nice boat) and to repeat the word after "joli" (in this case, "bateau"). We compared the time it took them to do so in a congruent condition (the article "le" has the same gender as the following noun, "bateau"), in a neutral condition as in "leur joli bateau" (their nice boat) where "leur" carries no gender information, and in an incongruent condition such as "la joli(e) bateau" where the gender marking "la" is incorrect.

We first tested the early bilingual group (they had started using their two languages, English and French, as early as five years of age, on average), and we found that they behaved like monolingual French speakers. They too had become sensitive to gender marking early in life and used it to speed up processing in perception.

The crucial question now became: Would late bilinguals (English speakers who had started speaking French on a regular basis at age twenty-five, some twenty-four years before we tested them) show the same effect as early bilinguals? If gender marking is indeed important during language processing, then they should have become sensitive to it. However, if there is a critical (or sensitive) period for taking into account gender marking, at least in perception, and if they acquired their gender-marking language after this period, then they should show little, if any, effect.

The results we obtained surprised us. Late bilinguals were not only totally insensitive to gender congruency ("le joli bateau") but also to gender incongruency (the ungrammatical "la joli(e) bateau"). It was as if they simply could not use the masculine "le" cue or the feminine "la" cue during the processing of those short phrases.

We investigated whether this was due to a slightly slower overall speed of response (it wasn't) or to their inability to use gender agreement when speaking French (in fact, they made very few gender errors in production). Their level of language proficiency was not at stake either – their oral comprehension of French was generally excellent after more than twenty years of daily use of the language.

It would appear therefore that certain processing mechanisms in a second language will never be acquired (or only partly acquired) after a specific point in time. Of course, late English–French bilinguals still recognize words perfectly, but recognition is neither facilitated by a congruent gender marking nor impeded by an incongruent one.

We could not resist concluding our study by extending Sir Winston Churchill's statement in the following way, "I have never mastered the gender of French nouns ... *be it in production OR perception.*"

Reference

Guillelmon, D. and Grosjean, F. (2001). The gender marking effect in spoken word recognition: The case of bilinguals. *Memory and Cognition*, 29, 503–511.

11.7 WHY ARE THEY TALKING SO FAST?

When we listen to a language we do not master well, we often feel that the speech rate is faster than that of our native language. Research has investigated whether there is evidence for this and, if so, how it can be accounted for.

Languages are spoken at about the same rate even though there is a lot of variability due to the speakers themselves, the situation, the topic being talked about, and so on. Many years ago, my University of Paris colleague, Alain Deschamps, and I measured the speaking rate of a group of English and French speakers in an interview situation. The average rates we found were quasi-identical: 176 words per minute for English and 174 words per minute for French.

Even when languages are totally different from one another, a spoken language on the one hand, and a sign language on the other, similarities are found if one examines the right level. Salk Institute Professor, Ursula Bellugi, and her colleague, Susan Fischer, found that when someone is signing, as compared to speaking, less signs are produced per minute than words. This makes sense as the hands-arms-body articulators are much larger in sign than the tongue-jaw-lips articulators in speech. However, and this remains a major finding of their research, when you count the number of propositions (basic ideas) per minute, the rate is identical in sign and speech.

Why is it then that when we listen to a language we do not master well, we feel that the rate is faster than in our native language? This leads to a general impression that speakers of language X (fill in your preferred second language) always talk fast. University of Geneva researcher, Sandra Schwab, and I examined this precise question in a study that was published in the journal, *Phonetica*.

We asked a group of native speakers of French, and a group of native speakers of German who had studied French for several years and used it occasionally, to listen to short stories in French read at a fast, a medium, and a slow rate. They were asked to estimate the rate of each story (using magnitude estimation) and to answer five comprehension questions.

The first thing we found was that, overall, second-language speakers did indeed give higher estimates than native speakers. But, more interestingly, the difference between the two groups was not the same at all rates. At a slow rate, the groups gave practically the same estimates. They started diverging at a normal rate (the estimates of the second-language speakers were higher), and they were quite different at a fast rate (here the second-language speakers gave much higher estimates). In sum, the faster the rate, the greater the difference between native and non-native speakers.

To start understanding why it is that we feel that speakers of a language that we do not master well speak faster, we examined the results of the comprehension assessment of the non-native speakers. We wanted to see if there was a relationship between the level of comprehension in a second language and the estimates of speech rate. A correlational analysis showed that there was. We found a significant negative correlation between comprehension scores and rate estimates: the lower the score, the higher the rate estimate. This was true when the stories were presented at a slow rate and at a medium rate. We didn't find the relationship at a fast rate: all non-native speakers found that rate extremely rapid however good their comprehension was.

So it would seem that our increased estimate of speech rate in a second language, at least when it is either normal or slow, could be due, in part, to the fact that we are trying to understand what is being said. The less we understand, the more we feel that the rate is high. Future studies will want to show how this estimate of rate evolves over time as oral comprehension improves. If there is progress, then estimates of speaking rate may start resembling those of native speakers, or at least of fluent bilinguals.

Reference

Schwab, S. and Grosjean, F. (2004). La perception du débit en langue seconde (Speech rate perception in a second language). *Phonetica*, 61, 84–94.

11.8 ASSESSING SPEECH PERCEPTION AND COMPREHENSION IN BILINGUALS

(Interview with Lu-Feng Shi)

When bilinguals need to have their speech perception and comprehension assessed clinically, how is it done? And what are the issues at stake?

Speech-language-hearing professionals often have to assess the speech perception and comprehension of bilinguals who suffer from a hearing or processing impairment. How they do so is an interesting topic that we know little about. One researcher who did a lot of work in the field was the late Dr. Lu-Feng Shi, Associate Professor of Communication Sciences and Disorders at Long Island University. He kindly accepted to answer a few of my questions, and I wish to thank him wholeheartedly.

What do speech-language-hearing professionals do in a clinic and who are those who seek their help?
In North America and some European nations, speech-language pathologists deal with speech and language disorders, whereas audiologists take care of hearing disorders. We work with a wide age range of patients, from infants

to older adults, more specifically with practically anybody for whom there is a breakdown in communication that causes functional limitation and/or participation restriction. Our primary goal is to enhance effective communication.

Can you give us some examples of patients that you assess?
Our clientele includes children who have speech, language, and hearing impairment (e.g., fluency and articulation disorders, language development issues, congenital hearing loss). As you can easily imagine, many are also bilingual. Adults typically have developed speech and language skills, so their communication difficulty is usually due to hearing impairment. When evaluating their hearing, we use tones as well as speech stimuli. As for our elderly patients, in addition to hearing loss, some are recovering from a stroke and may have motor speech issues. Here too, the patients' language background and in some cases their bilingualism have to be considered.

Are bilinguals assessed like monolinguals?
With monolingual clients, we present test items in their native language. For a bilingual client, things are more complicated. We know that a bilingual is not two monolinguals in one person (see Post 1.2), and therefore it is not adequate to compare the result of a test done in one language to the norm based on monolinguals in that language. Doing that has the potential of misdiagnosing the bilingual as having hearing or processing issues when that might not be the case.

Some might suggest that you allow for a few more errors during the assessment of bilinguals.
It's fine to accept that a normal-hearing bilingual client misrecognizes a few more words than the monolingual. We know his/her compromised performance is due to a language proficiency difference rather than a hearing/processing disorder. But most cases are not as clearly cut. What if a bilingual individual has both a hearing/processing disorder and a language proficiency issue? How much of the poor performance can be attributed to the disorder versus the difference in language proficiency? How can we then make a recommendation or set the goal for rehabilitation?

Should bilinguals be tested in all their languages then?
Ideally, bilingual clients should be evaluated in every language they use on a daily basis. After all, the goal is to enhance communication. If they

speak English at work but Spanish at home, then we should try to test them in both English and Spanish. But this is very hard in practice. To test a bilingual in two languages, we need a clinician who is equally proficient in both languages and who also understands the phenomenon of bilingualism. We also need two tests, one in English and the other in Spanish, for example, with comparable psychometric properties. We then need to administer each test in listening conditions that best simulate the situations in which these languages are used.

Couldn't an interpreter be used?
Yes, an interpreter can help us communicate with a client, but cannot help us judge the client's responses and score the test. Audiologists write down and score the responses to words or sentences in real time, so proficiency in the test language is essential. Moreover, bilingual clinicians should understand the culture each language is related to so as to be aware of the client's concerns and know how to best address them. There is also a trust issue here; as Leo Morales and his colleagues have shown, clients respond better to clinicians who share their cultural background.

Tell us more about test materials when assessing bilinguals.
I'm going to use English and Spanish again as examples. The most widely used test material in English includes a set of monosyllabic words which are prevalent in the language. By contrast, the most common words in Spanish have two syllables. These words have more phonotactic (syllable structure) and lexical cues and are therefore easier to recognize than those with one syllable. As such, I would expect poorer performance on an English word recognition test than a Spanish test in a perfectly balanced English–Spanish bilingual. If one is not aware of how these languages are structured, one might think the bilingual has a problem with English when that is not the case.

What about listening conditions?
In most clinics, speech recognition is only carried out in quiet, but ironically, even individuals with moderate hearing loss do not complain of difficulty with speech in a quiet room. To most, hearing becomes difficult in noisy situations such as in crowded places. Therefore, many scholars advocate testing clients in noise so as to better appraise their difficulty in real-life listening, in addition to testing them in quiet to get the baseline. The same goes for bilinguals;

only this time we are talking about four test conditions (quiet and noise for each language). That requires a lot of time not only for the clinician but also for the client. Whether a third-party insurer will pay for all this is anyone's guess.

If the ideal practice is not practical, what may be the second-best practice?

This is a very difficult question for which we don't yet have an answer. We have shown with Diana Sánchez that the performance of bilinguals in one language does not correlate with performance in the other, so it may be necessary to test in both languages if we are interested in getting the full picture. On the other hand, if for some clients from a given group, testing in both languages yields the same diagnosis and leads to the same set of recommendations, then perhaps it is adequate to just test in one language for diagnostic purposes.

What about rehabilitation?

We cannot assume that improving listening skills in one language automatically improves skills in another language. Each language has a unique set of phonemes and they are subject to the effects of hearing loss in a different way. English is notorious for highly confusable high-frequency, low-amplitude sounds such as /f/, /s/, and /θ/. English also allows clusters of up to four consonants, making correct recognition of each consonant in the cluster very difficult (e.g., the final consonants in "glimpsed"). Romance languages such as Spanish and Italian are more listener-friendly, in a way, as they have prominent vowels and limited cases of diphthongs and consonant clusters.

My guess therefore is that English–Spanish bilinguals may have more difficulty with English than Spanish speech as a result of hearing loss and thus require more rehabilitative effort in English, even if English is the stronger language of the two. This is an area in which more investigation is clearly needed.

So what are your conclusions on assessing bilinguals?

Without more research, I'll refrain from being too assertive. However, good clinical work is based on a sound rationale. As such, I would suggest that we test a client in one language if that alone can lead to a clear diagnosis. When rehabilitation is called for, then we may want to evaluate and follow up with both languages.

References

Morales, L. S., Cunningham, W. E., Brown, J. A., Liu, H., and Hays, R. D. (1999). Are Latinos less satisfied with communication by health care providers? *Journal of General Internal Medicine*, 14, 409–417.

Shi, L.-F. and Sánchez, D. (2010). Spanish/English bilingual listeners on clinical word recognition tests: What to expect and how to predict. *Journal of Speech, Language, and Hearing Research*, 53, 1096–1111.

12

The Bilingual Mind

INTRODUCTION

When people talk about the bilingual mind, one of the very first things they ask is what language bilinguals think in. It is only natural therefore that this topic be studied in Post 12.1. The answer is much more complex than one would have thought at first but also much more interesting.

Another topic often raised about the bilingual mind is counting and mathematical operations. In Post 12.2, Aneta Pavlenko presents the approaches used to study numerical cognition in bilinguals, the results obtained, and how to account for them.

An important aspect of the bilingual mind is memory, which is covered in Post 12.3. Both autobiographical knowledge and more general, factual, knowledge are guided by the bilingual's languages.

In Post 12.4, Aneta Pavlenko answers questions on how learning another language may reshape cognitive processes such as perception, categorization, memory, and self-perception. She also evokes the challenges of current research and the directions that will be followed in the future.

Post 12.5 shows how the topic of the bilingual mind can leave the academic domain and be of importance to other segments of society, in this case the judiciary. As will be seen, research on bilingualism and the bilingual mind played a role in the decision reached by the US Supreme Court in a case of bilingual juror exclusion.

The last four posts of this chapter concern what has been called "the bilingual advantage." It has been proposed by some that bilingualism strengthens certain cognitive processes, known as executive functions, and makes the bilingual brain more resistant to neurodegeneration. The posts were written over an eight-year period and reflect how things evolved rather dramatically over that time span.

Post 12.6, written in 2011, reviews the findings obtained concerning the cognitive effects of bilingualism, from very negative effects at the beginning of the past century, to largely positive effects at the beginning of this century. Post 12.7 discusses studies that seemed to show that bilingualism has a protective effect on the onset of dementia, but it does also mention some that did not.

By the time Post 12.8 was written, in 2016, the debate on the cognitive advantage of bilingualism had entered troubled waters with many researchers questioning its very existence. And finally, in Post 12.9, published in 2019, researcher Marc Antoniou helps us understand where things stand today as the debate rages on.

12.1 THINKING AND DREAMING IN TWO (OR MORE) LANGUAGES

Bilinguals are often asked about the language(s) they think and dream in. When analyzing their answers, we must not forget that thinking and dreaming can also be independent of language.

A question bilinguals are often asked is what language they think in. If they choose just one of their languages in their reply, then the reaction is often, "Ah, then it must be your stronger language" or even, "It must be the language of your inner being." The same kind of remark is made about the language(s) bilinguals dream in.

How true is this? The first thing to consider is that, in fact, thinking can be independent of language. When bilinguals are riding a bus, walking down the street, or exercising, their thoughts may not be in a particular language. Philosophers and psychologists have long acknowledged that thought can be visual-spatial or involve nonlinguistic concepts. Cognitive scientists Steven Pinker and Jerry Fodor, for example, propose that thinking occurs at first in "mentalese"; it is prelinguistic and occurs before the representations we are thinking about are turned into English, Spanish, or Chinese, for example.

But then why do we believe we think in a specific language? This is because language intervenes at a later stage while planning to speak, just as it does in our inner speech. Professor of applied linguistics, Aneta Pavlenko, defines the latter as subvocal or silent self-talk, that is, mental activity that takes place in an identifiable linguistic code and which is directed primarily at the self.

In a small survey I conducted with bilinguals and trilinguals in which I asked them which language(s) they thought in, a full 70 percent replied "both languages" or "all languages" (for trilinguals). They were either basing themselves on the planning stage leading to overt speech (the stage Berkeley psycholinguist Dan Slobin calls "thinking for speaking") or on their inner speech. Their answer is not surprising, then, since bilinguals use their languages for different purposes, in different domains of life, with different people (see a description of the Complementarity Principle in Post 1.5).

Thus, were I to think about something I wanted to say to an American friend, after the prelinguistic stage, it would be in English. Were I to think about a shopping list, it would be in French, as I live in a French-speaking region. Were I to think about what a colleague told me the other day, it would be in the language that the colleague used when we spoke.

University of London linguist, Jean-Marc Dewaele, has examined the factors governing language choice in inner speech. Among them we find the language that is dominant, when and where the languages were acquired, the bilingual's proficiency in these languages, the frequency of language use, and the size of the speaker's social network.

Are things any different when dreaming? Not really. In the small survey I undertook, almost as many bilinguals and trilinguals (64 percent in all) said that they dreamed in one or the other language, depending on the dream – when a language was involved, of course. Once again, the Complementarity Principle is at work here: depending on the situation and the person we are dreaming about, we will use one language, the other, or both.

One interesting aspect of dreams in bilinguals is that some people have reported speaking a language fluently in a dream when they are not actually fluent in that language. Linguist Veroboj Vildomec reported that a multilingual who spoke some Russian dreamed that he was speaking fluent Russian. But when he woke up, he realized that it had been in fact a mixture of Czech and Slovak, with a bit of Russian and not fluent Russian after all. Dreams are just that … and can do wonders to one's competence in a language!

References

Pavlenko, A. (2011). *Thinking and Speaking in Two Languages.* Bristol/Buffalo/Toronto: Multilingual Matters.

Grosjean, F. (2010). Personality, thinking and dreaming, and emotions in bilinguals. Chapter 11 of *Bilingual: Life and Reality.* Cambridge, MA: Harvard University Press.

12.2 WHAT LANGUAGES DO BILINGUALS COUNT IN?

Is it true that bilinguals always count in their first language? And if so, are bilingual children at a disadvantage if they study math in a second language? New brain studies suggest that bilinguals are more flexible than previously thought.

Post written by Aneta Pavlenko.

It is often said that bilinguals continue using their first language for simple arithmetic operations, such as addition or multiplication, long after they shifted to the second language in other domains. I am not an exception to this phenomenon – after two decades in the United States, I live, lecture, and write in English, but when it comes to balancing my checkbook, calculating a tip, or counting the number of reps at the gym, I often switch to Russian. Do others also count in their first language while living in the second, and if so, why? And what does this adherence mean for kids who study math in a second language or shift languages mid-way through the schooling process?

To study the relationship between bilingualism and numerical cognition, researchers commonly use experimental tasks that range from number recall to complex mathematical problems. They also use large-scale surveys that ask participants about their language preferences for everyday numerical activities, such as object counting, calculator use, telling time, memorizing telephone numbers, and figuring out discounts. The findings of more than three decades of research confirm that bilinguals who learned a second language in late childhood or adulthood favor their first language for mental computations. They are also faster at remembering numbers and solving mathematical problems in that language.

The first language advantage, however, is limited to speakers whose early schooling was in their home language. When kids are schooled in languages different from those of the home, they tend to favor the language of early schooling as the language of mental arithmetic. For the world's leading expert on numerical cognition, Stanislas Dehaene, this makes perfect sense. He argues that even the most fluent bilinguals favor the language of instruction because the laborious process of learning and reciting arithmetic tables imprints them as word sequences in the brain structures, and it is more efficient to automatically activate these sequences than to relearn arithmetic in a new language.

Yet the picture emerging from bilingualism research is significantly more complex. To begin with, mental arithmetic is not the only area where we deal with numbers – we also have to retrieve numbers from memory, such as dates, pin codes, or phone numbers. In my own case, the number of my old apartment in Kiev may pop out in Russian, while my social security number comes out in English. Such language dependence was also observed by an American psychologist, Elizabeth Spelke, who discovered that she could readily provide American friends with her summer address in France but not with her telephone number. Retrieving the number required that she say it in (non-native) French, visualize the numerals, and then mentally read them off in English.

Intrigued by this phenomenon, Spelke and her Russian-speaking graduate student at MIT, Sanna Tsivkin, conducted a training study with eight Russian–English bilinguals, who learned elementary arithmetic in Russian and favored Russian for everyday mental calculations. The participants were taught new numerical operations, new arithmetic equations, and new geographic or historical facts containing numerical information, in either Russian or English. When asked to recall these numerical facts and to solve problems or equations similar to those presented in the training, they performed faster and more efficiently in the language of the training.[1]

More recently, Nicole Wicha and her colleagues in San Antonio, Texas, came to a similar conclusion when they examined the relationship between bilingualism and math using event-related potentials. In their first study, they measured electrical activity in the brains of twenty-two

[1] See the next post for another example of the link between memory and language.

Spanish–English bilinguals performing basic multiplication calculations. All of the volunteers were college students who grew up in Spanish-speaking families but became proficient in English by the age of fifteen. They were asked to solve simple math problems, some of which were presented in digits and others in words, in both Spanish and English. The results confirmed the advantage for the language of instruction, but they also showed that some individuals responded faster in the language they used regularly and not in the language in which they initially learned basic math.

The researchers then repeated the experiment with fourteen elementary school teachers, who were bilingual in English and Spanish and had extensive experience of teaching arithmetic. Half of the participants taught in the same language in which they themselves learned math and the other half taught in a different language. The teachers were asked to judge the correctness of multiplication problems in each of their languages. Both groups were very fast in their responses, regardless of the language, but their brains appeared to respond faster to incorrect solutions in the language of teaching, regardless of whether it was the language of the speaker's early schooling.

These findings suggest that the language bilinguals count in may depend on the language of early schooling but the language of other numerical tasks depends on their subsequent experiences with language and math, so that some tasks may be handled faster and more efficiently in languages learned later in life. But, to add a bit of spice to the equation, there are also those who do not rely on words and vocalizations at all when dealing with math and prefer to think of mathematical relationships "in the language of math!"

References

Martinez-Lincoln, A., Cortinas, C., and Wicha, N. (2015) Arithmetic memory networks established in childhood are changed by experience in adulthood. *Neuroscience Letters*, 584, 325–330.

Salillas, E. and Wicha N. (2012). Early learning shapes the memory networks for arithmetic evidence from brain potentials in bilinguals. *Psychological Science*, 23, 745–755.

Spelke, E. and Tsivkin, S. (2001). Language and number: A bilingual training study. *Cognition*, 78, 45–88.

12.3 FORGOTTEN? TRY YOUR OTHER LANGUAGE

Recent research on the relationship between language and memory in bilinguals has produced some very interesting results. It would appear that both autobiographical knowledge and more general, factual, knowledge are guided by language.

Any bilingual will tell you that there are concepts that are best articulated in a particular language. In fact, when bilingual friends or acquaintances fumble for the right word or expression, how many times have we not heard, or proposed ourselves, "Try your other language." But words are just a small part of our knowledge. What about other forms of knowledge that we have stored in our memory?

Northwestern University researcher Viorica Marian has spent many years studying the link between language and memory. In one of her earlier studies, conducted with renowned cognitive scientist Ulrich Neisser, she interviewed a number of Russian–English bilinguals, in English and in Russian. They were given English prompt words in the English part of the study (e.g., "summer," "neighbors," birthday," etc.), and Russian prompt words (translation equivalents) in the Russian part. The task of the bilinguals was to describe an event from their own life that the prompt word brought to mind. They were also asked, after the study, to indicate the language they had spoken, had been spoken to, or were surrounded by, at the time that each recalled event took place.

What the researchers found was that the bilinguals accessed more Russian memories when interviewed in Russian than when interviewed in English, and more English memories when interviewed in English than in Russian. They concluded that the accessibility of autobiographical memories was improved when the language used at the time of remembering corresponded to the language in which the memories were initially formed.

But can the accessibility of general knowledge, and not just autobiographical knowledge, also be guided by language? In other words, is factual knowledge acquired in a particular language more likely to be recovered when the same language is used at the time of recall?

To study this, Viorica Marian and Margarita Kaushanskaya examined the retrieval of general knowledge in Mandarin–English bilinguals by means of three tasks: a multivalent task in which they tested the retrieval of multiple items in a category within each language, a bivalent task in which the questions asked had two possible correct answers, one in each language, and a univalent task where there was a single correct answer, in just one language.

For example, in the bivalent task, the bilingual participants were asked, either in Mandarin or in English, "In a famous love story, what were the names of two lovers who died because of family disapproval?" Another example, this time a request, again expressed either in Mandarin or English, was, "Name a statue of someone standing with a raised arm while looking into the distance." What the researchers found was that the participants were more likely to access information that had been encoded (learned) in Mandarin when interviewed in Mandarin (the encoding information was obtained by questioning the participants at the end of the experiment), and more likely to access information encoded in English when interviewed in English.

Thus, for the first question asked, the participants were more likely to say, Liang Shanbo and Zhu Yingtai when asked in Mandarin, and Romeo and Juliet when asked in English. Likewise, they answered more readily Chairman Mao when asked the statue question in Mandarin, and the Statue of Liberty when asked in English.

When the bilingual participants were given the multivalent task (they were prompted with "lakes," for example), the researchers found similar results. Mandarin responses such as Qinghai Lake, Lake Poyang, or Lake Tianchi were more likely to emerge during the Mandarin interviews and English responses such as Lake Michigan, Lake Ontario, or Lake Erie were more likely to be given during English interviews. As for the univalent task (where there was only one answer, encoded in only one language), even though language did not influence what particular memory was accessed, it did influence how quickly it was accessed.

The authors concluded that different types of knowledge are differentially sensitive to language-dependent memory, with language-dependent effects more likely when multiple alternatives are available for retrieval. Thus the bivalent and multivalent results could be due to the fact that whenever more than one correct answer is available, a selection mechanism relies on additional markings, such as the encoding language at the time of learning, to choose the answer.

So the next time you try to remember something, and you can't seem to do it in one of your languages, try changing language. *If* you are bilingual, of course. It might just work!

References

Marian, V. and Neisser, U. (2000). Language-dependent recall of autobiographical memories. *Journal of Experimental Psychology: General*, 129(3), 361–368.

Marian, V. and Kaushanskaya, M. (2007). Language context guides memory content. *Psychonomic Bulletin and Review*, 14(5), 925–933.

12.4 LANGUAGE AND THOUGHT IN BI- AND MULTILINGUALS[2]

(Interview with Aneta Pavlenko)

Learning another language may reshape cognitive processes such as perception, categorization, memory, and self-perception, and thereby reorganize the structure of the mind. Dr. Aneta Pavlenko answers questions about her book that addresses the intriguing relationship between language and thought in bi- and multilinguals.

Aneta Pavlenko, Professor at the University of Oslo, is the author of a groundbreaking book, *The Bilingual Mind*, on the intriguing relationship between language and thought in bi- and multilinguals. She is herself a speaker of many languages and has researched this topic for much of her career. She has very kindly accepted to answer a few questions about her book.

Your work is inspired by the writings of some renowned linguists and anthropologists such as Humboldt, Boas, Sapir, and Whorf. What role did they play exactly?

These scholars are commonly seen as proponents of linguistic relativity, the idea that different languages shape different worlds for their speakers. This idea is highly controversial and yet at the heart of the debate is a profound misunderstanding – and a deliberate misrepresentation – of Sapir's and Whorf's actual views. When we go back to their writings, we see that these multilingual scholars, interested in language

[2] The original title of this post was "The bilingual mind."

change, did not believe for a moment that language determines thought. If it did, both language change and successful second-language learning would have been impossible. In the book, I attempt to solve this linguistic whodunit, identify the real authors of the Sapir-Whorf hypothesis, and then return to the original questions raised by Humboldt, Sapir, and Whorf about what happens when we learn a new language.

What do you mean by the expression "the bilingual mind"?
I use the expression "the bilingual mind" to draw attention to the fact that most of the world's population is bi- or multilingual and to argue that this bi-/multilingualism matters for our understanding of human cognition. The process of learning and using language affects categorization, memory, perception, and self-perception; learning another language may reshape these processes and reorganize the structure of the mind.

You mention "language effects" in your discussion of the bilingual mind. Could you explain what you mean?
This term refers to demands individual languages place on our cognitive processes in terms of categorical judgments and allocation of attention. Some require us to mark whether the action is accomplished or still in progress, and others require us to say whether we personally witnessed particular events. Learning a new language requires us to allocate our resources differently and acquire new categorical distinctions and ways of parsing events.

You state that when one acquires a second language, cognitive restructuring takes place. Can you explain what this is?
Cognitive restructuring refers to self-reorganization of linguistic categories that takes place when we learn a second language. Take, for instance, English/Russian word pairs cup/chashka and glass/stakan. A Russian speaker learning English will begin by associating the English words "cup" and "glass" with the already existing representations of "chashka" and "stakan." But this can only take them so far because in English we call paper, plastic, and styrofoam containers for coffee on the go "cups" and in Russian they are "stakanchiki" (little glasses). To use English appropriately, the learner has to restructure the preexisting representations, in the case of "glass," for instance, shifting attention from shape to material. And this is just one simple example of the myriad of cognitive adjustments in lexical and grammatical categories that take place when we acquire a second language.

What are the main factors that account for this restructuring?
Cognitive restructuring is a very new direction in research on bilingualism. As a consequence, we are only beginning to understand the process and the factors that affect it. In my own view, the key factor involves language use in communication, in meaningful contexts, and in the presence of physical objects. The co-occurrence of form and meaning allows us to form new connections between words and their referents and to learn to pay attention to distinctions required by the second language.

How has your own multilingualism influenced your thinking on this topic?
First, my multilingualism provides me with experiential insights into what it means to live in two or more languages. Secondly, my other working languages – French, Spanish, Italian, Polish, Ukrainian, and my native Russian – offer access to a large body of literature that I can read in the original, which is particularly important in the case of Bakhtin, Luria, and Vygotsky who had been badly mistranslated into English.

In your book, you refer to a large amount of scholarly work, from many different sources, but you also call upon biographies, literature including poetry, as well as personal testimonies. Can you say a bit more about this?
Certainly. I deeply believe that our scholarship is only meaningful insofar as it can speak to real people and address their everyday problems and dilemmas. This is why I try to make connections between studies conducted in the experimental lab and autobiographical writing and poetry, which, in my view – and that of Vygotsky and Sapir – offers unprecedented access to people's inner worlds. The mixing also reflects my academic bilingualism. My training took place in two academic settings, Russian- and English-speaking, and while I write in English, I draw on the Russian academic tradition of interweaving research with fiction and poetry.

At one point in your book, you state that you are "irreverent by nature." How has this trait helped you in your work?
From the first day of graduate school, I never assumed that I should be buying into this or that theory and have continuously questioned the premises and foundations of our research enterprise. I suspect that this unruly behavior made me a pest and a nuisance to my professors, yet it also made me a better scholar because it led me to disrespect artificial boundaries between fields and paradigms. Conducting experimental research taught me healthy respect for the challenges of empirical science, while sociolinguistic theories equipped me with tools necessary for

critical evaluation of the scientific enterprise. Irreverence also makes me a better writer, or at least it makes writing more fun.

You sometimes show concern about the work of some psychologists, applied linguists, anthropologists, and even translators. Why is that?
In the case of psychology, my main concern is with the treatment of bilingual participants. Some researchers exclude bilinguals as "unusual" or "messy" subjects and others treat them as representative speakers of their first languages, brushing aside any potential effects of second language learning. In the case of linguistics and anthropology, my main concern is with the researchers' own bilingualism. Despite being linguists, we hold ourselves to an abysmally low standard as language learners. My concerns are reinforced by the many errors I see in the treatments of Russian in translation and in scholarly literature that sometimes does not even get the basic facts right.

Where do you see research on the bilingual mind going in the next ten years?
I see three main directions for research in the next decade. The first and the most straightforward will apply existing approaches to the study of other language combinations and different types of bi- and multilinguals. The second will examine whether language influences on cognition are also subject to plasticity effects; in other words, is there a critical period for learning to attend to categorical distinctions and motion trajectories in a native-like way? The third direction is to go beyond the study of acquisition of English, French, or German by immigrants and foreign language learners and to consider ways in which speakers of major world languages – including researchers – acquire languages spoken by small groups of people.

More generally, if you had one wish that could come true regarding bi- and multilinguals, what would it be?
This is an interesting and unexpected question. I guess, I would want people who speak more than one language to experience less anxiety about their languages, fewer concerns about perceived limitations and deficiencies, and more joy and pride. When I come to workshops and conferences in your homeland, Switzerland, I witness amazing presentations and exchanges taking place in German, French, and English. Yet I also see my multilingual colleagues and their students being concerned about the limitations of their English, deficiencies in their German, or the wrong accent in their French. To end with your words that became

a motto for my whole research agenda, a bilingual is not a sum of two monolinguals but a unique speaker/hearer in his/her own right. So let's take pride in our linguistic abilities and achievements.

Reference

Pavlenko, A. (2014). *The Bilingual Mind And What it Tells us about Language and Thought.* Cambridge: Cambridge University Press.

12.5 THE DAY THE SUPREME COURT RULED ON THE BILINGUAL MIND

The US Supreme Court is rarely asked to consider how the mind functions, let alone the bilingual mind. But it did so once in an intriguing case.

One day I picked up the phone and heard that characteristic sound that told me that I was receiving a transatlantic call. An American colleague from Northeastern University, Deborah Ramirez, introduced herself and asked me if I knew that the Supreme Court had mentioned my work in one of its rulings. Since she was preparing a paper on the case, we exchanged phone calls, emails, and faxes for a number of weeks. The story that emerged is fascinating.

On a Brooklyn street, back in 1985, Dionisio Hernandez fired several shots at his girlfriend, Charlene Calloway, and at her mother, Ada Saline. Calloway was wounded as were two men in a nearby restaurant. Fortunately, all the victims survived the incident.

In 1986, jury selection began for the trial, and it was during this *voire dire* episode that the prosecutor used his peremptory challenges to exclude some Spanish–English bilingual jurors. When the defense objected, the prosecutor explained that he was not certain the jurors could accept the interpreter as the final arbiter of what was said by the Spanish-speaking witnesses.

The prosecutor was basically asking these prospective jurors whether they could disregard everything that was said in Spanish and only take into account the translation that would be rendered in English. He stated, "They each looked away from me and said with some hesitancy that they would try, not that they could," and hence he excluded them.

This exclusion of jurors was appealed and went all the way up to the Supreme Court. The case is known as *Hernandez* v. *New York* (89–7645). In 1991, the Court affirmed the decision of lower courts, that is, it accepted the exclusion of these jurors. It should be noted that the appeal had taken the tack of stating that the exclusion had been discriminatory toward Latino jurors and not toward bilinguals in general.

Why is this case interesting? It is well known in psycholinguistics that any verbal information that is seen or heard is processed. For example, I can't ask you to count the number of letters in the following word without you also reading it: SNOW. (Yes, there are four letters in it, and yes, it is that substance that comes back every year in many countries of the world.) In addition, the information that is received is integrated with the information that preceded it as well as with the listener's general knowledge. This is true for monolinguals and for bilinguals, within and across languages.

So basically, the prospective bilingual jurors' answers were exactly the ones you would expect from bilinguals and were not idiosyncratic to specific bilinguals, as the Supreme Court alleged. They were going to have a hard time not listening to the witnesses when they spoke Spanish and they were also going to find it difficult not to integrate that information with the information given to them by the interpreter.

By asking bilingual jurors to disregard everything that was said in Spanish, the prosecutor and then all the appellate courts up to the Supreme Court were asking bilingual jurors to do something they simply could not do. In addition, by their decision, they were condoning the potential exclusion of bilingual jurors in later trials where testimonies would be given in a language other than English.

Is there a solution? In fact, there are two as mentioned by Deborah Ramirez in her paper: all jurors could be required to wear headphones during the testimony in a language other than English, or instructions could be provided to bilingual jurors regarding the resolution of discrepancies between the original testimony and the English interpretation.

I have contacted Deborah Ramirez several times over the years to ask whether things have changed since then. She has always written back to say that bilingual jurors can still be excluded for the very same reason as in the *Hernandez* case, and that indeed some are.

Reference

Ramirez, D. (1993). Excluded voices: The disenfranchisement of ethnic groups from jury service. *Wisconsin Law Review*, 3, 761–809.

12.6 WHAT ARE THE EFFECTS OF BILINGUALISM?[3]

Studies examining the effects of bilingualism tended to produce rather categorical findings in the past century. Today, it would appear that when differences are found between monolinguals and bilinguals, they are specific to a particular task and are rather subtle.

When I was preparing my first book on bilingualism some thirty years ago, I was confronted with opposing views on the effect of bilingualism on children. Studies in the first half of the twentieth century appeared to show that bilingual children had lower IQs and that they were outperformed by monolingual children in both verbal and nonverbal intelligence tests. Most of those studies concluded that bilingualism had a negative effect on the child's linguistic, cognitive, and educational development.

Midway through the last century, the opinions changed rather suddenly and researchers found that bilingualism was, after all, a real asset for the child. Many studies came to the conclusion that bilinguals are more sensitive to semantic relations between words, are better able to treat sentence structure analytically, are better at rule-discovery tasks, have greater social sensitivity, and so on.

Why was there such a discrepancy between the studies of the first and the second half of the century? We now know that one of the main problems lay in making sure that the monolingual and bilingual groups used in the studies were truly comparable in every aspect, apart from their linguistic skills. Even though studies in the latter part of the century controlled for many factors, a slight bias may have favored bilingual children at that time.

I returned to the question when I was preparing another book, *Bilingual: Life and Reality*. I contacted developmental psycholinguist Ellen Bialystok, the best-known authority in the field, and she kindly

[3] This post was written in 2011.

sent me papers to read and brought me up to date. What emerges from this research is that the differences between bilinguals and monolinguals, when any are found, are specific to a particular task and can be quite subtle.

It would seem that bilingualism enhances problem-solving where the solutions depend on selective attention or inhibitory control (abilities of the executive control system, according to Bialystok). This advantage would seem to continue throughout the bilingual's life span and appears to be present in elderly bilinguals.

The advantage shown by bilinguals – as discussed by Ellen Bialystok – is found also in certain metalinguistic abilities, that is, our capacity to analyze different aspects of language (sounds, words, syntax, etc.) and, if needed, to talk about these properties. But the advantage appears to be present only when selective attention or inhibitory control are needed to do the task. This is the case when a problem contains a conflict or an ambiguity such as counting words in a correct sentence, using a new (or made-up) name for an object in a sentence, judging that a sentence such as "apples grow on noses" is syntactically grammatical even though it contains a semantic anomaly, etc.

When the metalinguistic task requires the analysis of representational structures, then monolinguals and bilinguals obtain similar results. This occurs when the task is to explain grammatical errors in a sentence, substitute one sound for another, interchange sounds, and so on.

One domain where it would appear that bilinguals do less well than monolinguals is in vocabulary tests such as choosing a picture that illustrates the word spoken by the experimenter. This is not surprising, however, as bilingual children start being affected by the Complementarity Principle, which states that bilinguals usually acquire and use their languages for different purposes, in different domains of life, and with different people (see Post 5.8). When bilingual children are evaluated in terms of *both* their languages, then the results improve greatly.

So where do we stand today on the effects of bilingualism? Ellen Bialystok and Xiaojia Feng give a reply: "The picture emerging from these studies is a complex portrait of interactions between bilingualism and skill acquisition in which there are sometimes benefits for bilingual children, sometimes deficits, and sometimes no consequence at all." (p. 121).

In sum, we now have a fuller and more complex picture of what the differences are between monolinguals and bilinguals – when differences exist!

References

Bialystok, E. and Feng, X. (2010). Language proficiency and its implications for monolingual and bilingual children. In A. Durgunoglu and C. Goldenberg, eds., *Dual Language Learners: The Development and Assessment of Oral and Written Language*. New York: Guilford Press, pp. 121–138.
Grosjean, F. (2010). Effects of bilingualism on children. Chapter 18 of *Bilingual: Life and Reality*. Cambridge, MA: Harvard University Press.

12.7 DEMENTIA, LATER-LIFE COGNITION, AND BILINGUALISM[4]

A pioneering study that came out in 2007 showed that bilingualism has a protective effect on the onset of dementia. Since then, further studies have shown similar results but some have not.

In 2007, a pioneering study by Canadian researchers Ellen Bialystok, Fergus Craik, and Morris Freedman obtained results that were relayed around the world. It concerned the development of dementia, that is, disorders that impact memory, language, motor and spatial skills, problem-solving, and attention. They examined the medical records of a number of patients with dementia at a memory clinic in Toronto, half of whom were bilingual, and they found that the age of onset of the symptoms was 4.1 years later for that group than for the monolingual group. Basically, being bilingual had a protective effect in delaying the onset of dementia.

A few years later, the same researchers concentrated only on patients diagnosed with Alzheimer's disease – a common cause of dementia – and found similar results. In their conclusion, they were careful to underline that bilingualism does not prevent the development of the disease but that it appears to postpone the onset of its symptoms.

[4] This post was written in 2015.

Since that set of studies, other research groups have examined the topic in the hope of confirming that speaking two or more languages does indeed have a protective effect. Morris Freedman and eight other colleagues from three different countries reported on these studies in 2014. They compared the Toronto results with those of two other studies, one conducted in Hyderabad (India) and one in Montreal. They reported that in the Hyderabad study the age of onset of dementia in a large group of patients was strikingly similar to that of the first Toronto study: 4.5 years later in bilinguals than in monolinguals.

However, and this comes as a surprise, the Montreal study failed to show the same global effect. The study did show a significant protective effect for those who spoke at least four languages, but the benefit was only marginal for those with three languages, and there was no difference between those who spoke one or two languages, unless they were immigrants. What was even more surprising was that native-born Canadian bilinguals developed Alzheimer's disease earlier, and not later, than monolinguals.

Morris Freedman and his colleagues tried to make sense of these contradictory results. For example, they mentioned that the measure of the onset of dementia was different in Toronto and Hyderabad, on the one hand, and in Montreal, on the other. In addition, they questioned the way immigrants and nonimmigrants were defined in the Montreal study.

But the explanation may be more general than that. We have known for a long time that a person's cognitive reserve, that is the brain's resistance to cognitive decline due to aging, is associated with a number of factors such as childhood cognition, education, lifestyle including social and leisure activities, occupational status, and physical exercise. This explains why numerous websites dedicated to health mention exercise, mental stimulation, stress management, and having an active social life as ways, among others, of delaying dementia. So it could be, according to Morris Freedman and his colleagues, that "... bilingualism alone is insufficient to guarantee the postponement of dementia."

This realistic statement is a step back from what people (mainly the media) took away from the early studies conducted by Ellen Bialystok.

A combination of factors, instead of just one factor, would appear to have a protective effect.

Where does this leave bilingualism and its effect on later-life cognition, and not just on dementia? A study conducted by Thomas Bak and his colleagues in Edinburgh, on older citizens and not on demented patients, would seem to show that bilingualism does have a positive effect. So as to avoid the problem of different baseline characteristics in bilingual and monolingual groups (e.g., childhood intelligence), they gave a series of cognitive tests to people who had been originally tested at age eleven, some sixty years beforehand. When they compared the monolinguals and the bilinguals in the group, they found that bilinguals (the majority of whom had acquired another language after age eleven) performed significantly better than predicted from their baseline cognitive abilities, whereas monolinguals did not.

I asked Bialystok to comment on this result, and it is worth quoting parts of her answer:

> A prevailing problem in conducting research on bilingualism is the difficulty of disentangling cause and effect: did people develop certain skills because they were bilingual or did they become bilingual because of their advantages in those skills? As much as we try to control the research, that question persists. The study by Bak and colleagues goes a long way in addressing that issue. . . . It is not definitive evidence for causality, but it is the closest anyone has come to tracing the emergence of bilingual advantages in cognition to just the experience of being bilingual.

In sum, bilingualism would seem to have a positive effect on later-life cognition, as do other factors that have been known about for a much longer time.

References

Bialystok, E., Craik, F., and Freedman, M. (2007). Bilingualism as a protection against the onset of symptoms of dementia. *Neuropsychologia*, 45, 459–464.

Freedman, M., Alladi, S., Chertkow, H., Bialystok, E., Craik, F., Phillips, N., Duggirala, V., Bapi Raju, S., and Bak, T. (2014). Delaying onset of dementia: Are two languages enough? *Behavioural Neurology*, Article ID 808137, http://dx.doi.org/10.1155/2014/808137

Bak, T., Nissan, J., Allerhand, M., and Deary, I. (2014). Does bilingualism influence cognitive aging? *Annals of Neurology*, 75(6), 959–963.

Woumans, E., Santens, P., Sieben, A., Versijpt, J., Stevens, M., and Duyck, W. (2015). Bilingualism delays clinical manifestation of Alzheimer's disease. *Bilingualism: Language and Cognition*, 18(3), 568–574.

12.8 THE BILINGUAL ADVANTAGE: WHERE DO WE GO FROM HERE?[5]

The debate on the cognitive advantage of being bilingual has entered troubled waters with some researchers questioning its very existence. What does the future hold?

Over the last few years, we have been impressed by, and have reported regularly on, what has been called, "the bilingual advantage." It is the proposal that the experience of using two or more languages – selecting one, while inhibiting the other(s) – strengthens executive control (also called executive function). It is involved in such complex cognitive processes as attention, inhibition, monitoring, and so on (see Post 12.6). This bilingual advantage, which can be observed in various experimental tasks used with children and adults, has been reported to also have an impact on cognitive reserve. This is a protective mechanism against age-related cognitive decline and has been reported to delay the symptoms of dementia in bilinguals by a number of years (see Post 12.7).

As Aneta Pavlenko wrote, the early findings "captured our hearts and minds" and were a change from concerns about the disadvantages of bilingualism found in the literature in the first half of the last century[6]. But she asked whether the pendulum had swung too far in favor of bilinguals and reported on a heated debate that had started on this issue. Basically, many research teams, working with both children and adults, could not replicate the effect and doubted its veracity.

In mid-2015, researchers Kenneth Paap, Hunter Johnson, and Oliver Sawi published a very critical review paper of the field for the prestigious brain sciences journal, *Cortex*. In it, they question the very existence of the

<hr>

[5] This post was written in 2016.

[6] See Aneta Pavlenko's 2014 *Psychology Today* post, "Bilingual cognitive advantage: Where do we stand?" www.psychologytoday.com/intl/blog/life-bilingual/201411/bilingual-cognitive-advantage-where-do-we-stand

bilingual advantage and summarize their findings in the following way: "It is likely that bilingual advantages in EF (executive functions) do not exist. If they do exist they are restricted to specific aspects of bilingual experience that enhance only specific components of EF. Such constraints, if they exist, have yet to be determined."

Instead of simply publishing the paper, and letting it have the life of an ordinary article, the editors of *Cortex* asked twenty-one research teams in the area to write comments on it in a "Bilingualism forum." The short texts that appeared make for interesting reading and show how complex the debate really is. First, several authors express their despondency at the situation this particular field is in now. For example, Eric-Jan Wagenmakers from the University of Amsterdam writes: "... even the most dispassionate reader will feel depressed at the suggestion that the collective research effort on bilingual advantages in executive functioning has been a waste of time, effort, and resources. The presence of such research waste has profound negative ramifications that extend well beyond the research topic at hand. ..."[7]

One thinks here of the impact this will have on the scientific press that informs the layperson of advances in language research but also on the many websites and blogs that prone bilingualism and biculturalism and that hailed the earlier seminal findings, as we have done. Virginia Mueller Gathercole of Florida International University states this clearly, "One unspoken issue is undoubtedly some concern over the possible reversal of the growing positive press regarding bilingualism that the research on executive functions has engendered."[8]

The list of problems that emerge from the comments is extensive. It covers the publication bias that seemed to prevail (failures to replicate the original studies were either not proposed to journals or were not accepted) and problems with the experiments themselves such as the use of tasks that lack convergent validity, the existence of groups of participants that were far too small, the use of questionable statistics, and reporting only on the studies that gave positive results.

---

[7] Eric-Jan Wagenmakers (2015). A quartet of interactions. *Cortex*, 73, 334–335.
[8] Virginia C. Mueller Gathercole (2015). Are we at a socio-political and scientific crisis? *Cortex*, 73, 345–346.

Two problematic issues are repeated over and over again. The first concerns the lack of a clear explanation of how bilingualism affects executive control. For example, Barbara Treccani and Claudio Mulatti write:

one of the most serious faults of the literature on this topic (is) the lack of a clear, sound, well-grounded and broadly endorsed theory about how the mechanisms responsible for the management of the two languages would affect executive functions. The advocates of the bilingual advantage ... took for granted the existence of some relationship between the mechanisms that allow a person to handle two languages and those underlying the selection and control of other types of processes. However, the exact nature of this relation is usually not well specified and it is actually far from being clear.[9]

The other problem, already mentioned by researchers such as Virginia Valian, is that numerous factors affect the development and maintenance of executive control such as intelligence, education, lifestyle including social and leisure activities (playing music or exercising), and having an active social life. The whole problem of causality is posed therefore, and Raymond Klein even ventures that "it is just as likely that individuals with better executive functions were better able to master two languages."[10]

Should this line of research be abandoned and should researchers move on to something else? No, reply several commentators who then propose solutions for future research. The bilingual abilities of participants could be assessed far better, monolinguals and bilinguals should be matched on even more variables, different tasks should be used so as to obtain converging evidence, appropriate and sophisticated statistics should be called upon, failures to replicate a finding should be accounted for, and so on. In addition, longitudinal studies should be encouraged. As Ping Li and Angela Grant of Pennsylvania State University write, "Longitudinal designs allow us to track the same individual, regardless of his or her prior language history or cognitive

---

[9] Barbara Treccani and Claudio Mulatti (2015). No matter who, no matter how... and no matter whether the white matter matters. Why theories of bilingual advantage in executive functioning are so difficult to falsify. *Cortex*, 73, 349–351.

[10] Raymond M. Klein (2015). On the belief that the cognitive exercise associated with the acquisition of a second language enhances extra-linguistic cognitive functions: Is "Type-I incompetence" at work here? *Cortex*, 73, 340–341.

ability, across a period of time from no bilingual experience to low bilingual proficiency to high bilingual expertise. Simultaneously, cognitive control abilities can be measured at various time points across this period."[11]

The last word can be given to representatives of two research teams. Evy Woumans and Wouter Duyck write, "the discussion should not be about whether the bilingual advantage exists or not, but about what factors moderate its manifestation."[12] And Jared Linck states: "My expectation is that researchers will develop more specific hypotheses and employ refined methods, which will provide a more nuanced picture of the complex connections between cognitive processes and language experience."[13]

While this continuing research is taking place, and we await the results, we may want to study the many other advantages there are of being bilingual (see Post 1.4). Research on "the bilingual advantage" could then join a far broader enterprise, the scholarly study of the many benefits of living with two or more languages!

References

Paap, K. R., Johnson, H. A., and Sawi, O. (2015). Bilingual advantages in executive functioning either do not exist or are restricted to very specific and undetermined circumstances. *Cortex*, 69, 265–278.
Bilingualism Forum (2015). *Cortex*, 73, 330–377.

12.9 THE BILINGUAL ADVANTAGE: THREE YEARS LATER[14]

(Interview with Mark Antoniou)

The debate on the cognitive advantage of being bilingual rages on. Researcher Mark Antoniou helps us understand where things stand today.

Three years have now gone by since my last post on the topic (see Post 12.8), and numerous other studies have been undertaken. What better way

---

[11] Ping Li and Angela Grant (2015). Identifying the causal link: Two approaches toward understanding the relationship between bilingualism and cognitive control. *Cortex*, 73, 358–360.
[12] Evy Woumans and Wouter Duyck (2015). The bilingual advantage debate: Moving toward different methods for verifying its existence. *Cortex*, 73, 356–357.
[13] Jared A. Linck (2015). Methods matter for critical reviews too. *Cortex*, 73, 354–355.
[14] This interview was conducted in 2019.

to understand where things stand than to interview Dr. Mark Antoniou, Research Program Leader at Western Sydney University in Australia. He has published a review article on the topic, *The advantages of bilingualism debate*, and he is ideally placed to bring us up to date. We thank him wholeheartedly.

In the first pages of your review, two sentences stand out from the text: ". . . the field has now reached an impasse," and ". . . there is no consensus as yet on the relationship between bilingualism and cognitive benefits." Can you say a few introductory words on this?

The debate surrounding the bilingual advantage is very heated and fierce. It is also repetitive. Certain research groups consistently find support for a bilingual advantage, while other groups consistently find none. Those familiar with the literature are able to surmise whether the findings will be for or against the existence of a bilingual advantage simply by peering at the list of authors.

Your review covers three areas of research. The first concerns experimental evidence for a bilingual advantage in executive functions. Could you explain what is meant by "executive functions?"

Executive functions are cognitive processes that are used to control behavior in service of a goal. They include our ability to plan, direct attention, ignore distracting information, withhold habitual responses, be cognitively flexible, and juggle multiple tasks. Executive functions have been linked to success throughout life: academic achievement, positive behaviors, healthy relationships, and occupational success. It is thought by some that bilingual experience changes brain areas responsible for executive functions, and this leads to cognitive improvements in nonlinguistic processing.

Evidence has been found for a bilingual advantage in cognitive abilities, primarily in older adults, but there is also evidence against it. What are the problems that have led to this discrepancy?

There are many problems: differing definitions of bilingualism, misunderstanding the nature of bilingualism, misinterpretation of prior findings, studies plagued by methodological confounds, a publication bias that limited the chances of publishing null findings, and drawing conclusions that are not supported by the data. These problems may be found on both sides of the debate.

The second area of research you deal with concerns cognitive aging and the bilingual advantage. Why might bilingualism delay the onset of neurodegenerative disease such as dementia?
I'll focus on those researchers who have argued that bilingualism may indeed delay the incidence of dementia, but let's keep in mind that some passionately challenge this view. The truth is that we do not yet have a comprehensive theory that is capable of explaining the role of bilingualism.

A popular view is that over the course of a lifetime, a bilingual's two languages constantly interact and in order to manage this competition, a bilingual's executive function system, and the brain structures associated with it, will develop in ways that differ from a monolingual who faces no such pressures. Consequently, as we age and experience age-related cognitive decline, the bilingual brain is more resistant to the neurodegeneration that occurs. This is referred to as cognitive reserve, but the way that this works is not agreed upon either.

One possibility is that the brain structures stay healthier because they are more resistant to neurodegeneration. Another possibility is that when certain structures or connections between brain regions are damaged and disrupted, the bilingual brain is able to compensate by making use of alternative intact pathways. The challenge facing any theory seeking to reconcile these findings is that there exists evidence for each of these seemingly incompatible views.

In this area too, evidence has been found for and against the bilingual advantage. You state that the cause may be that some studies are prospective whilst others are retrospective. What is meant by this?
Retrospective studies are historical in nature. They involve examination of medical records and attempt to understand the causes of neuropathology after the fact by examining relationships between demographic date, and other data, and diagnosis. Such studies were the first to support the claim that bilingualism may delay the incidence of dementia. They have been criticized by some as being methodologically flawed but not all these criticisms stand up to scrutiny.

Prospective studies involve recruiting a sample of participants and following them longitudinally over some period of time. Studies on dementia incidence typically involve recruiting a large initial sample, following those individuals over many years, and taking note of which people were later diagnosed with dementia and comparing whether differences can be observed between mono- and bilinguals. They too are limited by methodological confounds.

In the third area of research, brain plasticity resulting from bilingualism, the results are clearer. What are they?

Studies that examine structural changes in the brain resulting from long-term bilingual language use present results that are particularly compelling. Bilingualism unquestionably changes both gray and white matter in numerous brain structures distributed across a wide network, and many of these structures are associated with executive functions. Although we know that bilingual and monolingual brains differ, it is less clear how differences in brain structure relate to performance on experimental tasks.

One message that emerges from your review is that bilingual advantages are unlikely to extend to all bilinguals under all circumstances. Could you explain this?

Recent work has moved away from comparing separate groups of monolinguals and bilinguals, but has instead come to the realization that bilinguals also differ from other bilinguals in terms of their patterns of language learning and use. We are starting to see studies treat bilingualism as a continuum. Such designs allow one to explore bilingual variables that may affect cognitive abilities.

You end by stating that "the bilingual advantage debate is likely to roar on" and you give a few leads as to where this research could go. Please explain.

It is roaring on as we speak and new papers are published regularly. We can already see the direction in which the field is heading. Studies are being conducted with larger sample sizes to make them more solid. There is a move away from using bilingualism as a categorical variable, as we saw above, and towards examining a monolingual-bilingual continuum. Such designs make it possible to ask questions regarding "how much bilingual experience is needed for an advantage to emerge?" The goal would be to predict which types of bilinguals would be more likely to show an advantage in a given domain and which would be less likely.

This said, we still have some way to go before we can reconcile those on opposite sides of the debate concerning the cognitive consequences of bilingualism.

Reference

Antoniou, M. (2019). The advantages of bilingualism debate. *Annual Review of Linguistics*, 5, 395–415.

13

The Bilingual Brain

INTRODUCTION

Research on the bilingual brain uses many approaches such as doing experiments with EEG (electroencephalogram), employing brain imaging techniques, and studying multilingual aphasia. These will be touched upon in this chapter.

Post 13.1 presents studies, using neuroimaging techniques, that show how the nature of the languages used, as well as the type of bilinguals studied, have an impact on the results found.

Posts 13.2 and 13.3 cover a long interview with an expert, Dr. Ping Li, who explains how the bilingual brain uses the same neural structures as the monolingual brain but in different ways. He covers a number of issues such as how learning a second language impacts different areas of the brain, how very different languages, such as English and Chinese, engage distinct neural representations, and how individual differences play a role.

Posts 13.4 and 13.5 concern aphasia – language and speech impairment due to brain damage – in multilinguals. Post 13.4 relates the case of a man who had a stroke and when he recovered he could no longer communicate with his wife in the language they had spoken together for some twenty years. Instead, he used another language linked to an emotional episode he had lived through in his earlier years.

Post 13.5 examines the impairment and recovery patterns of multilinguals who suffer from aphasia, and concentrates on those who experience nonparallel recovery of their languages. We present the factors that may explain differential recovery and discuss whether the languages not recovered are lost or inhibited.

Finally, Post 13.6 is exceptional in that a patient with aphasia takes part in an interview on what she is living through. She evokes the moment when she had her stroke, the state of her languages just after it, and what she is doing in order to recuperate her languages.

13.1 STUDYING THE BILINGUAL BRAIN WITH NEUROIMAGING TECHNIQUES[1]

Neuroimaging techniques are allowing researchers to better understand how the brain organizes and processes the languages of bilinguals. Studies are described that show how the nature of the languages used, as well as the type of bilinguals studied, have an impact on the results found.

In 1978, researchers Martin L. Albert and Loraine K. Obler wrote a highly influential book, *The Bilingual Brain*, which gave great momentum to the neuropsycholinguistic study of bilingualism, but also offered, as it happens, a very catchy title to talk about it. For the next twenty years, researchers concentrated on such topics as bilingual aphasia (see Posts 13.4 to 13.6) and the lateralization of languages in bilinguals. Various experimental techniques involving listening, reading, and finger tapping were used to see if the involvement of each hemisphere (left and right) was the same or not in monolinguals and bilinguals, and, for the latter, whether this depended on the type of bilingualism. Unfortunately, clear and definitive answers were never obtained, despite what is stated in the more popular press and in some general public books.

With the advent of neuroimaging techniques such as event-related potentials and functional magnetic resonance imaging, much more sophisticated research could be undertaken in an attempt to understand how the brain organizes and processes the bilingual's languages. In this post I will describe a research project initiated by Dr. Ping Li (interviewed in the next two posts) that lasted some seven years and involved researchers from the United States, Hong Kong, China, and the United Kingdom.

In a first study, Li and his coauthors wanted to find out whether verbs and nouns in Chinese are represented in the same way in the brain as are their counterparts in English: verbs in the frontal region of the brain and nouns in the posterior region. The authors noted that verbs and nouns in Chinese do not contain grammatical markers as do similar words in English and

---

[1] The original title of this post was "The bilingual brain."

other Western languages. In addition, many Chinese verbs can occur as subjects, and nouns as predicates. Finally, Chinese has a much higher number of ambiguous words than English that can be used either as a noun or a verb (e.g., "huihua" means both to draw and a drawing).

Native speakers of Chinese took part in a functional magnetic resonance imaging study in which they were presented with the written version of two-character Chinese words as well as nonwords (lexical items that looked like words but weren't). They were asked to decide whether what they saw was a real word or not. The results the researchers obtained were that nouns and verbs in Chinese were not confined to specific brain regions, as in English; rather they activated a wide range of overlapping areas, in both the left and the right hemispheres. The authors explained the involvement of the right hemisphere (language is usually lateralized in the left hemisphere in right-handers) because of the visual features of Chinese characters and the lexical tones carried by Chinese words.

Having shown that very different languages, in this case English and Chinese, have different neural representations for nouns and verbs, the interesting question became: What about bilinguals who store and process these two languages? Researcher Alice H. D. Chan of the University of Hong Kong along with six other researchers, among them Ping Li, addressed this question. Their participants, this time, were early Chinese–English adult bilinguals who had started to learn each language before the age of three on average. They were asked to do the same task as above, first in one language and then in the other.

The researchers found that Chinese nouns and verbs involved activation of common brain areas (thus replicating the first study) whereas English verbs engaged many more regions than did English nouns. They concluded that under specific conditions, bilingual learners may deal with word information of the two languages separately. Thus, when word class is an important marker during language development, as it is in English, early bilinguals will acquire this language-specific property. In sum, the bilingual brain is highly plastic.

But is this true of late bilinguals? A third study, this time headed by researcher Jing Yang also of the University of Hong Kong, along with two other researchers including Ping Li, answered this question. The participants they used were native Chinese adults who had begun to learn English at age twelve on average. They too showed no significant differences in brain activation for nouns versus verbs in Chinese (once again replicating the earlier study) but, to the surprise of the researchers, they showed little neural differentiation of nouns and verbs in English, unlike the early bilinguals.

The authors concluded that when a second language is acquired later, such as in adolescence, the linguistic experience one develops for one's native language can shape the neural representation of the second language. This said, they noted aspects of their data that seemed to show that with more linguistic exposure to English, and hence improved language proficiency, the late bilinguals may yet develop neural sensitivity to noun-verb differences in their second language.

These three studies are a fine example of how modern imaging approaches can contribute to our understanding of how the bilingual brain organizes and processes languages, and how the degree of overlap of languages, as well as age of onset of the second language, play an important role at the neuropsycholinguistic level.

References

Li, P., Jin, Z., and Tan, Li. H. (2004). Neural representations of nouns and verbs in Chinese: an fMRI study. *NeuroImage*, 21, 1533–1541.

Chan, A. H. D., Luke, K.-K., Li, P., Yip, V., Li, G., Weekes, B., and Tan, L.-H. (2008). Neural correlates of nouns and verbs in early bilinguals. *Annals of the New York Academy of Sciences*, 1145, 30–40.

Yang, J., Tan, L.-H., and Li, P. (2011). Lexical representation of nouns and verbs in the late bilingual brain. *Journal of Neurolinguistics*, 24, 674–682.

13.2 WHAT IS DIFFERENT IN THE BILINGUAL BRAIN? I

(Interview with Ping Li)

Recent research has shown that the bilingual brain uses the same neural structures and resources as the monolingual brain but in different ways. Dr. Ping Li explains.

Research on the bilingual brain has gone through several stages over the years: the study of aphasic polyglots, experimental work on language lateralization in bilinguals, and now brain imaging studies that examine language processing and neural structures and connections between them (see Post 13.1). One of the leading researchers in this field is

Dr. Ping Li, Professor of Neurolinguistics and Bilingual Studies at the Hong Kong Polytechnic University. He works on the neural and computational bases of language representation and learning and has kindly accepted to answer a few of our questions. We wish to thank him wholeheartedly.

Before addressing the issue of what is different in the bilingual brain, as compared to the monolingual brain, can you quickly go through what is clearly similar?
It may be helpful to say at the outset that we are talking about the human brain, bilingual or not, which is the only brain that can learn and use complex natural languages for communication. No brain of any other species on our planet has language like ours, despite claims that other animals may also have sophisticated communication systems.

Against this backdrop, then, the similarities between the bilingual and monolingual brains will be more important than the differences. For example, given the physical constraints of the human brain – its neuro-anatomical substances – we must be using more or less the same neural structures to learn and use different languages, whether these are English, Chinese, French, or Spanish. In other words, we cannot imagine that each of the world's 7000+ languages occupies a different part of the brain. Now, this is not to deny that different languages will engage the neural structures in different ways, a position I myself dearly embrace and which you described elsewhere (see Post 13.1).

Does evolution also play a role?
From an evolutionary perspective, human language has had a long history – at least one hundred thousand years – and has evolved into a very complex communicative system. Evolution has determined that something as complex as human language simply cannot be supported by a single area in the brain. Rather, a great deal of brain resources needs to be dedicated to language. Recent neuroimaging evidence shows that language processing involves not only the classical Broca's and Wernicke's areas but the entire brain, from frontal to temporal to parietal lobes.

Concerning this, note that there is an area in the brain that we can call "the visual cortex" (for visual processing), but there is no such area that we can call "the language cortex," to the disappointment of some who look for a "language gene" or a "language area." Because of this, there is also no "monolingual cortex" or "bilingual cortex." The most plausible scenario, as has been argued by David Green and his colleagues, is that the brain uses the same neural structures and resources to handle different languages, but in different ways, even in the same individual.

For many years, we were led to believe that bilinguals were language lateralized differently than monolinguals? Is there any truth to that?
Although the idea of different brain lateralization patterns for bilinguals versus monolinguals made sense initially, like many intuitively appealing ideas, the more we know about the linguistic brain, the more unlikely this view has now become.

I want to illustrate my point with one simple example. Take monolingual English speakers who learn Chinese and acquire lexical tone, an essential aspect of the language for listening and speaking Chinese. Now, we know that native Chinese speakers typically use the left hemisphere to process lexical tones (although the right hemisphere is also engaged to some degree), given that tones are phonological units marking different word meanings (for example, /pa/ means "squat" if pronounced in Tone 1 and "crawl" in Tone 2).

Native English speakers learning Chinese initially treat such tonal differences simply as acoustic variations (high pitch in Tone 1 and low-then-high pitch in Tone 2) and use the right hemisphere to process them. But once they are fluent bilinguals, they start to treat these tonal differences as phonological, and not just acoustic, variations. The difference between Tone 1 vs. Tone 2 is now just as important as that between /ba/ and /pa/. Hence, there is a stage where bilinguals shift from relying on the right hemisphere to the left hemisphere, as lexical tones become linguistically meaningful to them.

Tell us more about the use of the right hemisphere.
I mentioned above that even native Chinese speakers use the right hemisphere to some extent, so the story is even more complicated. In one of our recent studies, we found that comprehension of Chinese idioms by native speakers engages the right hemisphere much more strongly than we previously thought based on data from figurative language processing. This is because the understanding of Chinese idioms requires a lot of historical, social, and cultural background knowledge

and the right hemisphere plays a huge role here in integrating such knowledge.

So, the dichotomy between monolinguals vs. bilinguals with regard to left-vs.-right brain lateralization, without regard to specific linguistic features or components, does not seem to be a fruitful direction for future work.

Over the years, what differences in neural structures and connections have clearly emerged between monolinguals and bilinguals?
From what has been said so far, we should be careful when we speak of "the monolingual brain" versus "the bilingual brain," because language is complex and the brain is complex. This said, being a bilingual does have significant implications for the brain, both for how the brain represents and processes the two or more languages (function) and for how the brain changes as a result of learning languages (structure).

Bilingual experience, as compared with other types of experience, is somewhat unique in terms of neuroplasticity, that is, functional and physical changes in the brain induced by activities performed regularly. For example, given how complex language is, you cannot learn a new language in a day despite what various commercial products claim for speedy language learning. If you are serious about learning, you have to, at the very least, remember thousands of words (lexicon), learn the sound system (phonology), acquire the writing system (orthography), learn the complex grammar (syntax), and learn the subtle ways to express yourself (pragmatics).

To learn all of these components of language, you need to consistently use many parts of the brain. For example, the lexicon engages the frontal and parietal cortical regions, phonology uses your frontal and temporal regions, orthography uses your occipital and temporal-parietal regions, syntax engages your frontal and subcortical regions, and pragmatics relies on both the left and the right hemispheres.

What impact does this have on the bilingual brain?
When you spend a couple of weeks, months, or even years learning a second language, the net effect of this effort is that your entire brain is exposed to, and trained by, the auditory and visual features of the language (see the Chinese tone example above).

Neuroscientists have discovered that when bilingual brains are compared with monolingual brains as a whole, specific brain regions are more active when doing specific linguistic tasks (phonology, orthography, syntax). These regions also become strengthened in terms of the amount/volume of neural substances, that is, gray matter and white matter.

Thus, a recent trend in the neurosciences of bilingualism is to study how these areas become better connected in the bilingual's brain. For example, in one of our studies we showed that students learning Chinese for only six weeks display a more integrated neural network that connects the superior temporal gyrus with the frontal and parietal cortex, and this contrasted with students who have not learned Chinese within the same time period.

References

Green, D. W. (2003). Neural basis of lexicon and grammar in L2 acquisition: The convergence hypothesis. In R. van Hout, A. Hulk, F. Kuiken and R. Towell, eds., *The Interface Between Syntax and the Lexicon in Second Language Acquisition.* Amsterdam: John Benjamins, pp. 197–208.

Grosjean, F. and Li, P. (2013). *The Psycholinguistics of Bilingualism.* New York, NY: John Wiley & Sons, Inc.

Li, P., Legault, J., and Litcofsky, K. A. (2014). Neuroplasticity as a function of second language learning: Anatomical changes in the human brain. *Cortex,* 58, 301–324. DOI: 10.1016/j.cortex.2014.05.001

Li, P. (2015). Bilingualism as a dynamic process. In B. MacWhinney and W. O'Grady , eds., *Handbook of Language Emergence.* Malden, MA: John Wiley & Sons, pp. 511–536.

13.3 WHAT IS DIFFERENT IN THE BILINGUAL BRAIN? II

(Interview with Ping Li)

Dr. Ping Li continues explaining how the bilingual brain uses the same neural structures and resources as the monolingual brain but in different ways.

In Part I (see Post 13.2), Dr. Li answered a first series of questions on the bilingual brain. Here we continue the interview, and are grateful to him for devoting his time to our questions.

Could we go back to the bilingual experience and the impact it has on neuroplasticity, that is, how it can lead to functional and physical changes in the brain?

Yes, another unique aspect of how the bilingual experience impacts the brain is related to the fact that bilingual speakers often have to change the language they are using and have to monitor this, not to mention intertwining their languages in the form of code-switches and borrowings. These processes, it has been suggested, result in positive brain changes in the frontal and subcortical brain regions (due to inhibition of the unwanted language(s)) and in the anterior cingulate cortex (due to monitoring).

Although the specific brain mechanisms underlying these processes are still being debated, it is safe to say, given the available evidence from recent neuroimaging studies, that learning a new language and becoming a bilingual is a good choice for neuroplasticity, particularly in light of the uncertainties associated with the question of which type of cognitive experience is better for the brain.

It should be noted also that the language-learning experience impacts many areas in the brain, in both the left and the right hemispheres – as we previously alluded to regarding how complex language is – whereas other types of cognitive experience (like juggling, doing jigsaw puzzles, etc.) may be beneficial to limited brain regions, such as the occipital cortex for vision, the motor cortex for movement, and the hippocampus for memory.

So what can be concluded concerning the bilingual experience?
It helps to shape the brain, even if such brain changes may not be revolutionary when evaluated against the grand spectrum of the evolution of the human brain (see Post 13.2). Such changes come about precisely because of the frequency, intensity, and duration of the bilingual experience. Scientific studies have shown that the extent of brain change is positively correlated with the level of proficiency gained in a second language.

Generally speaking, for all cognitive experiences – learning and using a language being one of them – the more often you perform the task, the more you will see brain changes; and the longer you work on it, the stronger will be the effects. Indeed, there has been work showing that if one stops learning a language or performing a cognitive task, the gained brain changes, such as increases in gray matter volume, will return to pre-learning or pre-training levels. So, "use it or lose it" and "no pain no gain" are all true when it comes to the positive effects of neuroplasticity.

Since there are many types of bilinguals, do some bilinguals resemble monolinguals in neural structures and/or connections while others are very different? If so, what factors are behind this?
This is a hugely important issue at the core of psychology: how do we identify the factors underlying individual differences in the learning and representation of knowledge? This question is also related to my earlier point that we cannot categorically describe "the bilingual brain" versus "the monolingual brain": rather, there is a continuum from being monolingual to being bilingual.

As you yourself have pointed out elsewhere, bilinguals use their two languages to a different extent, in different contexts, for different purposes, and with different people (see Post 1.5). Underlying these volatile experiences of bilingualism are the different behavioral and brain patterns, such as which area of the brain becomes activated and which areas are better connected with one another. The many different shades of the term "bilingualism" also make it exceedingly difficult to find two bilinguals who are exactly the same in every aspect of their language history or behavior. We may also need better tools and methods to study individual differences in bilingual learning and representations.

Can you be a bit more specific as concerns your own area of expertise?
I can see at least three dimensions along which we identify individual differences when we compare bilingual and monolingual brains. The most obvious factor is the age at which a second language is learned. If you learn a new language late in your life, your brain patterns are more likely to be similar to a monolingual's in your native language, whereas they will be more different from those of native speakers of your second language. Work from my lab and that of many others has demonstrated this, and a great deal of theoretical thinking has gone into this in the past.

There are also the linguistic features of languages that differ vastly from one another (phonology, orthography, syntax, etc.), and researchers are only beginning to understand the impacts of these differences on the bilingual as well as the monolingual brains. There is recent evidence that distant languages, such as English and Chinese, are more likely to engage distinct neural representations in the bilingual individual, as compared with languages that are more similar to one another.

Finally, individuals have very different cognitive abilities before any new language is acquired, including their working memory and cognitive control abilities. How these kinds of individual differences impact the monolingual versus the bilingual brain is largely unknown. Only a few recent studies have started to investigate this. The hope is to identify individual differences and predict how such differences may underlie the monolingual and bilingual brains.

Where do you see the bilingual brain sciences going in the next few years? Your colleague, Professor Arturo Hernandez, in an earlier post[2] thinks we should examine how age of acquisition, language proficiency, and language control help shape the bilingual brain. What do you think?
While I share Arturo Hernandez's view that these are significant aspects, my own perspective is that the neuroscience of bilingualism should move beyond just looking at these factors. New emerging methods in behavioral studies, computational modeling, and brain imaging are helping us to address new and exciting interdisciplinary questions.

I predict, for example, significant progress in the understanding of individual differences and bilingual language representation and learning. I also see emerging new work in identifying cross-language similarities and differences using computational and neuroimaging techniques, and these could certainly impact bilingualism research. Finally, what brain effects are attributable to language learning versus to other cognitive experiences will be yet another very fruitful direction of research in the near future.

We will also need a better understanding of the issue of domain-general vs. domain-specific cognitive capacity and effects of transfer across domains. Work along these lines is actively pursued by many labs including our own.

On a more practical level, what does work on the bilingual brain bring us? I'm thinking here of the assessment and treatment of aphasic patients, bilinguals who suffer from dementia, and so on.
I see translational work being done in the sciences of learning that may be relevant to your question. In particular, I think that over the next few years, new research will emerge to link the lab with the classroom, to bridge basic research with pedagogical practice, and to connect virtual- and real-world learning experiences.

[2] www.psychologytoday.com/intl/blog/life-bilingual/201409/understanding-the-bilingual-brain

In the same spirit, researchers need to address the questions you raise and connect bilingual brain studies with the practical applications of treating bilinguals who suffer from cognitive and linguistic disorders. Integrating neuroscience with learning and cognition is a task for all those interested in the brain-behavior-cognition relationship. Hence, jumping on this bandwagon is not a luxury but a necessity for researchers in our field.

References

See the four references at the end of Part I.

13.4 THE MAN WHO COULD NO LONGER SPEAK TO HIS WIFE

This is the case of a multilingual man who had a stroke and who, upon recovery, could no longer communicate with his wife in the language they had spoken together for some nineteen years. A possible reason relates to a very emotional episode he had lived through in his earlier years.

Communication with language(s) is so much part of our lives that we take it for granted – at least, those of us who are not language scientists. However, when it breaks down, we suddenly realize how crucial it is to our existence. Here is an example taken from well-known case studies of multilingual aphasia.

A forty-four-year-old man who had suffered from a stroke was referred to Dr. Mieczyslaw Minkowski of Zurich, Switzerland. His mother tongue was Swiss German and his second language was Standard German, which he had learned at school. (Note that Swiss German is not intelligible to Standard German speakers.) He had also learned a little French in his school years. At the age of nineteen, he went to France where he worked for some six years. During his stay, French became his everyday means of communication and he quickly became fluent in it.

At age twenty-five, he returned to Switzerland and worked as a railroad conductor and then as a trader. He married a childhood friend and settled in Zurich. Together they spoke Swiss German as they did with their two children, their friends, and their acquaintances.

When the man had his stroke, some nineteen years after having returned to his native country, he lost consciousness for several hours.

On recovery, it was found that his language abilities were impaired – he suffered from aphasia. He recovered comprehension of his three languages within a day or two but his speech was altered severely. To everyone's surprise, when he started to speak, first producing a few words, then more and more, it was in French only, a language he had rarely used since his return! His wife could not understand him as she didn't speak French and so, his children, with their poor school French, had to act as interpreters between the two!

His French improved quite quickly and then he began to slowly recover his second language, Standard German. As for Swiss German, it did not reappear until four months after his stroke. Two months later, his best language was still French; German was improving quite rapidly, but he still spoke Swiss German in a very hesitant manner.

It was only sometime later, during the Christmas vacation, that his Swiss German suddenly became almost fluent, as did his German. But then his French started to regress! This continued, and in time he could no longer describe in French what he had read; he had to use German or Swiss German.

McGill University linguist Michel Paradis termed this type of recovery pattern from aphasia "antagonistic" – one language regresses (in this case, French) as the others progress (German and Swiss German). French was the first language the patient recovered; then, as German and Swiss German progressed, French started to lose ground. At the end of the observation period, he had lost almost all fluency in that language.

In Post 13.5, I give examples of other nonparallel recovery patterns from aphasia. I also go over the factors that may account for which languages are recovered. What is interesting here, though, is to try to understand why French, which was not the person's mother tongue or most used language, should have been recovered first.

Dr. Mieczyslaw Minkowski was one of the first researchers to propose psychosocial factors to account for the language recovery of aphasic patients. In order to explain the restitution of this man's languages in the reverse order in which he had learned them, and used them, he questioned him on his earlier life. The patient reported that the most beautiful years of his life had been those spent in France in his early twenties. And his great love had been a French woman with whom he had lived for some time. On his return to Switzerland, he had remained a staunch francophile, and he stated that his preferred language was French even though he rarely used it.

This case study reminds us of the myth that I have already discussed that bilinguals express their emotions in their first language (see Post 10.1). According to researcher Aneta Pavlenko, things are much more complex than that. The relationship between emotions and bilingualism plays out differently for different individuals. This is true when language abilities are unimpaired, as it is when they are impaired, as we have just seen here.

Reference

Gitterman, M. R., Goral, M., and Obler, L. K . (2012; eds.). *Aspects of Multilingual Aphasia*. Bristol: Multilingual Matters.

13.5 IMPAIRMENT AND RECOVERY PATTERNS IN MULTILINGUAL APHASIC PATIENTS[3]

Researchers have long been interested in multilinguals who suffer from aphasia, that is, language and speech impairment due to brain damage. The 200 or so published cases of nonparallel impairment and recovery are both fascinating and instructive.

In Post 13.4, I described the case of a multilingual man who had a stroke and who, upon recovery, could no longer communicate with his wife in the language they had spoken together for some twenty years. He suffered from multilingual aphasia.

Researchers are increasingly interested in the bilingual brain. Recent imaging techniques have greatly facilitated their work and the field of cognitive neuroscience of bilingualism is very active (see Posts 13.1 to 13.3). An older branch of the field studies multilingual aphasic patients, that is, those bilinguals or multilinguals who suffer language and speech impairment due to brain damage.

There are an increasing number of case studies published on the subject and according to CUNY Graduate Center specialists Loraine

---

[3] The original title of this post was "The man who could no longer speak to his wife. Part II."

K. Obler and Youngmi Park, the impairment patterns generally found is that there is the same kind of aphasia in all of the person's languages. In addition, the degree of impairment is proportional to the proficiency level the patient had in each language prior to the incident.

Most aphasic patients show parallel recovery of their languages, that is, the progress they make, albeit sometimes rather slow, is the same in all of their languages. There are, however, some 200 or so published cases today of differential impairment and recovery. McGill University linguist, Michel Paradis, organized them into a number of categories. One of the most frequent is selective recovery during which the patient never regains one or more languages. For example, a professor of physics whose mother tongue was Swiss German and whose second language was German moved to the French-speaking part of Switzerland when he was thirty. From then on, French became his most used language. At age forty-four, he had a stroke and the first language to reappear was French. However, his mother tongue, Swiss German, never returned, unfortunately.

In another type of recovery, differential recovery, the languages are differently impaired at the time of injury and are restored at the same or different rates. Here is an example: a Pole who spoke Polish (his mother tongue) as well as German and Russian was hit by a piece of shrapnel during the war. When he came to, his Russian was least impaired, his Polish was impaired in production, and his German was the most impaired. During recovery, he made most progress in Russian due to the Russian surroundings he lived in as well as the therapy he received in Russian.

Successive restitution, another recovery pattern, occurs when one language does not begin to reappear until another has been restored. A Swiss German mechanic had a motorbike accident and became aphasic. When language production was restored, he could speak only German (his second language after Swiss German). He made progress in the language due to therapy in that language. It is only when German was almost completely restored that he started to speak his first language, Swiss German.

Another pattern of recovery is the object of the preceding post. It has been termed antagonistic: one language regresses as the other progresses. In the case described, French was the first language recovered; then as German and Swiss German progressed, French started losing ground. Even more spectacular is alternate antagonism that corresponds to a "come and go" pattern of recovery. Michel Paradis reported on a case of a nun in Morocco, who had a moped accident and became totally aphasic. She went through stages of recovery where she spoke one language quite well but the other was dysfluent, and then, a few weeks later (sometimes even a few days later), the reverse would be true – the fluent language became dysfluent and vice versa.

Researchers who have examined these and other nonparallel recovery patterns have attempted to account for the factors that explain the order in which the languages are recovered. Here are a few that have been proposed over the years: the earliest language learned, the language most used just before the injury, the patient's affective and emotional state just prior to and after the injury (see Minkowski's explanation of the case described in Post 13.4), the language used in therapy following the injury, the language that the person also writes and reads in, and so on, not to forget the age of the patient and the severity of the injury.

It is probably a combination of several of these factors that can explain the nonparallel recovery of languages. All this becomes even more complex when patients show a different type of aphasia in each of their languages.

One final point pertains to the languages that are not recovered. Most researchers seem to agree that they are not lost but that they are inhibited, or more precisely that the control mechanisms that allow for language choice inhibit a language. The evidence for inhibition rather than loss comes from aphasic patients who may still understand a language but may no longer be able to speak it, from the cases of alternate antagonism where languages come and go over short periods of time, and from the many instances of multilingual aphasia where all the languages are finally recovered.

Reference

Gitterman, M. R., Goral, M., and Obler, L. K . (2012; eds.). *Aspects of Multilingual Aphasia.* Bristol: Multilingual Matters.

13.6 MULTILINGUAL APHASIA: A PERSONAL TESTIMONY

(Interview with Isabelle K.)

Language and speech impairment due to brain damage is a very difficult experience some people have to live through. Here an aphasic patient gives us her personal testimony.

Dr. Valerie Lim, a speech-language therapist in Singapore, contacted me to tell me that she had a multilingual aphasic patient, Isabelle K., who was willing to be interviewed. I was thrilled as a personal testimony can be of interest to others recovering from aphasia, their family members and friends, and the general public. It can also be motivating for the person herself who is struggling to recuperate her language(s). I am truly grateful to both Isabelle for her testimony and to Dr. Lim who put us in touch with one another.

Isabelle, please tell us a bit about yourself and your multilingualism. First, which languages did you speak as a child, with your parents and grandparents?
My father was Japanese and my mother Swedish. Although I was born in Sweden, we lived in Japan until I was eleven. English was the common language between my parents, and so it became the language at home. In my early years, my mother spoke English with me but then she started teaching me Swedish when I was seven. With my father, I spoke English and a bit of Japanese. As for my Japanese grandparents, my sister and I would communicate with them only in Japanese as they could not understand English.

What about the languages you used during your schooling?
At age six, I went to an international school in Tokyo where my classes were all in English, except for Japanese classes. I learned French when I was eleven years old but only really improved it as an adult.

English got a definite boost when I went to boarding school in the UK between the ages of eleven and eighteen and then to Oxford University for my undergraduate studies. I also went back to Japan over the summer all these years to see my grandparents.

For postgraduate studies from the ages of twenty-three to twenty-six, I went to the Stockholm School of Economics to do a master's degree in economics and finance. During those three years, my Swedish improved significantly.

Currently, which language(s) do you use with your husband and at work?
My husband is a French-speaking Belgian but we have always spoken in English together since we met in London and lived there for many years. We lived in Paris from 2010 to the end of 2012, so my French improved but I am not fluent in it by any means.

As for my work, English is my main language, although I am on disability leave currently. I use Japanese about once a year when I fly to Japan for my work.

Two years have gone by since your stroke. Can you first tell us what happened on the day that you had your accident?
On August 22, 2017 at 1.30 pm – I remember the moment so well – I was working in my office in Singapore and I had a severe stroke. I had had the worst headache during the morning, and was sitting at my desk finishing a conference call when I fell to the floor and I could no longer speak. I remained calm but I needed an ambulance immediately.

I had suffered an ischemic stroke, that is, an artery in the brain had become blocked. Almost the entire left side of the brain where the speech function is located was affected. The significant and rapid brain swelling led the doctors to perform a decompressive craniectomy – part of the skull was removed – which saved my life. After a few days I regained consciousness only to discover that the right side of my body was paralyzed (hemiplegia) and I could not utter a single sound.

How did you become aware that you had become aphasic? Which languages could you no longer speak?
I could not speak aloud any one of my languages when I woke up in the intensive care unit. I had completely lost the connection between my brain and my vocal cords. I could not utter a single sound! I was also suffering from speech apraxia (inability to coordinate speech muscles), and dysarthria (slurring of speech) given my paralysis on the right-hand side of my body, including my face and mouth.

My family was quite stressed but inside me I thought to myself that my speech would definitely come back. My husband, after a lot of research, pushed the doctors to try out music therapy with me. And because of it, on the day of my birthday a few weeks later, my voice came back and

I could sing happy birthday in English! The doctors could then make a diagnostic and confirmed a strong aphasia as well as the apraxia.

How about speech comprehension of your different languages? Was it hindered too?
Aphasia affected my expressive functions significantly, but my comprehension was not as affected. Based on the conversations around me when I was in hospital, I could understand English and 40 percent of French. Five weeks later, I realized I was able to comprehend conversational Swedish when I skyped my mother, and eight weeks later I was able to understand my Japanese neighbor when I came home from hospital.

Comprehension often comes back first. What about language production apart from English which came back first?
I recovered Swedish about a year ago and Japanese about eight months ago. I heard French every day, since my husband was speaking French with business colleagues and friends on the phone, and even though I now understand 60 percent of French, I can only say a few words in it.

And your ability to read and write? Did it suffer too?
Yes, it did. Initially, while I was still at hospital for my stroke, I was able to read in English but I did not write at all well. My writing in English has improved progressively since then – my therapy takes place in that language – but I still cannot write as I could pre-stroke. Swedish was the second language to come back, and I can now read at 90 percent and write at 60 percent. Japanese is only coming back slowly after two years, but it is far from the level I used to have pre-stroke.

Not being able to express oneself is extremely distressing. How did you live through this difficult time?
I was frustrated but I was not distressed. I have been quite lucky so far to have the strength to keep fighting every day without being too depressed. I guess it is also because I am so happy to be alive and every day is a gift. But it is indeed quite difficult to be one day a multilingual professional and the next day not being able to communicate properly with other people.

Were there moments when you felt that you were not making any further progress?

Many a time – I felt that my speech was not making any improvements, or only marginal improvements. It was about a year and a half ago, I confided in my husband that I was not making the progress I needed to and he comforted me by saying that my speech would come, slowly and surely. In the last three months, my speech has been more rapid, more accurate, and more diverse. It is a marathon and every day is another opportunity to make a little progress.

What are your remaining problems today?
Although I have improved, speaking English is still slow. When I am perky, I can now say 70–75 percent of what I want to say pre-stoke. This is already much better than fifteen months ago, when I was only able to say 25–30 percent of what I wanted to. But when I am tired it slides down to about 50 percent. As they say, once you have completed 90 percent of the journey, there is still half of the way left!

All cases of aphasia are different from one another but would you have a few words of advice for aphasic patients who are just starting therapy, and for those who surround them and take care of them?
Start your speech therapy soon. Never give up – however long it takes. Your brain is making new connections every day, but it can take a long time in aphasic patients. Try new things, for example, read out loud, use music therapy which is excellent, and cognitive function therapy helps too.

Finally, those who are caring for us should keep having words of encouragement such as, "It is awfully hard to do what you are having to do after the stroke, but keep it up, and in a couple of years reap the benefits. Even if you cannot speak perfectly, well done!" Dr. Valerie Lim has been very encouraging. She has accompanied me from the beginning in my speech recovery journey and I want to thank her.

14

Special Bilinguals

INTRODUCTION

Special bilinguals have both a regular and a unique relationship with their languages. Some, such as teachers, translators, and interpreters, make a living from their extensive knowledge and careful use of their languages. Others, such as airline pilots and traffic controllers, or foreign correspondents, do not have to reflect on them as much but cannot do their jobs without their other language(s) and specific skills. And others still, such as bilingual writers, express their art in a second or third language, or in both their languages. This chapter is a tribute to all these bilinguals.

Post 14.1 examines the bilingualism of teachers of a second language who share many similarities with regular bilinguals, but who are also characterized by a number of differences.

The three posts that follow concern those who earn their living by translating or interpreting. Post 14.2 examines the particular skills and resources needed to be a translator. This entails understanding the original text in the source language, and having the necessary transfer skills and appropriate linguistic, stylistic, and cultural skills in the target language.

Posts 14.3 and 14.4 concern interpreters. In Post 14.3, it is shown that interpreters are often taken for granted, and yet they are accomplishing one of the most difficult tasks humans can undertake. And in Post 14.4, an interpreter, Iain Whyte, tells us about his profession, his background, and the different types of interpreting that he does.

The three posts that follow concern occupations that often require special forms of bilingualism. Post 14.5 is the interview of an American foreign correspondent in Paris, NPR journalist Eleanor Beardsley. She explains how in her reporting she has to constantly keep in mind those back in the United States who do not know French or the culture of the country she is working in.

For Post 14.6, an expert, Judith Burki-Cohen, explains how pilots and air traffic controllers communicate in a language that is often not their own. Post 14.7 discusses sleeper agents who have to develop linguistic and cultural skills rarely required of regular bilinguals.

The last three posts concern bilingual writers. Writing is one of the most demanding skills that is acquired, and writing literary works is an art that only a handful of people ever master. And yet, there are some very special bilinguals who write literature in their second or third language, as shown in Post 14.8, and there are those who even write in two languages (Post 14.9). Finally, Post 14.10 is an interview with Eva Hoffman, the acclaimed bilingual author of *Lost in Translation*, a book that launched a new genre, the language memoir.

14.1 TEACHERS OF A SECOND LANGUAGE[1]

Teachers of a second language share many similarities with regular bilinguals, but they are also characterized by a number of interesting differences. In addition, they help lay the foundations of interlingual and intercultural communication among their students.

I have always been fascinated by how second/foreign/world language teachers juggle between their lives as bilinguals and their profession as teachers of a language, culture, and literature. This may come from the fact that I started my career teaching English to French students and that I too had to handle this duality.

Those who teach a language other than the country's main language(s) are usually bilingual in that they use their two (or more) languages on a daily basis. But they are special bilinguals in a number of ways.

First, some may not often use the language they teach outside the classroom since they may not have a need for it in everyday communication. Regular bilinguals usually have several domains of use for their different languages.

Second, most language teachers have insights into the linguistics of the language that regular bilinguals simply do not have. They have to explain German morphology and word order, the rules of the past participle in

---

[1] The original title of this post was, "Teaching and living with two or more languages."

French, the difference between "ser" and "estar" in Spanish, and so on, when a regular bilingual would have a hard time doing so. Any normal bilingual who has replaced a language teacher knows firsthand how difficult it is to suddenly explain a complicated aspect of a language that she usually speaks without giving it a second thought.

A third difference is that language teachers have both their languages active when they teach – they are in a bilingual mode (see Post 3.1). Thus, as they are using one of their languages overtly in class (e.g. Spanish), they also have their other language (e.g. English) ready to intervene in case someone asks a question in it or produces a code-switch (see Post 3.4). But some may not allow themselves to intermingle their languages overtly and they may well correct those who do.

This is an interesting predicament. So as not to "set a bad example," they may avoid code-switching or borrowing themselves even though this could facilitate communication. However, outside of school, and in private, they may well do so. This said, I have known some language teachers who refrain from intermingling languages completely in everyday life so as not to slip into this mode when they are teaching.

A fourth difference is that they are usually true admirers of the second language they teach – at least of its standard variety – and they have a real love for its culture(s). They convey this passion to their students some of whom become fascinated in turn. This may lead the latter, one day, to visit a country where the language is spoken and even to live in it. The enthusiasm many teachers show is not the norm in regular bilinguals who spend less time thinking and talking about their languages and their cultures. Everyday aspects of life are simply too demanding of their time and attention.

Finally, many language teachers simply do not believe they are bilingual. This is true of many regular bilinguals but maybe more so in the case of teachers. They hold a very strict view of what it means to be bilingual such as to have complete and equal proficiency (spoken and written) in your two or more languages, having no accent in them, and even having grown up with all languages.

When I speak to language teachers who feel this way, I try to convince them that they are indeed bilingual even though they do have specific characteristics. I also tell them that despite the demanding job that they do daily, they are laying the foundations of interlingual and intercultural communication among their students – something they can certainly be proud of.

Reference

Grosjean, F. (2010). Special bilinguals. Chapter 13 of *Bilingual: Life and Reality*. Cambridge, MA: Harvard University Press.

14.2 TRANSLATORS AND THE ART OF TRANSLATION[2]

It is worth stepping back a bit to reflect on what it means to be a translator, the art of translation, and its link to bilingualism.

There is a longstanding myth that bilinguals are born translators. In fact, apart from everyday language, bilinguals are not particularly good translators. Why is that? One reason is that they acquire and use their languages for different purposes, in different domains of life, with different people (see Post 1.5).

Unless they have domains of life covered with two languages, or they acquired the language they are translating into (the target language) in a manner that puts the emphasis on translation equivalents, they may be missing the required vocabulary.

Bilinguals may also not be sufficiently fluent in one of the languages involved and may not have the stylistic varieties and the expressions needed for a quality translation. In addition, they may lack the cultural knowledge linked to a language that would facilitate, for example, their understanding of the original text or message.

Translators must have a complete set of translation equivalents in the other language, at least in the domains concerned. They must also know the two languages (or dialects) fluently, at all linguistic levels, and they must avoid all the usual translation traps such as false friends and literal translations. Set expressions can be a nightmare to translate for those who are not careful enough. Thus, if the French expression, "Je me raconte des histoires," is translated literally into English as, "I'm telling myself stories," the

---

[2] The original title of this post was, "Desperately seeking a final translation."

French meaning is not conveyed; it should have been translated as, "I'm kidding myself."

Translators must express in one language, in as faithful a way as possible, the meaning and the style of the text in another language. This entails understanding fully the original text in the "source language" and having the necessary transfer skills, as well as the linguistic, stylistic, and cultural skills in the target language to produce a correct translation.

Very little room is left for the translator's own intuition or creativity. He or she must follow the original text as closely as possible and render it in correct prose in the target language.

Translators are very much special bilinguals, and translation is definitely a difficult bilingual skill. It is no wonder then that there are specialized schools where students learn to translate professionally such as the Monterey Institute of International Studies in California.

One of the requirements for entry to these schools is to have excellent language skills in two or more languages. Lengthy training then transforms the "regular" bilingual into a certified translator. Another extended training period is needed to form a professional interpreter, as we will see below.

14.3 THOSE INCREDIBLE INTERPRETERS

We often take the work of interpreters for granted, and yet they are accomplishing one of the most difficult linguistic skills humans can undertake. They are special bilinguals par excellence.

Have you ever sat down in an interpreter's booth, put on the headphones, and tried to interpret the incoming speech? I did when I was a young and rather naive student who thought that being bilingual meant one could interpret simultaneously. No sooner had I started than problems arrived. As I was outputting the first sentence, the second one was already coming in but I hadn't paid enough attention to it. I remembered its beginning but not its ending. Very quickly I fell behind and I just couldn't say anything more after a few minutes!

Many years later I still remember the scene vividly and because of it, but also because of my own research on the perception and production of speech, I have the utmost respect for interpreters and the training they have to go through to do their job well.

Interpreters come in various types (community, conference, sign language), and interpreting itself is diverse in that it can be consecutive or simultaneous. I will take two extreme cases of interpreting that differ in many aspects including age: bilingual children who act as interpreters and adult simultaneous interpreters.

Many children who belong to minorities (immigrants, migrant workers, Deaf people) act as successive interpreters as well as cultural intermediaries between their communities and the outside world. Despite the fact that they have no training in community interpreting, their natural abilities never cease to impress us. Stanford University professor Guadalupe Valdés examined the strategies adopted by Spanish–English bilingual youngsters and found they used a number of strategies to convey essential information, including tone and stance. They were also able to compensate for linguistic limitations. Valdés concluded that the traits and abilities they exhibited were characteristic of exceptional cognitively competent children.

Authors Brian Harris and Bianca Sherwood, some years prior, had described a young Italian girl (BS) who, before she was four, was already interpreting between the Abruzzi dialect and Italian. She then acquired Spanish when her family moved to Venezuela, and English when they moved to Canada. In no time at all she was interpreting from, and to, these languages for her parents: phone calls, conversations, messages, radio and TV programs, etc. In addition, she quickly developed diplomatic skills, softening her father's outbursts when bargaining with non-Italians. Her father once told her to call his interlocutor a nitwit; she calmly said, "My father won't accept your offer!"

Some of these childhood interpreters sometimes find themselves, as adults, in the role of professional interpreters after having followed intensive training in schools such as those in Monterey or Geneva. (Of course, many other interpreters have not had to go through this kind of childhood experience although many do grow up bilingual.)

In addition to having all the skills of translators (see the preceding post), professional interpreters must have all the linguistic and cognitive skills that allow them to go from one language to the other, either simultaneously or successively. For example, simultaneous interpreting involves careful listening, processing, and comprehending the input in the source language, memorizing it, formulating the translation in the target language, and then articulating it, not to mention dual tasking, that is, letting the next sequence come in as you are outputting the preceding one. Researcher David Gerver has reported that simultaneous interpreters overlap speaking one language while listening to another up to 75 percent of the time!

Interpreters must activate the two languages they are working with. They have to hear the input (source) language but also the output (target) language, not only because they have to monitor what they are saying but also in case the speaker uses the target language in the form of code-switches. However, they must also close down the production mechanism of the source language so that they do not simply repeat what they are hearing, as they sometimes do when they get very tired!

Given these processing requirements, in addition to knowing translation equivalents in numerous domains and subdomains (e.g. business, economic, medical), as well as stylistic variants, it is no wonder that interpreters, like translators, are considered special bilinguals. As the saying so rightly states:

It takes more than having two hands to be a good pianist.

It takes more than knowing two languages to be a good translator or interpreter.

References

Valdés, G. (2003). *Expanding Definitions of Giftedness: The Case of Young Interpreters from Immigrant Communities*. Mahwah, NJ: Lawrence Erlbaum.

Grosjean, F. (2010). Special bilinguals. Chapter 13 of *Bilingual: Life and Reality*. Cambridge, MA: Harvard University Press.

14.4 AN INTERPRETER TELLS US ABOUT HIS PROFESSION[3]

(Interview with Iain Whyte)

Language interpreters accomplish one of the most difficult linguistic tasks humans can undertake. How do they do it?

---

[3] The original title of this post was, "Those incredible interpreters, Part II."

I have always been fascinated by language interpreters. After a first post on the topic (see the previous text), what better way to come back to it than to find out about the profession by interviewing an interpreter. Iain Whyte, who heads an interpreting and translation agency in the Paris region, grew up speaking both English and French. He has been active all of his life as a language professional, be it in the written or the spoken modality, and has very kindly accepted to answer my questions.

In what way did growing up bilingual and bicultural help you become a professional interpreter?
I was born in India of a French mother and a British father, and lived there for about nine years. My parents used the one person–one language approach (see Post 6.4) and when we left, I was fully bilingual, although slightly more dominant in English due to my English schooling there. I then spent the next ten years in boarding schools in England but lived in France four months of the year where my parents had settled.

I went to university in France, first Paris Nanterre University and then Sciences Po, the Paris-based research university in the social sciences, and had no problem fitting in. The grounding I received there in politics and economics, and my fluency in my two languages, were a good starting point to provide translating and simultaneous interpreting services to business corporations, NGOs, local governments, and so on.

We have all seen photos of interpreters in booths or at the back of conference rooms doing simultaneous interpretation. What is involved and how difficult is it?
It involves interpreting what a person is saying in real time, that is, as the person is speaking. It requires a high degree of concentration, which explains why we work in teams of two or three, each team-member doing a 20- to 30-minute shift before handing over to a colleague. You have to get used to speaking and listening at the same time, a skill you gain through practice and experience. It calls for concision and clarity of expression, as well as synthesizing and analytical skills. Obviously, being specialized in the topic or area of expertise involved is a necessity.

What other aspects of simultaneous interpretation are special?
You have to be quick at finding equivalences for expressions and sayings. You have to keep up with the speaker no matter how fast he or she speaks,

and identifying in part with the speaker is important. One of the most difficult challenges is interpreting jokes, whose power often lies in a play on words which is difficult or sometimes impossible to render in another language.

Can you explain what consecutive interpreting is and how it is done?
During consecutive interpreting, the speaker stops every one to five minutes, usually at the end of a "paragraph" or complete thought, and the interpreter then steps in to render what was said into the target language. A key skill involved is note-taking, since few people can memorize a full paragraph in one hearing without loss of detail. Many professional interpreters develop their own "ideogramic" symbols, which allows them to take down not the words but the thoughts of the speaker in a sort of language-independent form.

Consecutive interpreting is more laborious than simultaneous interpreting as it slows the proceeding down. All participants in a meeting have to wait for the interpreter to stop speaking before they can resume their exchange. In addition, for those who understand both languages, source, and target, it means hearing the discourse twice.

What is whispered interpreting (chuchotage) and how is it different from the above?
Whispered interpreting is the same as simultaneous interpreting but it does away with any equipment such as a booth, microphone, and headset. The interpreter sits next to his/her client(s) and literally whispers the interpreted message.

Many interpreters have a source and a target language (e.g. English into French). Is that your case or do you interpret as easily in both directions?
Because of my family background and linguistic experience as a child, I'm able to interpret as easily in both directions. This sometimes gives me a competitive advantage over others, particularly when clients don't know into which language (e.g. English or French) the interpretation will be required.

How do you prepare yourself before taking on an interpreting job?
First of all, I accept interpreting assignments only in my domains of expertise. In addition, my clients usually provide me with preparatory material such as presentations, PowerPoint slides, reading lists, speaker

profiles, statistics, and so on. I also make a point of keeping abreast of the latest developments in my areas of expertise by reading the generalist and specialist press.

Some speakers are easier to interpret than others. Can you tell us what aspects of speech output facilitate your task?
The speaker's rate of speech flow is important: it mustn't be too slow or too fast! In fact, we interpreters have the same concerns as ordinary listeners regarding the clarity, pace, and quality of the speaker's discourse. The speaker's ability to summarize his or her thoughts clearly and concisely from time-to-time is also much appreciated.

With the advent of modern communication technology (video and voice interaction over the web), how has your job changed?
We can now interpret meetings online without having to travel, and we can do so at any time of the day and night, for example, interpret a speech by Donald Trump given at 2 a.m. French time (8 p.m. US time)! And during conferences and events, our interpreting also benefits people who are not physically present in the same venue.

Tell us about the work you do for France 24, the international news and current affairs television network based in Paris?
It involves interpreting during live radio or TV broadcasts while the event is actually taking place (state ceremonies/visits, parliamentary debates, speeches, etc.). It also involves interpreting pre-recorded material, notably interviews with celebrities, politicians, and so on. It requires good background knowledge of international and domestic politics and of the personalities involved. Round-the-clock availability and quick responsiveness to ongoing events are also necessary.

You have also interpreted for well-known politicians including former French President François Hollande and current President Emmanuel Macron. How stressful is it?
It is no more stressful than interpreting "ordinary" people, but we are clearly aware of the risk of causing a *faux pas* or even a diplomatic incident if we use the wrong terms and generate misunderstandings!

Finally, what is a typical interpreting nightmare you have?
My worst nightmare is a speaker who thinks he/she is speaking clearly but is, in fact, not clear at all. These are the kind of moments when you have

to be creative and give a semblance of sense to something that is devoid of meaning. Fortunately, this happens rarely!

14.5 LINGUISTIC AND CULTURAL CHALLENGES OF FOREIGN CORRESPONDENTS

(Interview with Eleanor Beardsley)

Foreign correspondents navigate, linguistically and culturally, between the country they are working in and the country they are reporting to. Here is how they do it.

Foreign correspondents join a long list of special bilinguals. They lead their lives with two or more languages – like regular bilinguals – but their work also puts them in a unique relationship with their languages and cultures. They have to keep in mind those back home who will listen to them, or read their articles, most of whom may not know the language or the culture of the country they are working in. Eleanor Beardsley, National Public Radio (NPR) correspondent in Paris, is a well-known and much-appreciated voice on radio in the United States. She has kindly accepted to answer a few of our questions and we thank her wholeheartedly.

You are bilingual in English and French and have lived in France for many years. What are the advantages this brings you as a foreign correspondent?
The advantages of being bilingual are that you can read all the newspapers, listen to the radio, watch TV, talk to people, and really know what's going on in a society. Also you can travel to other countries with completely different cultures (where people also speak that language) and it's like having a direct entry into it.

An example of this was when I covered the Tunisian revolution. I arrived on the last day of the dictator, my first time in the country, but was able to talk to everyone because they spoke French. It was very strange finding myself operational and being able to converse and communicate with people in what would have ordinarily been a foreign, Arabic-Muslim society.

Are there any disadvantages at all in being bilingual/bicultural when compared to foreign correspondents who are not anchored as fully in a foreign language and culture?
I don't think there's really a disadvantage except perhaps that things begin to seem normal as you "go native." So maybe you don't recognize

a story that someone who is very foreign to the place would recognize. Certain cultural and societal differences no longer stand out as much.

When you travel as a journalist and you don't speak the language, you usually have an interpreter. Which is fine too because sometimes as a complete outsider you can have interesting ideas for stories and things hit you in a different way. And of course we can't speak every language!

How hard is it to prepare a report on something typically French (e.g. the almost monarchical political system in France) for a US audience that may not know anything about it?
It's not too hard. I just try to imagine how to make it interesting for a US audience that doesn't know the subject. I ask myself what would make it relevant for them. Usually I try to compare things to something similar in the United States. If I am trying to understand a topic, I usually start with a good interview with someone who knows the field. I find this person often by following French media. A good interview often gets you into a topic and gives you further ideas about it. And then things build up and you can think of a scene to put in your story, and so on.

Are there some topics your "French side" would love to report on but you don't as you know that they wouldn't be well received back in the States?
There aren't really any reports that would not be well received in the United States, but they might just be a bit pointless. On the other hand, there are some things I feel myself wanting to talk to the French about. For example, if I were a journalist targeting a French audience, I would do a story on the absurdity of closing down the country – public schools, businesses, government – for religious holidays, and at the same time touting your secularism.

Now, this story might fall flat in the United States. However, I did allude to it in a piece I did on the excess of school vacations in France. I did that one for American audiences. But the people who seemed to appreciate it the most were expats living in France!

Are there still some things about France where you need help deciphering them after so many years?
There are still plenty of things I don't know about France, but I usually just ask a question and then begin to research it. I don't think I really need help deciphering things. At this point, I feel I know how the French think and what they think about different topics. In addition, as my

husband is French I can always ask him! Or even my eleven-year-old son who is growing up French and American.

When recording your reports, you have to deactivate your French as best as possible. Do you find this difficult to do?
I don't have to deactivate my French when I record, but there are some words or expressions that we have in English that are French in origin and these I now find very difficult to say. Like "déjà vu." This is because the "vu" is mispronounced in English – we pronounce it as "vous" (we don't have the French "u" sound). So I have to choose – do I say it the French way or the American way? If you say it the American way, the meaning is "already you" instead of "already seen." But it would sound weird to say it the correct French way with Americans. On the other hand, I don't have a hard time with "savoir faire" because it sounds about the same in both languages. So usually I tailor my pronunciation to my audience.

Of course, if you do insert French into your reports on purpose (e.g. to talk about something typically French), how do you then get your audience to understand what you have just said (e.g. translate, explain, etc.)?
If I put French in my report, I usually have to translate it. Sometimes listeners like to hear you speak French, they like to hear you interacting in the foreign language. But it's usually translated or explained, unless it's something obvious like "Bonjour Monsieur" or "Merci beaucoup." And with names, sometimes I don't pronounce French names to an English-speaking person as I would to a French speaking person.[4]

Have friends and colleagues back home ever told you that after so many years you are starting to "sound French" in your radio reports, both in content and form? If so, how do you take it?
I love this question! No, no one has ever told me I sound French when speaking English. However, when Americans hear me speaking French they think I sound French! But a native French speaker always knows I'm not French. What I usually get is a polite, "Do I hear a little accent?" It becomes a compliment when someone thinks I'm Canadian from time to time. But mostly they ask me if I'm English or American.

Something I get a lot from Americans is: "Do you have a southern accent in French?" This is because I'm from the South and have a southern accent in

---

[4] On the topic on how to pronounce borrowings and foreign names, see Post 3.5.

English. I always tell people that when an English speaker is speaking French you can't tell the difference between someone from Great Britain and the United States – it's the Anglo accent that comes through!

14.6 BILINGUALISM IN THE SKY: PILOTS AND AIR TRAFFIC CONTROLLERS

(Interview with Judith Burki-Cohen)

English is the international language of civil aviation and so many airline pilots and controllers have to communicate in a language other than their own. An expert tells us what the implications are.

There are some 100,000 commercial flights each day in the world which means that literally millions of interactions take place between pilots and air traffic controllers, very often in a foreign language since English is the international language of civil aviation. This entails a special form of bilingualism as it is very domain-specific and has to be optimal at all times. How does it take place? How efficient is it? Are there breakdowns and if so, what are they due to? What still needs to be improved? Dr. Judith Burki-Cohen, formerly a senior scientist at the US Department of Transportation's Office of the Secretary, Research and Technology has worked extensively on these questions and has very kindly accepted to be interviewed. We thank her wholeheartedly.

What percentage of communication between pilots and air traffic controllers involves English as a foreign language for one or both parties would you say?

In non-English-speaking countries, near 100 percent, because few air traffic controllers and only some pilots are native speakers of English. In countries where English is the official language, it will depend on the percentage of international flights or international student pilots. This will vary according to region.

Who is responsible for making sure that both air traffic controllers and pilots are sufficiently proficient to talk to one another in English?

The civil aviation authorities in each country, which are affiliated with the International Civil Aviation Organization (ICAO) headquartered in Canada. For all pilots and air traffic controllers, it requires proficiency in aviation phraseology. Since March 2011, the ICAO also requires general English language proficiency for pilots and controllers flying internationally or interacting with international flights.

Is English always respected or do pilots and controllers who share the same language, for example, a German pilot speaking to a German controller, slip into their native language?
Well, they really shouldn't. One important reason is the so-called party line, that is a source of information for pilots and for air traffic controllers. The airspace is divided into sectors that communicate on the same radar frequency. As a pilot, I can increase my situation awareness by listening to who else is on the same frequency. This tells me who is near me and whether they encounter any weather that I should know about. I may even catch an air traffic controller's mistake, such as clearing me for the same runway as another airplane.

Pilots and controllers speaking in languages other than English deprive non-English-speaking pilots flying in the same airspace of the information in the party line, and they thus diminish their situation awareness.

Flying is the, or one of the, safest ways of travelling so communication in English, even though it is in a foreign language for many, seems to work very well. What are the procedures that are in place to make it so efficient?
The most important aspect is the strictly regulated phraseology and communication procedures that aim at avoiding misunderstandings. That is why it is so critical that all pilots and air traffic controllers adhere to these procedures, which afford multiple occasions to catch errors.

One procedural requirement, for instance, is careful "readback" by the pilot of what the controller has said, and "hearback" by the controller. The latter is supposed to listen to the pilot's readback and catch any readback errors.

Of course errors can go unnoticed, especially in a congested airspace. Efforts are underway to shift routine conversations to "datalink" via satellite, where air traffic controllers can communicate with pilots via text messages.

There are some instances where communication between pilots and air controllers break down though. Can you tell us how much is due to faulty English as compared to other reasons?

In addition to readback and hearback errors, there are many reasons why communication breakdowns happen. Faulty English is just one of them and restricted to areas with international flights or pilots. Use of nonstandard phraseology may or may not be due to lack of English proficiency. There are also stuck microphones that block an entire frequency and there is frequency congestion where a pilot cannot get a word in.

Another problem is airplane callsign confusions, where a pilot may take a clearance for another airplane with a similar sounding callsign. Certainly, all these issues are not helped with lack of English proficiency as a compounding factor.

How important is accent in communication breakdown since a controller and a pilot might each have a different English accent? Would you have an example of an incident due to this?
There are certainly complaints from both pilots and controllers, and incidences where accents may have played a role. A quick search of an official reporting system in the United States for "foreign accent" yields just ten reports filed in the past ten years. However, there are many unreported incidents involving pilots flying into non-English-speaking territory, pilots using airports with foreign students, pilots communicating with non-native-English-speaking crew, and of course air traffic controllers communicating with international flights or pilots.

Not only may pilots and air controllers have different first languages influencing their English but they might also come from different cultures. How does this affect communication?
You may be thinking of the 1990 Avianca crash near JFK airport, where 73 of the 158 passengers died. This is a perfect example of James Reason's Swiss Cheese Model, where several "holes" in the system have to line up to result in an accident. Yes, the Avianca copilot may have been intimidated by the controller's assertive manner, and a certain "macho" culture may have prevented him from successfully communicating the seriousness of the situation. This is all conjecture, however.

The facts are that the crew did not use the correct phraseology, which would have required them to declare a fuel emergency and request an emergency landing. Also, the crew had failed to obtain weather information before and during the flight and were unaware of the serious weather around JFK airport. Thus, they did not have enough fuel to handle the resulting delays at this notoriously busy airport. Moreover, the captain missed the first approach and had to go around for a second try. Finally, a less busy controller might have further inquired after hearing the nonstandard phrase "we're running out of fuel," especially with an international crew.

A few years ago, you gave specific recommendations for how air traffic controllers should talk to foreign pilots speaking English. What were they? Controllers should be aware that international pilots may be less familiar with the phraseology or that regional phraseologies may differ. Controllers should be especially careful with numbers, and stick to giving them in single digits instead of grouping them, that is, "eight" "three" instead of "eighty three." Grouping occurs differently for different languages (three and eighty in German, or four times twenty and three in French). Units for weights, distances, barometric pressure, etc., may also be different in different countries.

Controllers should speak "staccato," that is, break the instruction up into its component words by inserting short pauses. Recognizing where one word ends and the next begins is notoriously difficult for listeners of a foreign language. And of course controllers should pay extra attention to complete and correct readback. Finally, keeping instructions short will facilitate correct readback and save time over trying to cram too much information into one clearance.

References

Gladwell, M. (2008). The ethnic theory of plane crashes. Chapter 7 of *Outliers: The Story of Success*. New York: Little, Brown & Co.
International Civil Aviation Organization (2010). *Manual on the Implementation of ICAO Language Proficiency Requirements*. Montreal, Canada: ICAO.

14.7 SLEEPER AGENTS AS SPECIAL BICULTURAL BILINGUALS[5]

Sleeper agents, that is, spies who have been infiltrated into a target country, are very special bicultural bilinguals. They have to develop linguistic and cultural skills that are rarely required of regular bilinguals.

We are all intrigued by the story of sleeper agents, that is, spies who have been infiltrated into a target country and who "go to sleep" before

[5] The original title of this post was, "The linguistic and cultural skills of sleeper agents."

being activated. In 2010, we read about Anna Chapman and some ten other members of her spy ring who were expelled back to Russia. But before them, there were others.

George Koval, for example, in the middle of the last century, took part in the development of the atomic bomb in the Manhattan Project at Oak Ridge. Having grown up in the United States, he spoke fluent American English. His family emigrated to the Soviet Union during the Great Depression and that is where he was recruited by their largest foreign intelligence agency, the GRU. He then came back to the United States and managed to spy for the Soviet Union for close to ten years.

Sleeper agents such as Koval appear to be ordinary citizens, but they are in fact very special bicultural bilinguals. Their language fluency must be similar to that of native speakers in every way and they must have no trace of a foreign accent. This is quite exceptional as the majority of bilinguals have an accent in at least one of their languages (see Post 1.7).

Sleeper agents must also restrict themselves to using just one language in all situations (English in our case). This is quite different from regular bilinguals who use their two or more languages for different purposes, in different domains of life, and with different people. Sleeper agents cannot revert to their other, hidden, language and so they have to acquire the vocabulary, the expressions, and the levels of language for every domain of life in just one language.

These agents have to avoid code-switching and borrowing even when they are with other bilinguals and the situation is conducive to intermingling languages (see Post 3.4). And when they are with monolinguals, they have to carefully monitor what they are saying and avoid false friends (similar words with different meanings) as well as other language traps (e.g. translating something literally from their other language).

The kind of permanent monitoring they have to do on their language output is extremely demanding, and it becomes even more so during moments of stress and emotion when regular bilinguals might well slip into their other language.

On the cultural side, sleeper agents are trained to behave fully as nationals of the country they are spying on. They must put aside every aspect of their other culture and behave monoculturally in their "host" culture. For example, Koval played baseball and was very good at it.

Unlike regular biculturals who combine and blend aspects of their two or more cultures (see Post 9.1), sleeper agents must be "pure" members of the culture they are living in. At no time must the attitudes, beliefs, values, and behaviors of their other culture filter through.

As for their cultural identity, they have to pretend to identify fully with the culture they are living in, and they have to show this in their everyday behavior. Regular biculturals can choose to identify solely with culture A, solely with culture B, with neither A nor B, or with both A and B (see Post 9.2). Sleeper agents do not have this choice overtly even though, covertly, they continue to identify fully with their original culture.

With time, though, and despite the strict instructions they have received, some sleeper agents do start identifying, in part at least, with their host culture. And some few actually shift from being sleeper agents to becoming double agents. If used correctly by the intelligence services of the "host" country, they can do incredible damage to their original country. But here we leave the domain of language and culture and enter the very murky waters of counter-espionage.

References

Grosjean, F. (2010). Linguistic traps await deep-cover spies. *The Guardian*, July 13, 2010: www.guardian.co.uk/education/2010/jul/13/deep-cover-language

Grosjean, F. (2010). Special bilinguals. Chapter 13 of *Bilingual: Life and Reality*. Cambridge, MA: Harvard University Press.

14.8 AMAZING BILINGUAL WRITERS I

Writing is one of the most demanding skills that is acquired, and writing literary works is an art that only a handful of people ever master. And yet, there are some very special bilinguals who write literature in their second or third language, and sometimes even in two languages.

There are many writers who are bilingual or multilingual but they usually write their works in their first language, or in their most proficient writing language when they changed language dominance in their childhood. This is the case of Richard Rodriguez, the author of *Hunger of Memory*, whose first language was Spanish but who writes in English, his dominant language. It is also the case of Eva Hoffman, of *Lost in Translation* fame, who moved to Canada from Poland when she was thirteen and who uses English as her literary language (see her interview in Post 14.10).

Some authors, however, decide to write in their second or third language, even though they have good writing skills in their other language(s). This was the case of Joseph Conrad, the author of classics such as *Lord Jim*, *The Secret Agent*, and *Nostromo*. He was born in Poland where he spent his youth before living in France for four years. He then joined the English merchant navy and traveled the world until age thirty-five. It is then that he became a full-time novelist – in English, his third language!

Frederick Karl, one of his biographers, tells us that he decided not to write in Polish, his first language, in order to separate himself from his father as well as from his own first culture. Neither the Poles nor the British understood why he had chosen English, and Conrad had to live with a well-known bicultural dilemma – being categorized as a member of the other culture by each of the cultures concerned (see Post 9.2).

Even though Conrad had a very strong accent in English which prevented him from lecturing publicly (see Post 1.7), he wrote wonderful prose in English which required practically no editing. Even so, he belittled his English and wrote, "In writing I wrestle painfully with (this) language which I feel I do not possess but which possesses me – alas!"

A more recent bilingual author who wrote in her second language only was Ágota Kristóf. She left Hungary during the 1956 uprising along with her first husband and their four-month-old baby girl. They came to settle in Neuchâtel, Switzerland, and for a number of years she worked in a local watchmaking factory. She was totally monolingual in Hungarian when she arrived but she went back to school and studied French.

Kristóf started her literary career some twelve years after having arrived, first by writing poems in French. She then wrote her first novel, *The Notebook*, in French also, the story of twin brothers lost in a country that is torn apart. It was a real success and it has been translated into numerous languages. This was the beginning of a long career as an author of novels, short stories, and plays – all in French!

When we read biographies or interviews of bilinguals who write in their second or third language, we sometimes find evidence that some did try out writing in their first language. One such writer was Jack

Kerouac, the much-acclaimed author of *On the Road*. Kerouac's first language, and only language until age six, was French. He came from a French Canadian family that emigrated to Lowell, Massachusetts, and with whom he spoke the Quebec French variety, joual. His manuscript, *Sur le Chemin*, was written shortly after his 1951 best seller (it is in fact a different story). It was never published in French but Kerouac did translate it into English as *Old Bull in the Bowery*. The original French version was only discovered in 2008.

Unlike these bilingual authors – and there are many others such as André Aciman, Ha Jin, Andreï Makine, Dai Sijie, Ahdaf Soueif, and Xu Xi – who have remained faithful, for the most part, to just one language, there are some authors who actually write in their two languages, as we will see in the next post.

References

Grosjean, F. (2010). Bilingual writers. Chapter 12 of *Bilingual: Life and Reality*. Cambridge, MA: Harvard University Press.

Karl, F. R. (1979). *Joseph Conrad*. New York: Farrar, Straus and Giroux.

Interview of Ágota Kristóf: www.hlo.hu/news/agota

14.9 AMAZING BILINGUAL WRITERS II

A handful of bilingual authors write literature in two languages, not just one. Some write their first works in their first language and then move on to their second language, others do the reverse, and some actually combine the two languages in the same work.

We saw in the previous post that some bilingual authors write literature in their second or third language despite the fact that writing is one of the most demanding skills ever acquired. What is even more amazing is that other authors write their works in two languages, not just one.

Many of these authors go from writing in their first language to writing in their second or third language, usually after having emigrated. For example, Vladimir Nabokov, born in Russia in 1899, started by writing in Russian (e.g. *Mashenka, The Gift*) before becoming famous in the English-speaking world for his novels written directly in English (e.g. *Bend Sinister, Lolita*).

A similar itinerary was followed by Nobel Prize winner, Samuel Beckett, who was born in Ireland but who moved to France permanently at age thirty-one. His first novel, *Murphy*, was written in English but after World War II, he started to write in French (e.g. *Molloy*).

Hunter College Professor Elizabeth Beaujour has analyzed why authors such as these shift over to writing in their second or third language. The first reason is obvious – it is to gain a wider audience, even if the émigré community is quite large in their new country. A second reason is that bilingual authors are rarely happy with the translations that are done of their works. They either redo the translations themselves, even though the process is particularly tormenting for many of them, or they write new works directly in their second or third language.

And a third reason is quite simply that different aspects of life require different languages (see Post 1.5). Writing a novel in the "wrong language" (e.g. a story in Russian that takes place in the United States) is particularly difficult, as Nabokov himself experienced.

There are also those bilingual writers who start to write in their second language and then, a few years later, revert to writing in their first language, something they had not done before. Canadian and French author, Nancy Huston, is such a person. After having moved to France from North America in 1973, she wrote her first book, *Les Variations Goldberg*, in French. The reason she gives is that her mother tongue, English, was "too emotionally fraught at the time." She continued writing in French for a number of years and then decided to write a novel in English, *Plainsong*. It came out twelve years after her first book in French.

Huston explains her return to English by her need to tell stories, "wholeheartedly, fervently, passionately . . . without dreading the derisive comments of the theoreticians." She now writes in both her languages and translates her works both ways.

Elizabeth Beaujour has found that bilingual authors, in the twilight of their career, are no longer satisfied keeping their two languages separate. They make sure that their works are published in both languages (as did Beckett and as does Huston currently), and they have bilingual characters who speak their languages and shift from one to the other quite freely.

Today, in fact, there is an increasing number of authors who write bilingually, even at the start of their career. Thus, Junot Díaz, a winner of the Pulitzer Prize in 2008 for *The Brief Wondrous Life of Oscar Wao,* brings a lot of Spanish into his English prose. And Susana Chávez-Silverman, a Hispanic American author, uses a blend of English and Spanish that is higher than normal in her books such as *Killer Crónicas.*[6] She states that she remains bilingual in her writing so as not to have to choose between her two languages.

Among other authors who write in their two languages we find: André Brink (Afrikaans, English), Ariel Dorfman (Spanish, English), Claude Esteban (Spanish, French), Romain Gary (French, English), Julien Green (French, English), Milan Kundera (Czech, French), and Jonathan Littell (English, French).

This said, as Elizabeth Beaujour writes, it is still rare for bilingual or polyglot writers to create work that has the same weight in more than one language. Those that do are truly exceptional people!

References

Grosjean, F. (2010). Bilingual writers. Chapter 12 of *Bilingual: Life and Reality.* Cambridge, MA: Harvard University Press.
Beaujour, E. (1989). *Alien Tongues: Bilingual Russian Writers of the "First" Emigration.* Ithaca, NY: Cornell University Press.

14.10 LOST IN TRANSLATION

(Interview with Eva Hoffman)

Lost in Translation evokes different things to different people: a movie, an episode in TV series, a novel, a song, and so on. But for those interested in bilingualism, biculturalism, and second language learning, it is a language memoir of considerable importance that created a new genre. Its author, Eva Hoffman, answers questions about her much-acclaimed book.

Back in 1989, Eva Hoffman published her first book, *Lost in Translation,* a memoir about immigration, language loss, second language acquisition, and discovering a new land and a different culture. Her autobiography was to have a worldwide success – the Nobel prize winner Czeslaw Milosz called it "graceful and profound" – and it helped launch a new genre, the

---

[6] Susana Chávez-Silverman reading extracts of *Killer Crónicas*: https://uwpress.wisc.edu/books/2616-audio.html

language memoir. We asked Eva Hoffman if she would answer a few questions for us on the fifth anniversary of our *Psychology Today* blog. She very kindly accepted to do so and we wish to thank her wholeheartedly.

More than a quarter of a century has gone by since you published *Lost in Translation*. How do you consider it now after all these years and the success it has had?
Occasionally, I've had to go back to it and reread parts of it – and I find that I have a double reaction: One is to wonder who wrote it; and the other is to think, "This is pretty good." The success of the book was initially entirely amazing to me. When I was writing it, I didn't know if it would be published, or whether anyone would understand, or care about, the experience I was trying to describe – the internal journey involved in emigration, and the process of translating yourself into another language and culture.

But since then, of course, emigration and other cross-national movements have become one of the central phenomena of our time; and it seems that I identified something about that experience which many others understand – perhaps in part, because I was writing about it innocently, so to speak; that is, by trying to capture my own perceptions as directly as possible, without thinking about previous literary models, or worrying about the book's reception. What can I say, I was lucky.

Your book was presented as a "classically American chronicle of upward mobility and assimilation," but it is also a narrative of becoming bilingual and bicultural in adolescence. Is there any reason you do not use these words in your text: "bilingual" appears only once, as does "bicultural?"
The book is about the process of *becoming* bilingual and bicultural – rather than having achieved these conditions. But also, I didn't want to start with these external labels – I wanted to talk about their meanings from within.

The account you give of your first day at school with your sister has marked many readers, especially those who have experienced something similar. Do you feel things have changed in the half century that has gone by?
Yes, it is half a century, or a bit more ... And yes, I feel things have changed enormously. We have become much more aware of cultural difference, and how important our first language and culture is to our identity – how deeply raveled it is with our basic sense of self. I don't think

there are many schools now where children are forcibly yanked out of their first names – although I'm sure these rites of passage can still be difficult for immigrant children.

You state about the time you were monolingual in Polish: "The more words I have, the more distinct, precise my perceptions become ..." Does it apply even more as a bilingual since you do have more words now if you combine both languages?
Hmmm . . . I'm not sure it works quite like that. What I was talking about in that passage was a certain relationship to language – a relationship in which words seemed to correspond to things and to name them directly (this is partly an illusion which we all have to grow out of). Polish at that point made the world vivid, as English did not. On the level of sheer vocabulary, English is a fantastically rich language – and so is Polish, for that matter. Both are rich in salty, colloquial, culturally particular expressions.

So yes, sometimes I reach for a phrase in the other language, to express a particular tone or vein of humor, perhaps more than for specific words. And of course, since those first stages of emigration, I have acquired an adult vocabulary – of politics, for example, or literary criticism – which I didn't have then; and which to a large extent, I had to translate from English to Polish.

Toward the end of your book, you write about your Polish and English: "Each language modifies the other, crossbreeds with it, fertilizes it. . . . I am the sum of my languages." Do you share the idea that a bilingual is not two monolinguals in one person?
I think perhaps we need to distinguish between functional and internal bilingualism. You can speak two languages very well, but not incorporate them into your psychic life. But if both languages are deeply incorporated into your psyche – your consciousness, and perhaps deeper layers as well – then hopefully you do become one, linguistically integrated person. For me, one crucial moment in my trajectory was when I started dreaming in English. Later still, I had a dream in English which I had originally had in Polish; that was the moment when I understood I had become truly internally bilingual.

Again, at the end of your book, you state, ". . . I begin to trust English to speak my childhood self as well. . . ." Now that you have gone back to Poland so often, and have so many contacts there, is the reverse true, that is you trust Polish to speak your adulthood self?

Yes, that was a gradual process as well – as I mentioned, I learned certain parts of the Polish vocabulary after I'd had them in English; but also, as I have come to use Polish more frequently – and to write e-mails in it! – it has become a more fluent language for my adult perceptions and self.

What was your own sense of the accuracy and authenticity of the translation of your book into Polish, *Zagubione w przekładzie?* **Were there moments when you felt that English and Polish refer to incommensurable realities?**
Yes, there were such moments – although they did not have to do with the accuracy of the translation, but rather with the tenor of the two languages. Written Polish is very grammatically precise and, in comparison to American English, quite formal. So one of the things I was missing in the translation was the flexibility, the looseness of American English. Indeed, one of the surprises of reading *Lost* in Polish was to see just how Americanized I had become – in my cultural references, but also, in this informality of expression.

Do you still enjoy Polish poetry and if so, is there a difference in the ways in which you respond to verses in Polish and English?
I read Polish poetry much more rarely – so when I do, I am perhaps more freshly struck by its beauty. But my responses to English poetry are now also very primary and (with some poems!) intense.

You moved to England in 1993 and have lived and worked there for many years. Could you state, as you did at the very end of your work about the United States, "I am here now" and, if so, what does it mean for your triculturalism?
My semi-joking formulation for this is that London is my midway point between Manhattan and Cracow. It's a good synthesis, and I'm certainly here to stay.

Reference

Hoffman, E. (1989). *Lost in Translation: A Life in a New Language.* New York: Dutton/Penguin.

15

Reminiscing

INTRODUCTION

This chapter contains three posts in which I reminisce on a few events that I lived through during my career studying bilingualism and bilinguals.

Post 15.1 relates my interview with one of the greatest minds of our time, Noam Chomsky. The topics concerned whether there is a difference between monolinguals and bilinguals, whether you can lose a first language or not, the permanent influence of a second language on a first language, and why it is that bilinguals have been studied much less than monolinguals by theoretical linguists.

Post 15.2 is an interview with me conducted by Aneta Pavlenko to celebrate my fifty years in the field of bilingualism. I answer questions regarding my upbringing, the countries I lived in, the bilingual's language modes, how the field of bilingualism has changed over these years, and the areas I would suggest younger colleagues delve into.

Finally, Post 15.3 relates my travails in preparing and writing my French book on bilingualism, *Parler plusieurs langues: le monde des bilingues.* It was a far bigger challenge than I could have imagined, but it also allowed me to get some insight into the reported difficulties bilingual authors have writing in their two languages, or translating their work from one language to the other (see Posts 14.8 and 14.9).

The book contains other posts written from a personal perspective, but since they fit in well with the different topics found in this work, they can be found in the respective chapters. In them I relate how I changed language dominance several times during my life (Post 4.1), how my boys spent their first years as monolinguals before becoming bilingual (Posts 6.8 and 5.10), the support I received from an exceptional bilingual and bicultural couple when I was a young faculty (Post 10.7), how I maintain contact with the four cultures that have influenced me (Post 9.5), and the letter I wrote to my newborn grandchild who was born to be bilingual (Post 10.8).

15.1 REMEMBERING AN INTERVIEW WITH NOAM CHOMSKY[1]

It is rare that you have the opportunity to sound out one of the great minds of our time on a scientific topic that you are interested in. This happened to me when I interviewed Noam Chomsky on bilingualism.

A few years after having written my first book on bilingualism (*Life with Two Languages: An Introduction to Bilingualism*), I contacted Professor Noam Chomsky at MIT to ask him whether he would be kind enough to give me a bit of his time to talk about bilinguals and bilingualism. He very kindly accepted and the interview took place in his office in the now-famous Building 20 at MIT.

I was still a young academic at the time and I was touched that such an illustrious linguist would spend some time with me discussing a topic that has always intrigued me. As I am writing this post, many years later, I feel all the more honored to have had this moment with him.

Noam Chomsky started off by saying that he knew very little about bilingualism but as our conversation continued, he clearly showed that he had given it some thought. Four topics marked the interview. The first was that Noam Chomsky was not convinced that there is a sharp difference between monolingualism and bilingualism. As he stated: "I'm about as monolingual as you come, but nevertheless I have a variety of different languages at my command, different styles, different ways of talking, which do involve different parameter settings."

I kept coming back to this first point throughout the interview (for me, bilinguals *are* different from monolinguals) and a bit later on when I asked him whether shifting styles is really the same as shifting languages, he did add, "It's different in degree, very different, VERY different in degree, so different in degree that you could call it a difference of quality. Because, after all, degree differences do turn into quality differences." For Noam Chomsky, the really interesting question is how a particular system of the mind can be simultaneously in several different states, and whether this is unique to the language faculty. He believes that it isn't.

A second topic we spent some time on concerned whether you can lose a first language in adulthood. Noam Chomsky didn't think you could

---

[1] This post was originally entitled, "Noam Chomsky on bilingualism."

and argued that there is some sort of residual storage. He took the example of a sixty-year-old man who hasn't spoken German since age twenty and who no longer seems to be able to use it. The real test for him would be to see how quickly he could relearn it. He was convinced that the person would learn German a lot faster than if he were starting from scratch and he added that he would probably learn it with the right pronunciation, the right nuances, and so on. As he stated, "My guess is that you can't really erase the system."

A third topic concerned the permanent influence of a second language on a first language in a prolonged language contact situation. In Post 3.9, I described a set of studies my colleagues and I had conducted that seemed to show that a second language (French) can have a real impact on a first language (Spanish in this case) when the former is used much more than the latter for an extensive period of time. We had used acceptability judgments and had found quite a large influence of French on Spanish, the first language of the adult immigrants we tested. They had arrived as adult Spanish monolingual speakers twenty years before.

For Noam Chomsky, however, the native language competence of the immigrants had not in fact been changed. Rather, it was their cognitive style that was now different. He suggested that when you move into a foreign language environment, your standards on grammatical acceptability are lowered because you are confronted with many ways of saying things, in the one or the other language, or in both. This change in cognitive style may thus explain the way you react to your native language, but it should not influence your knowledge of your native language.

In our research, we subsequently used a translation task and we obtained similar results which made us think that the impact of a dominant language, over a lengthy period of time, can be quite profound even on the first language competence of adult native speakers. This work was done several years after the interview, though.

Finally, I asked Noam Chomsky why linguists, most notably theoretical linguists, had spent so little time studying bilingualism. After all, wasn't half the world's population bi- or multilingual? He did not play down the interest of understanding people who know and use several languages but he thought that theoretical linguists should start with simple cases, that is, with monolinguals. For him, the argument is the same as for chemists who study H_2O and not other types of water that contain other substances. To understand the latter, you have to start with the former. As he stated, "The only way to deal with the complexities of the real world is by studying pure cases and trying to determine from them the principles that interact in the complex cases." This is taken for granted in the physical sciences, according to him, and it should also be in the nonphysical sciences.

Our meeting lasted about an hour and I came away with some answers but also additional questions and a few doubts. This said, I felt honored to have spent a short moment with one of the great thinkers of our time, and I still feel that way so many years later.

15.2 FIFTY YEARS IN THE FIELD OF BILINGUALISM[2]

(Interview with François Grosjean)

François Grosjean started his blog in 2010 and more than 2.2 million readers have visited it since then. But who is this rather discreet researcher known the world over?

Interview conducted by Aneta Pavlenko.

2017 marks a special anniversary for François Grosjean – fifty years in the field of bilingualism. His concepts and ideas now form the foundations of the field and his books have inspired numerous others, myself included. But how much do we know about their enigmatic author? To learn what makes François tick, I conducted an "anniversary interview."

Your recent book, *A la recherche de Roger et Sallie* (2016), is dedicated to your unconventional parents and their career in international espionage. You clearly share your parents' love of travel and discovery but did Roger and Sallie share your interest in languages?

I explain at the beginning of my autobiography, *A Journey in Languages and Cultures: The Life of a Bicultural Bilingual*,[3] that I did not grow up with my parents. I first lived with a foster mother in a small village near Paris and then I spent ten years in boarding schools, in Switzerland and England. My father knew some English since he spent a year in

---

[2] The title of this post was originally, "What you didn't know about François Grosjean." It was published in August 2017.

[3] Published by Oxford University Press in 2019.

England during World War II and was part of the Double Cross system run by MI5. But after that, his English quickly withered away and he was basically monolingual.

My English mother, on the other hand, became trilingual as an adult, first adding French to her repertoire and then Italian. When my first book on bilingualism came out in 1982, I sent her a copy. Many years later, I inherited all her documents – I had been estranged from her since the age of sixteen – and I found the book with annotations. I took it that she too was interested in what it means to live with two or more languages.

Many readers assume that you grew up in multilingual Switzerland, yet you were raised as a monolingual speaker in France until the age of eight. How did you become bilingual and Swiss?
This might sound astonishing, but when I was eight, my mother abducted me from my foster home – my parents had divorced and my father had visiting rights – and she took me to Switzerland. There she put me in an English boarding school and within a year I was bilingual in French and English. I stayed there for six years, in contact with the cultures of the other boys, mainly British and American. She then decided that the school wasn't strict enough, and she transferred me to a boarding school in England. I didn't come back to Switzerland, apart from a few vacations, before the age of forty. But it was meant to be part of my mosaic of cultures and I now live here.

You first got interested in bilingualism during your studies in France and England, and then deepened your interest during your time as an academic in the United States. What is it about these three largely monolingual environments that prompted you to look at bilingualism of all things?
Maybe it was precisely because of the monolingualism in these countries that I wanted to discover who I was – a bilingual and bicultural person. My MA thesis in Paris fifty years ago was the beginning of a long journey trying to understand those of us who live with two or more languages, in one or several cultures. It also led me to develop my holistic view of bilingualism which states that the bilingual is not two monolinguals in one person (see Post 1.2). And then I worked on what it means to be bicultural, something that I needed to do to come to grips with who I was (see Post 9.1).

One of the key concepts you pioneered is the notion of mode, monolingual vs bilingual, but is it truly possible for bilinguals to be in the monolingual mode?

The language mode concept explains how bilinguals, in their everyday interactions, keep their languages separate or let them intermingle depending on a number of factors (see Post 3.1). When in a monolingual mode, only one language is used and the others are deactivated, mainly because you do not need them, or you cannot use them, at that particular time. The question is whether they can be totally deactivated.

Experimental data show that this can indeed be the case based on various linguistic and psycholinguistic factors (for an example, see Post 11.1). And on a more personal level, most bilinguals have been through the experience of being "shocked" to hear someone utter a word or sentence from a language they know but did not expect from that person. This can even lead to momentary comprehension difficulties until the other, deactivated, language kicks in.

What do you see as some of the key changes and breakthroughs of the past fifty years, in academic research and in the attitudes towards bilingualism in the world at large?
When I first started working on bilingualism, the researchers in the field were few and far between, and the books and publications rather sparse. The language sciences concentrated on monolinguals as they had done for many years before. Since then, things have changed dramatically, and bilingualism research is extremely widespread and very exciting. There are even academic journals dedicated just to bilingualism. One that I helped found, *Bilingualism: Language and Cognition*, now has the third highest impact factor in 180 linguistics journals!

As for attitudes toward bilingualism, there has been a rather strong shift from insisting on the dangers of bilingualism to lauding its advantages. One must be careful not to go too far here, though, as both you and I have stated in our posts.

What do you think are the most critical questions for the new generation of researchers? If you were to begin your research from scratch in the year 2017 what do you think you would study?
There are probably two areas, among others, I would encourage younger colleagues to delve into. The first is better understanding the psycholinguistics and neurolinguistics of code-switching and borrowing – what is often known as language mixing (see Post 3.4). These are areas that are not yet well studied experimentally and I think new studies could reveal many fascinating things.

The other area concerns biculturalism and how it impacts on bilingualism. Studies have rarely divided up their bilingual participants into those who are monocultural – remember that many bilinguals are members of just one culture – and those who are bicultural. Interacting frequently with two or more cultures will no doubt have a profound impact on how languages are stored and are processed.

What are your current projects and what should we be looking forward to in the years to come?
I am currently finishing a book with Dr. Krista Byers-Heinlein on speech perception and comprehension in bilingual adults and children. I'll then work on a book relating my own journey in languages and cultures and how it has influenced my research over the years. It has been an amazing adventure and I look forward to sharing it with others.

References

Grosjean, F. (2010). *Bilingual: Life and Reality*. Cambridge, MA: Harvard University Press.

Grosjean, F. (2016). *A la recherche de Roger et Sallie*. Hauterive, Suisse: Attinger.

Grosjean, F. (2019). *A Journey in Languages and Cultures: The Life of a Bicultural Bilingual*. Oxford: Oxford University Press.

Grosjean, F. and Byers-Heinlein, K. (2018). *The Listening Bilingual: Speech Perception, Comprehension, and Bilingualism*. Hoboken, NJ: Wiley.

15.3 A BILINGUAL CHALLENGE: WRITING A BOOK IN YOUR OTHER LANGUAGE

Writing a book in one language is something special but writing another book, on the same subject, in your other language is even more special. Here is my personal testimony of this bilingual challenge.

Bilingual writers have always fascinated me, and I marvel at those who write in their second or third languages (see Post 14.8). I am also amazed at those few who write their works in two languages (see Post 14.9). Never did I imagine that I would get to live that very experience for a few months.

My usual working language is English (see Post 4.1) and apart from a few academic papers and a statistics primer written with a French colleague, I have not written in French, certainly not a full-scale book.

More than a year ago, however, I signed a contract with a leading Parisian publisher to do just that thinking that it would be child's play. After all, I am fluent in both English and French, I've been working on bilingualism, the topic of my new book, for such a long time, and I was going to address a general public.

I soon realized though that it would be a challenge. First, during the preparation stage, I had to read up on bilingualism in the French-speaking world ("la Francophonie"), which comprises some thirty countries that have French as an official language (sometimes shared with other languages). Assessing the degree of bilingualism in these countries wasn't an easy task as their censuses do not systematically ask about bi- or multilingualism, if they ask about languages at all. For example, neither France nor Belgium asks language questions whereas other countries such as Canada and Switzerland do (see Post 2.2).

I also had to find studies in French on the various aspects of bilingualism that I would be dealing with as I couldn't expect my future readers to read the ones written in English that I usually refer to. In addition, there are aspects of bilingualism that interest the French-speaking world more than in English-speaking countries such as the opinions people have of their languages and of multilingualism. I also had to find examples of bilingual language behavior such as code-switching and borrowing in which French was involved. And finally, I had to make sure that I had all the appropriate translation equivalents of the concepts I would be dealing with throughout my book.

But all that was the easy part! The actual writing process was far harder than I had imagined even though I write French without any problem and have lectured in that language for the last twenty years. I quickly realized that my writing style, very much influenced by my years of writing in English, simply had to become more French. I usually write short sentences with few clauses but written French requires far longer sentences with many subordinate clauses. In addition, written French usually takes on an impersonal, rather formal, tone. For example, I simply didn't feel I could give personal examples the way I do in English.

I also left out people's testimonies which have their place in nonfiction prose in English. Thus, at the beginning of my book *Bilingual: Life and Reality*, I describe the many bilinguals I had met on a particular morning – the baker's wife, my garage mechanic, even children in the local day-care across from where I live. I didn't feel this would be appropriate for French-speaking readers, and so I opted to start with the bilingualism of famous French people such as Napoleon (his first language was Corsican and he only learned French at age six), the famous researcher and Nobel laureate, Marie Curie, who was originally Polish but had done all her work in France, as well as the bilingual writer Samuel Beckett, also a Nobel prize winner, who wrote his books in both English and French.

On the level of vocabulary, written French has a tendency to use unfamiliar, rather specialized, terms that must not be repeated too soon after having been used. Writers have to find ways around this either by using pronouns or finding synonyms. The problem though is that specialized words don't have exact synonyms and one is loath to use words with slightly different meanings. And, of course, I had to be careful to avoid false friends which are near homographs in English and French but with different meanings (see Post 3.8).

After a while, I found my French stride and wrote my book in four months. As I was doing so, though, my mind would often go back to bilingual authors who have written about the difficulties of writing in their two languages, or of translating their work from one language to the other. In both cases, they find that they produce very different books. Having now finished my book, entitled *Parler plusieurs langues: le monde des bilingues*, I know exactly what they mean; it is very different from the one that I wrote on the same topic in English a few years before!

References

Grosjean, F. (2010). *Bilingual: Life and Reality*. Cambridge, MA: Harvard University Press.
Grosjean, F. (2015). *Parler plusieurs langues: le monde des bilingues*. Paris, France: Albin Michel.

Index